D1288913

WITHDRAWN

a visual mixtape

VOL. 01: THE SYMPHONY

BLAXIS

COVER ILLUSTRATION BY
JASON REEVES

VOL. 01 PLAYLIST

one nation

b, r & d

I'M WATCHI ALL. T WAY.

wildfire

consonance

PUBLISHER – JIBA MOLEI ANDERSON
DIRECTOR OF MARKETING – ROCHON PERRY
ART DIRECTOR – La MORRIS RICHMOND
COPY EDITOR – JUDE W. MIRE

purge

4 Pages 16 Bars: A Visual Mixtape Volume One: The Symphony is published by Blaxis Publishing, an imprint of Cedar Grove Books, Inc. 3500 West Armitage Avenue #2R Chicago, IL, 60647, USA. On the internet: http://www.griotenterprises.com; all artwork, the distinct likenesses thereof, and all related indicia are TM and © 2015 their respective creators, all rights reserved. The stories, characters and incidents presented in this publication are fictional. Any resemblance to persons living or dead is purely unintentional. All other material, except where noted, is TM and © 2015 Blaxis Publishing. Except for purposes of review, no portion of this publication may be reproduced or reprinted in any way without the express written permission of the copyright holder(s). Printed in the USA.

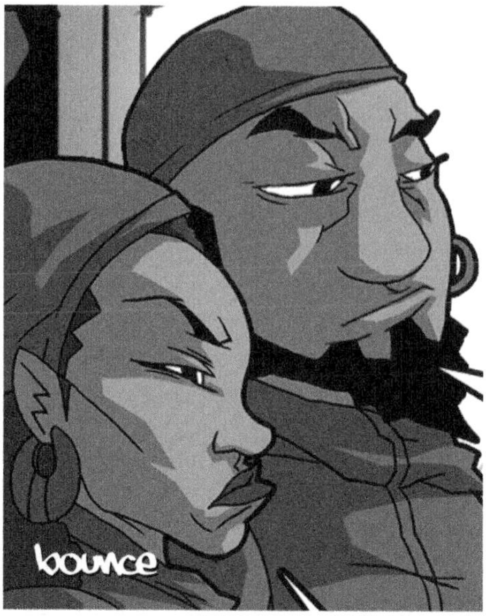
bounce

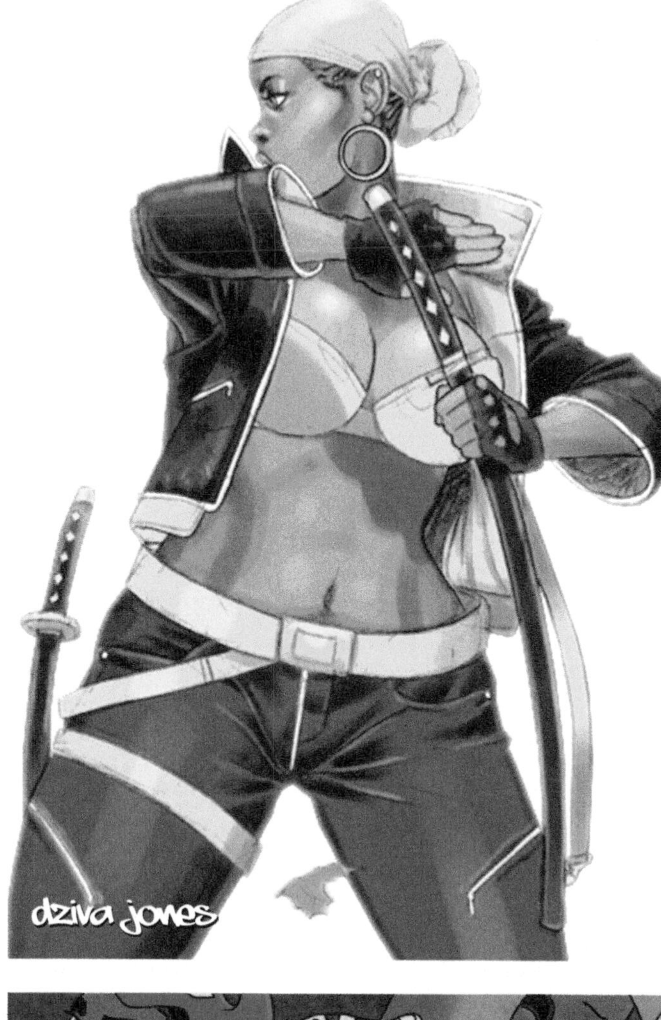
dziva jones

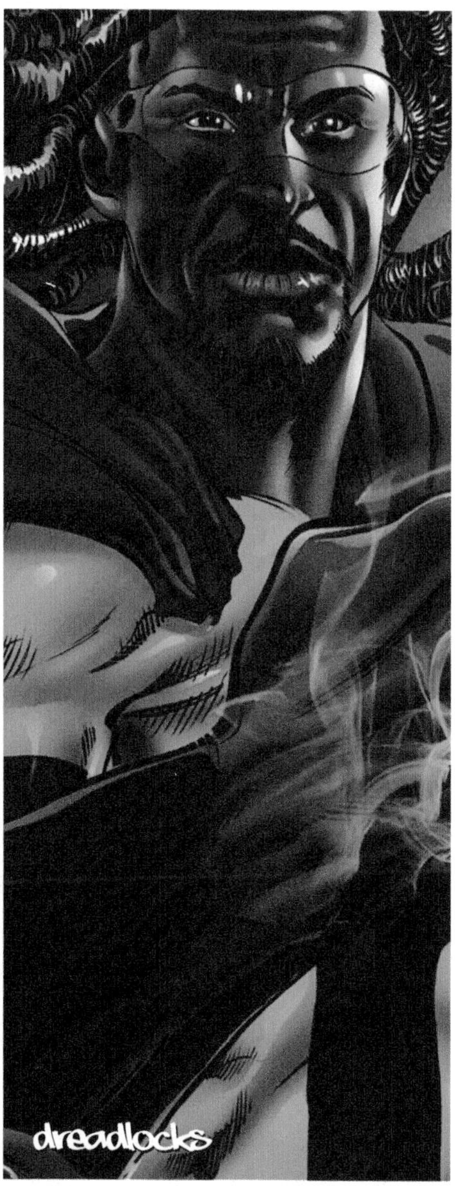
dreadlocks

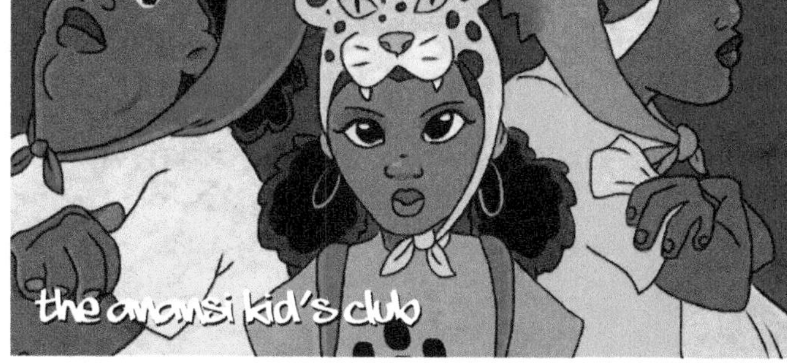
the anansi kid's club

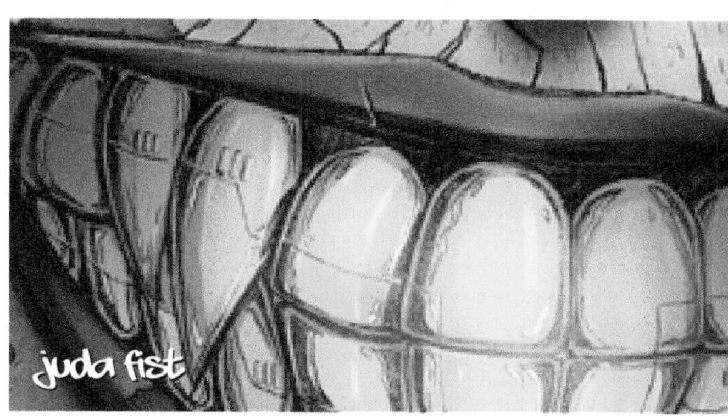
juda fist

for jackie ormes

THE FIRST AFRICAN AMERICAN WOMAN CARTOONIST
CREATOR OF TORCHY (1911 – 1985)

comics are hip hop

BY JIBA MOLEI ANDERSON

"It was all a dream, I used to read Wizard Magazine…"

- Paraphrasing 'Juicy" by
The Notorious B.I.G

Pssst… Guess what?

Comics are **Hip Hop**.

Of course, if this were written in the 20s, I would have said, "Comics are the **Blues**." If this were written in the 40s, then Comics would be akin to **Jazz**. In the 50s, Comics would be considered **Rock and Roll**…

You get the idea.

Comics started out as a sort of *gutter* hybrid art form of image and text, which (for the most part) were crudely drawn, crudely written disposable fair printed on cheap paper for the unwashed masses, mostly children, to enjoy.

Comics were *hood*. Back in the day, nobody who considered themselves *true* artists or writers would claim comics as a legitimate art form. Artists wouldn't claim comics, using that work as a stepping-stone while they pursued "legitimate" work from advertising agencies.

Hell, Stanley Lieber created the pen name **Stan Lee** initially to distance himself from comic book work for the day when he would write *The Great American Novel*.

Comics are *dangerous*. Along with Jazz, along with Rock and Roll, along with Hip Hop, Comics were once, and according to some, still considered the bane of existence; a poison of the mind that would lead to delinquency, crime, homosexuality, and murder. **Frederic Wertham** made his bones by putting the fear of comics into the hearts and minds of good, hard-working, American folk with his ode to ridiculousness *Seduction of the Innocent*.

Comics are *gully*. They have the ability to tap into our base instincts.

They allow some to engage in power fantasies of strength, sexual illusion and dominance, fulfilling wishes to be overly-muscled, gritted teeth savage demigods who can kill with impunity, cruelly reducing women to disposable plot devices only useful for fulfilling carnal needs or a tool for motivation in their mutilation or death by exotic and tragic means.

The Comic Book industry knows *beef*. From the eternal struggle for dominance by **DC** and **Marvel** to the conflict between **Milestone Media** and **Ania** (a rift that echoed the East Coast/West Coast war without the death of its representatives), to the dearth of flame wars pertaining to every aspect of comics in social media, it's a wonder that we've never seen scuffles on par with the **Source Awards** at the **San Diego Comic Con**.

At the same time, Comics are *conscious*. Comics can uplift. Comics can inspire. Comics can show us at our absolute best. We love **Superman**, **Batman**, **Wonder Woman**, the **Black Panther**, **Storm** and many others because they illustrate who we want to be. Two Jewish men for the purpose of punching Hitler, and the ugliness of Nazism, in the face, created **Captain America**. **Spider Man** shows that an ordinary schlub could rise from his nebbishness and become a hero because, of course, with great power comes great responsibility. The **X-Men** fight for equality in a world where not only are they not wanted, but are outright persecuted for being different.

Like Hip Hop, Comics are *experimental*, have different styles, represent different regions, and are global. **East Coast** is different from the **West Coast**, which is different from the **Midwest** and the **Dirty South**, yet no matter if you rock **Nas** or **Rakim**, **NWA** or the **Souls of Mischief**, **Common** or **Eminem**, **Outkast** or **T.I.**, it's still representing the culture that is Hip Hop. By the same token, no matter if you're **Justice League** or **Avengers**, **Hellboy** or **Saga**, **Blade of the Immortal** or **Archie**, you're still knee deep in that comic book culture.

MOTOR CITY BLACK AGE OF COMICS CON
ILLUSTRATION BY SHAWN ALLEYNE

ETEKA: RISE OF THE IMAMBA BY BEN HINSON
ILLUSTRATION BY DERYL BRAUN

Comics and Hip Hop share the mastery of *elements* in order to be truly down in the game. The practitioners of Hip Hop are the **MC**, the **DJ**, the **B-Boy** & **B-Girl** and the **Graffiti** artist. The practitioners of comics are the **Writer**, the **Penciller**, the **Inker**, the **Colorist** and the Letterer.

And, just like Hip Hop, *money* has come in and changed the game. Before 2008, one could say that **DC** and **Marvel** were in the same boat as **Dark Horse**, **Image**, **Dynamite**, **IDW**, **Boom**, etc. Even though DC and Marvel were "bigger labels," they were still in the comic book family.

Like Hip Hop, Comics had cinematic success well before recent memory. For instance, one may be able to call the 1978 **Superman** film the **Beat Street** of comic books movies. Furthermore, Comics and Hip Hop have borrowed from each other as well as had moments of symbiosis (i.e. the **Wu-Tang Clan**, MCs using their rap monikers like secret identities, rappers creating comic books, **Brotherman**, etc.). Real talk, 1997's **Blade**, in tone, attitude and execution, was as close to a Hip Hop influenced comic book movie you were gonna get.

However, once **Iron Man** and **The Dark Knight** made big money, the Mouse (**Disney**) bought Marvel, the Rabbit (**Warner Brothers**) doubled down on DC and changed the whole game. Now we've got the **Corporate Two** trying to dominate, and sublimate, an industry that thrives on innovation and diversity. For them, it's not about creating good stories, but exploiting IP.

Same thing happened in Hip Hop. Before **Dr. Dre's** classic **The Chronic**, you could have **A Tribe Called Quest**, **EPMD**, **Salt N Pepa**, **Public Enemy**, **Arrested Development**, **2 Live Crew**, **MC Hammer** and more rock the airwaves and all be considered Hip Hop. After The Chronic, it became all about blunts, guns, sex and "keeping it real." It became all about the clothing deal or schilling products before even getting the record deal. It became less about speaking your truth and more about fattening your bank account…

In other words, Hip Hop became more about **Drake** and less about **Kendrick Lamar**.

Still, just like real Hip Hop, real Comics *endure*. Like Hip Hop, Comics have the **mainstream** and the **underground**. Like Hip Hop, the underground, or **independent** scene of Comics is where true innovation and experimentation exists. That's where you'll find cats grinding out with passion, creating their own labels and selling their wares out of the *trunks* of their *digital* cars (POD, websites, **Comixology**, **Drive Thru Comics**, **Kickstarter**, etc.) searching for that fan with discernable taste to purchase what they have to offer.

And, just like Hip Hop, the work is diverse, dangerous, gully and uplifting. These Comics represent our base fears and our wildest dreams.

Remember when **Nas** said, "All I need is on mic?" The Comic creator could say, "All I need is one pen, or one pencil, or one stylus…"

This is where the future exists. This is where we exist. We are **4 Pages | 16 Bars**, and we came to rock the house.

Protect ya neck.

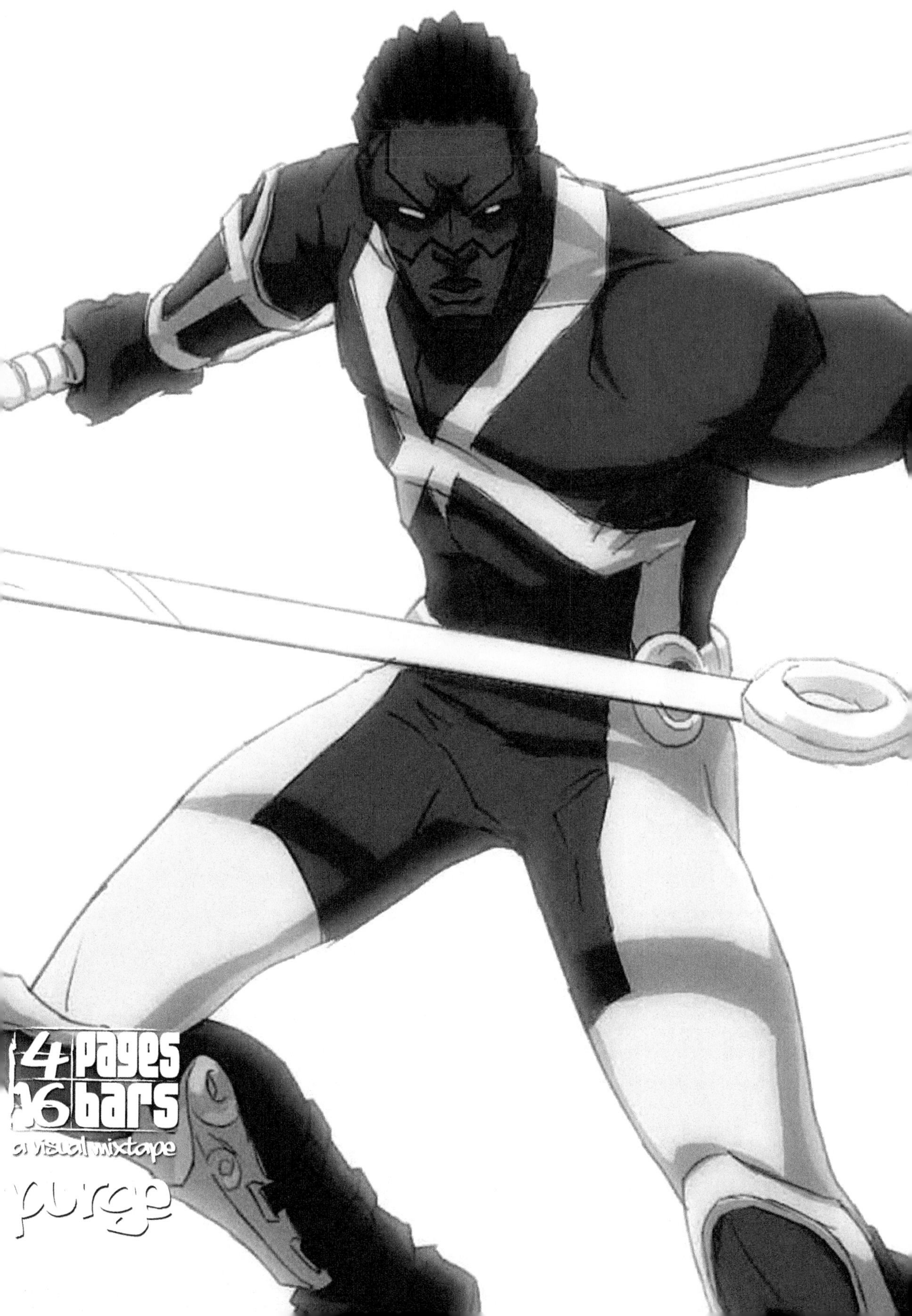
4 pages
16 bars
a visual mixtape
purge

COVER ILLUSTRATION BY
KRISHNA ANDBALRAM BANERJEE

INTERIOR ART BY
ROB HAYNES & KRISHNA ANDBALRAM BANERJEE

PIN-UP ART BY
GUS VASQUEZ & JAY REED

Roosevelt Pitt is the creator of *Purge*.

Purge began its run in July of 1995 with the now defunct
ANIA Comics, a group of African American comic creators
who banded together to publish Afrocentric stories. However,
the creators of Purge jumped ship after their first issue in favor
of self-publishing. Under their new name of **Amara Entertainment**,
Purge began anew.

The series featured the title character, a successful businessman, who felt an
uncontrollable desire to return to his old neighborhood and help where the
police couldn't. As Purge, he could fight crime as he felt it should be fought—
at the criminals' own level. Purge felt that the only lessons that criminals could
learn were violent ones. He used a souped-up motorcycle for transportation
and was an expert in hand-to-hand combat.

Currently, Pitt is working on all-new Purge adventures, to be released in 2015.

website: charlesthechef.net

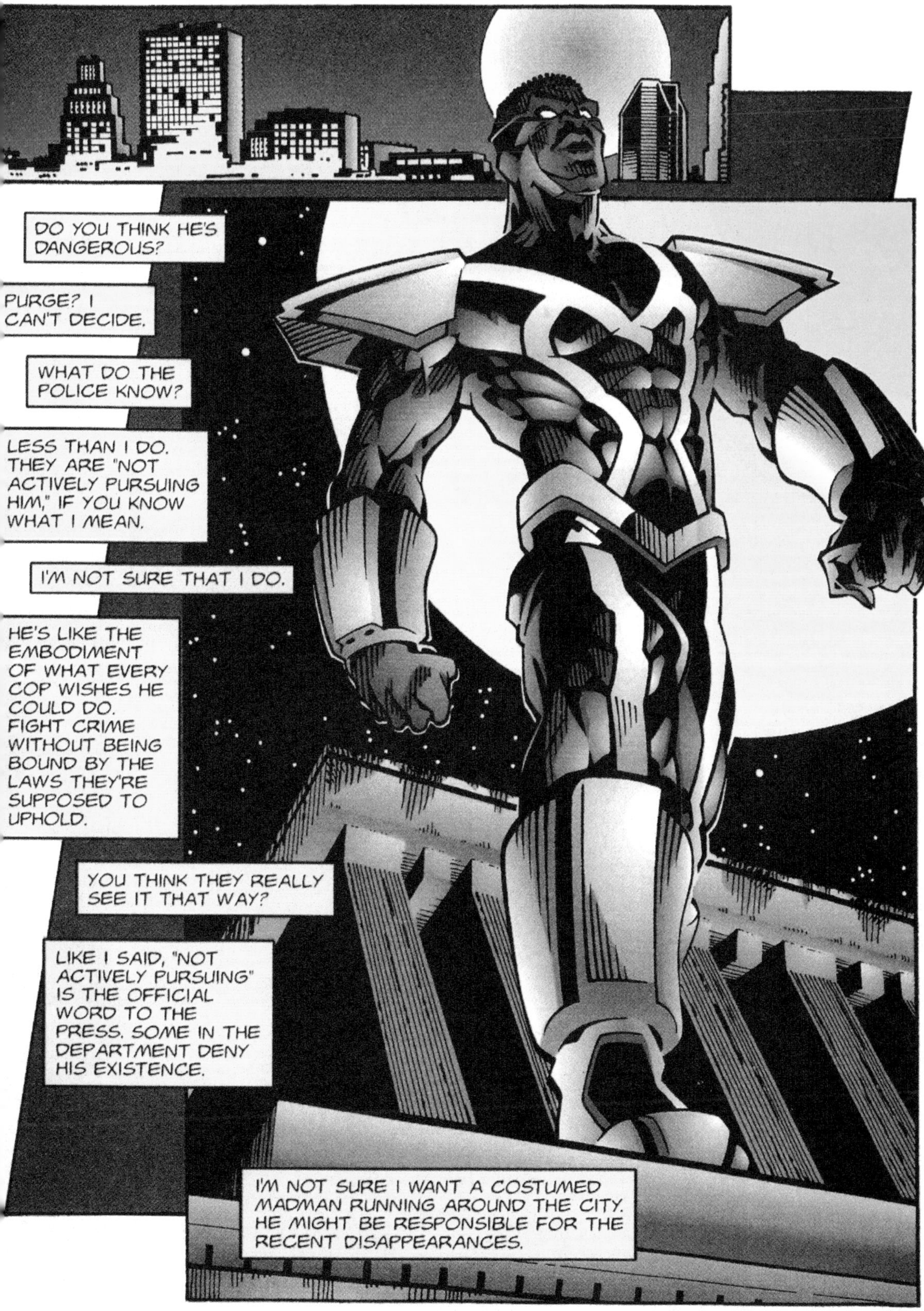
DO YOU THINK HE'S DANGEROUS?
PURGE? I CAN'T DECIDE.
WHAT DO THE POLICE KNOW?
LESS THAN I DO. THEY ARE "NOT ACTIVELY PURSUING HIM," IF YOU KNOW WHAT I MEAN.
I'M NOT SURE THAT I DO.
HE'S LIKE THE EMBODIMENT OF WHAT EVERY COP WISHES HE COULD DO. FIGHT CRIME WITHOUT BEING BOUND BY THE LAWS THEY'RE SUPPOSED TO UPHOLD.
YOU THINK THEY REALLY SEE IT THAT WAY?
LIKE I SAID, "NOT ACTIVELY PURSUING" IS THE OFFICIAL WORD TO THE PRESS. SOME IN THE DEPARTMENT DENY HIS EXISTENCE.
I'M NOT SURE I WANT A COSTUMED MADMAN RUNNING AROUND THE CITY. HE MIGHT BE RESPONSIBLE FOR THE RECENT DISAPPEARANCES.

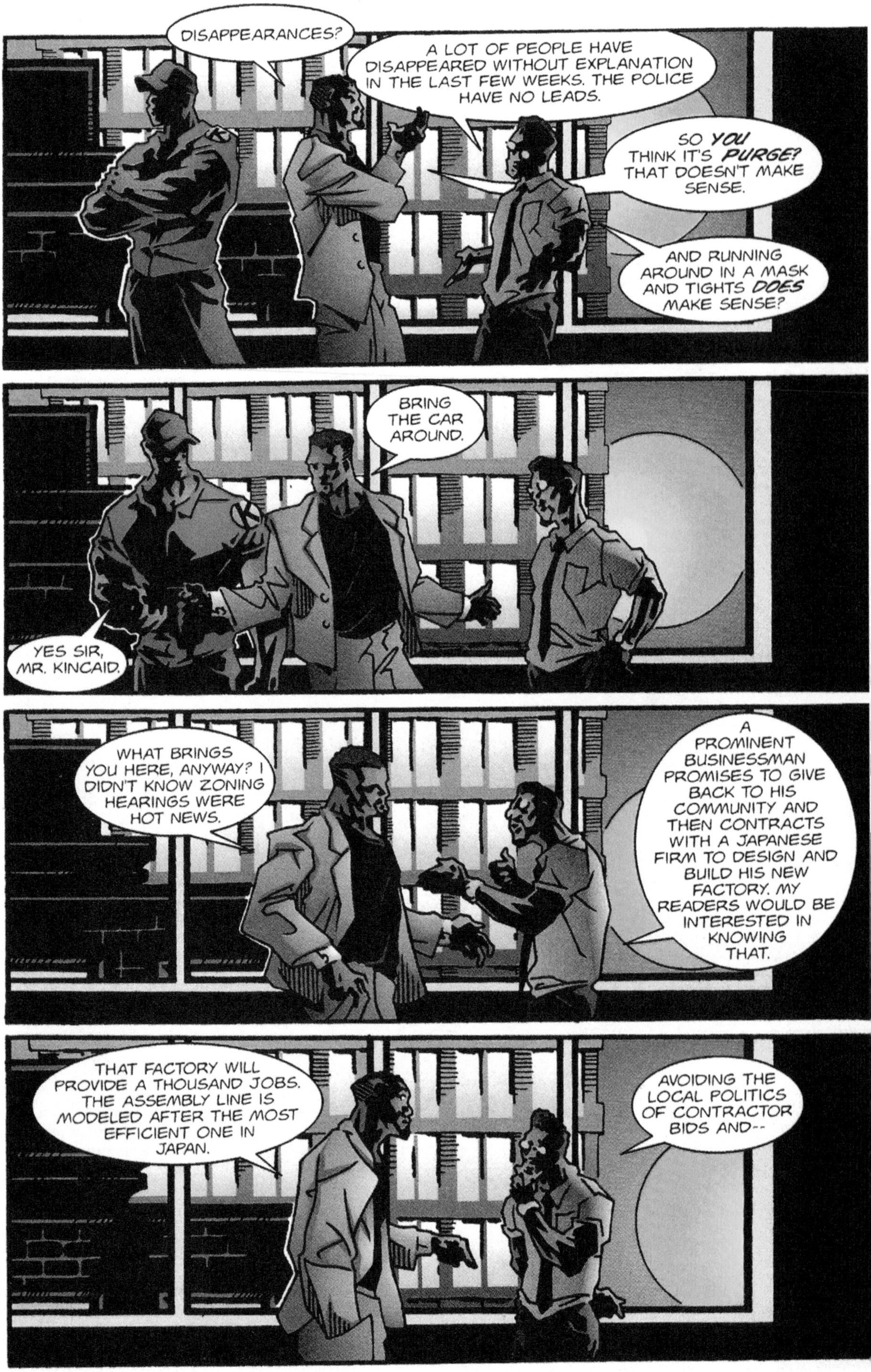
DISAPPEARANCES?
A LOT OF PEOPLE HAVE DISAPPEARED WITHOUT EXPLANATION IN THE LAST FEW WEEKS. THE POLICE HAVE NO LEADS.
SO *YOU* THINK IT'S *PURGE?* THAT DOESN'T MAKE SENSE.
AND RUNNING AROUND IN A MASK AND TIGHTS *DOES* MAKE SENSE?
BRING THE CAR AROUND.
YES SIR, MR. KINCAID.
WHAT BRINGS YOU HERE, ANYWAY? I DIDN'T KNOW ZONING HEARINGS WERE HOT NEWS.
A PROMINENT BUSINESSMAN PROMISES TO GIVE BACK TO HIS COMMUNITY AND THEN CONTRACTS WITH A JAPANESE FIRM TO DESIGN AND BUILD HIS NEW FACTORY. MY READERS WOULD BE INTERESTED IN KNOWING THAT.
THAT FACTORY WILL PROVIDE A THOUSAND JOBS. THE ASSEMBLY LINE IS MODELED AFTER THE MOST EFFICIENT ONE IN JAPAN.
AVOIDING THE LOCAL POLITICS OF CONTRACTOR BIDS AND--

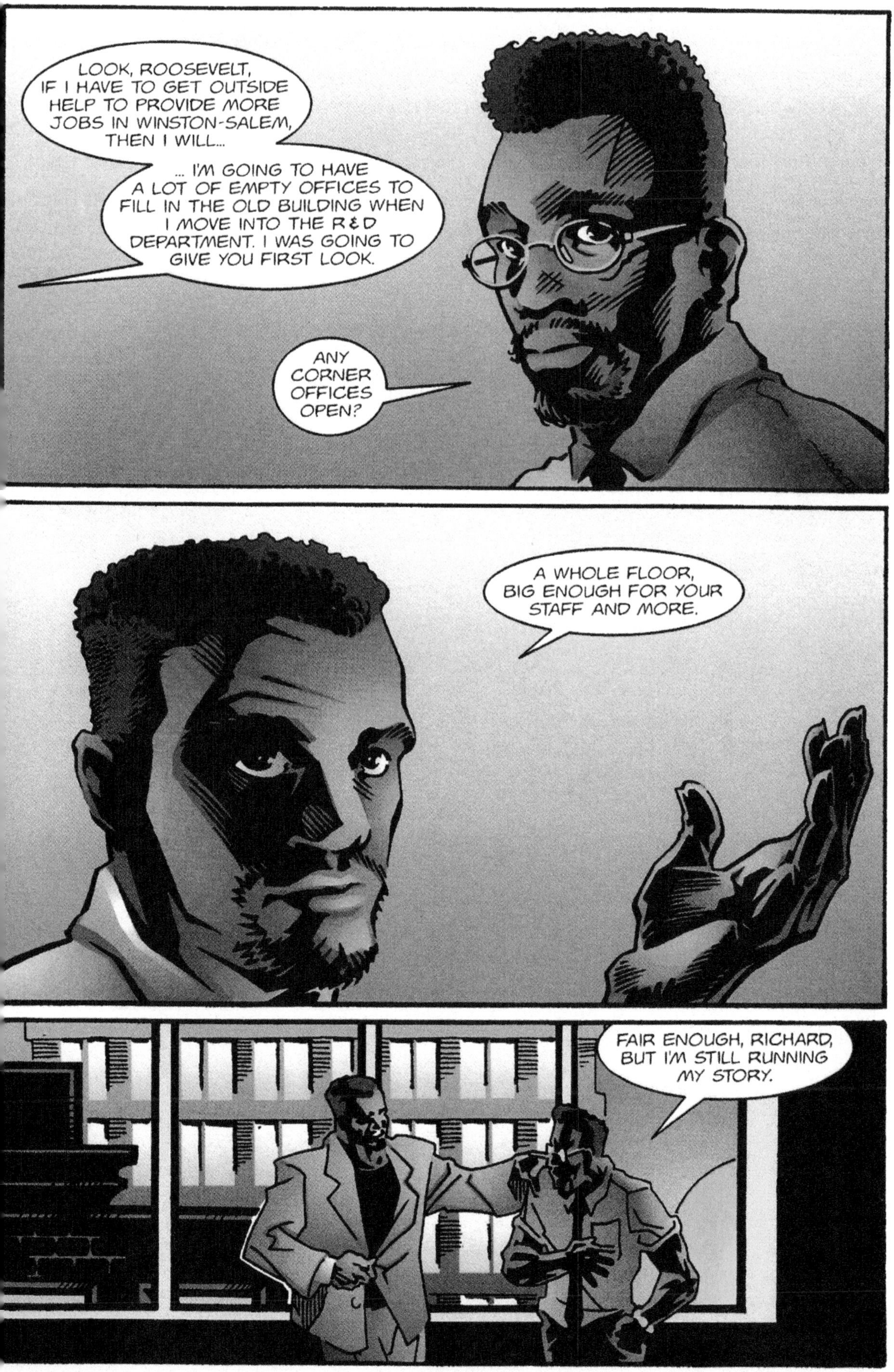
LOOK, ROOSEVELT, IF I HAVE TO GET OUTSIDE HELP TO PROVIDE MORE JOBS IN WINSTON-SALEM, THEN I WILL...
... I'M GOING TO HAVE A LOT OF EMPTY OFFICES TO FILL IN THE OLD BUILDING WHEN I MOVE INTO THE R&D DEPARTMENT. I WAS GOING TO GIVE YOU FIRST LOOK.
ANY CORNER OFFICES OPEN?
A WHOLE FLOOR, BIG ENOUGH FOR YOUR STAFF AND MORE.
FAIR ENOUGH, RICHARD, BUT I'M STILL RUNNING MY STORY.

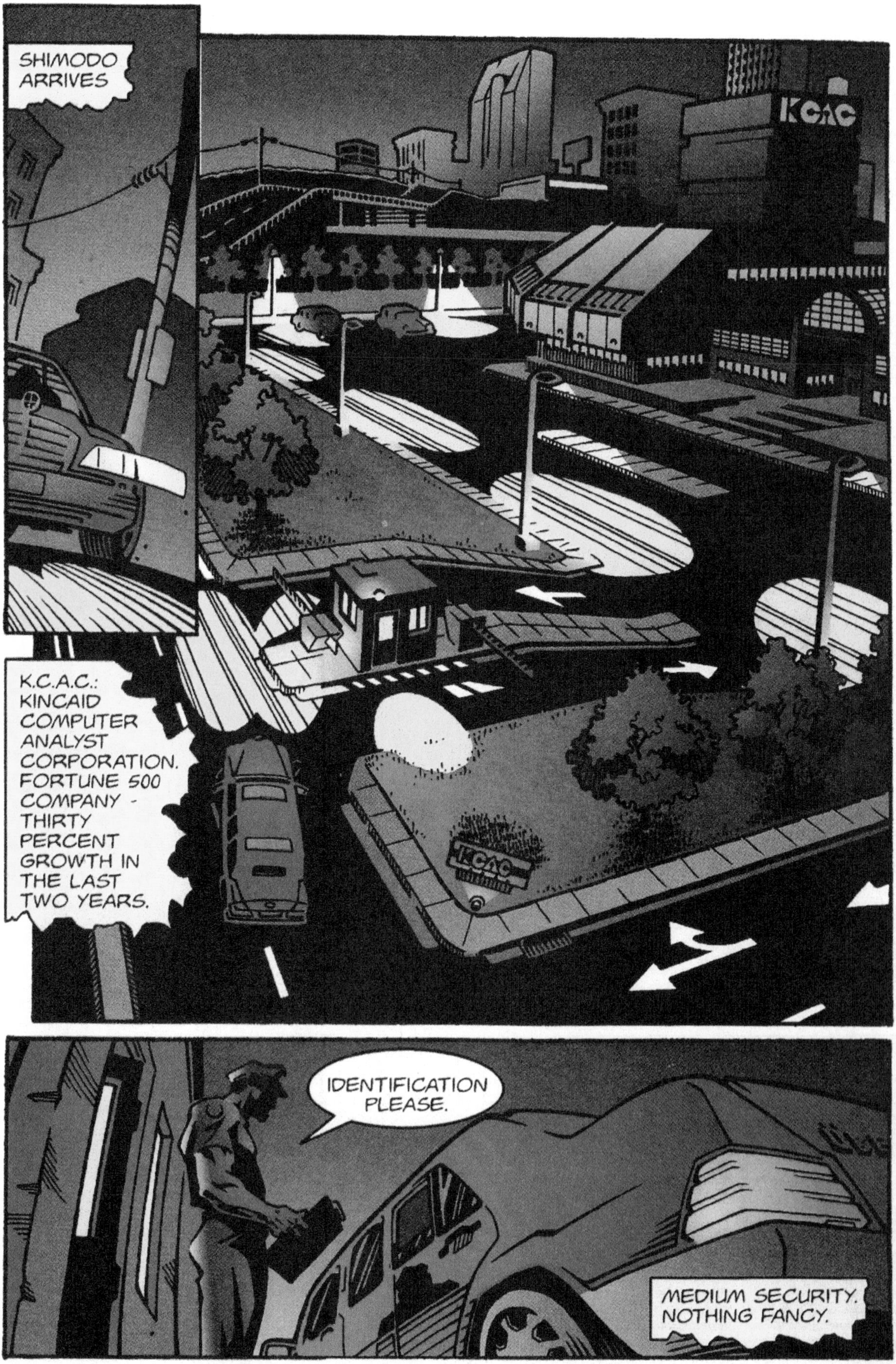

SHIMODO ARRIVES
K.C.A.C.: KINCAID COMPUTER ANALYST CORPORATION. FORTUNE 500 COMPANY - THIRTY PERCENT GROWTH IN THE LAST TWO YEARS.
KCAC
IDENTIFICATION PLEASE.
MEDIUM SECURITY. NOTHING FANCY.

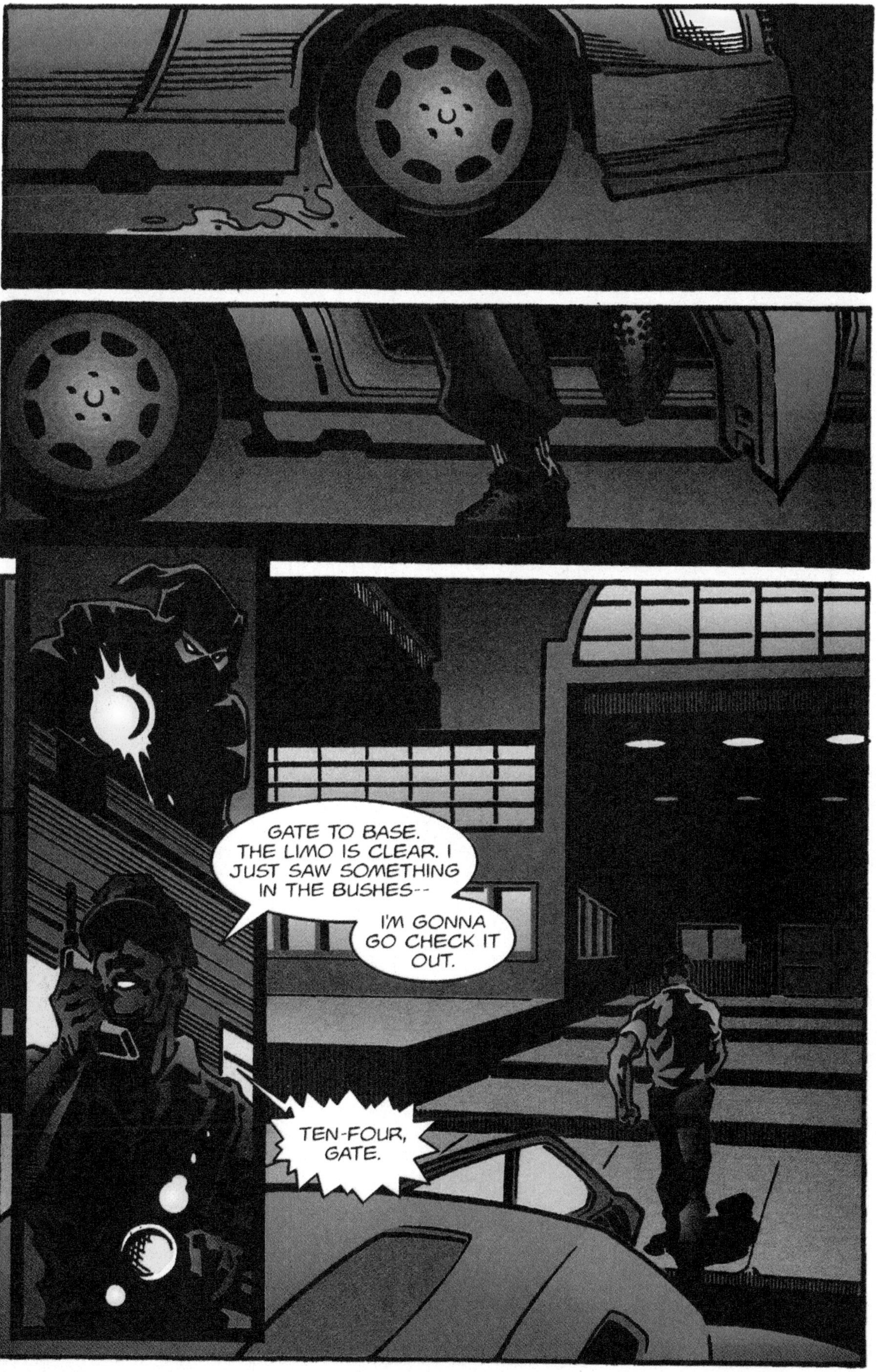
GATE TO BASE. THE LIMO IS CLEAR. I JUST SAW SOMETHING IN THE BUSHES--
I'M GONNA GO CHECK IT OUT.
TEN-FOUR, GATE.

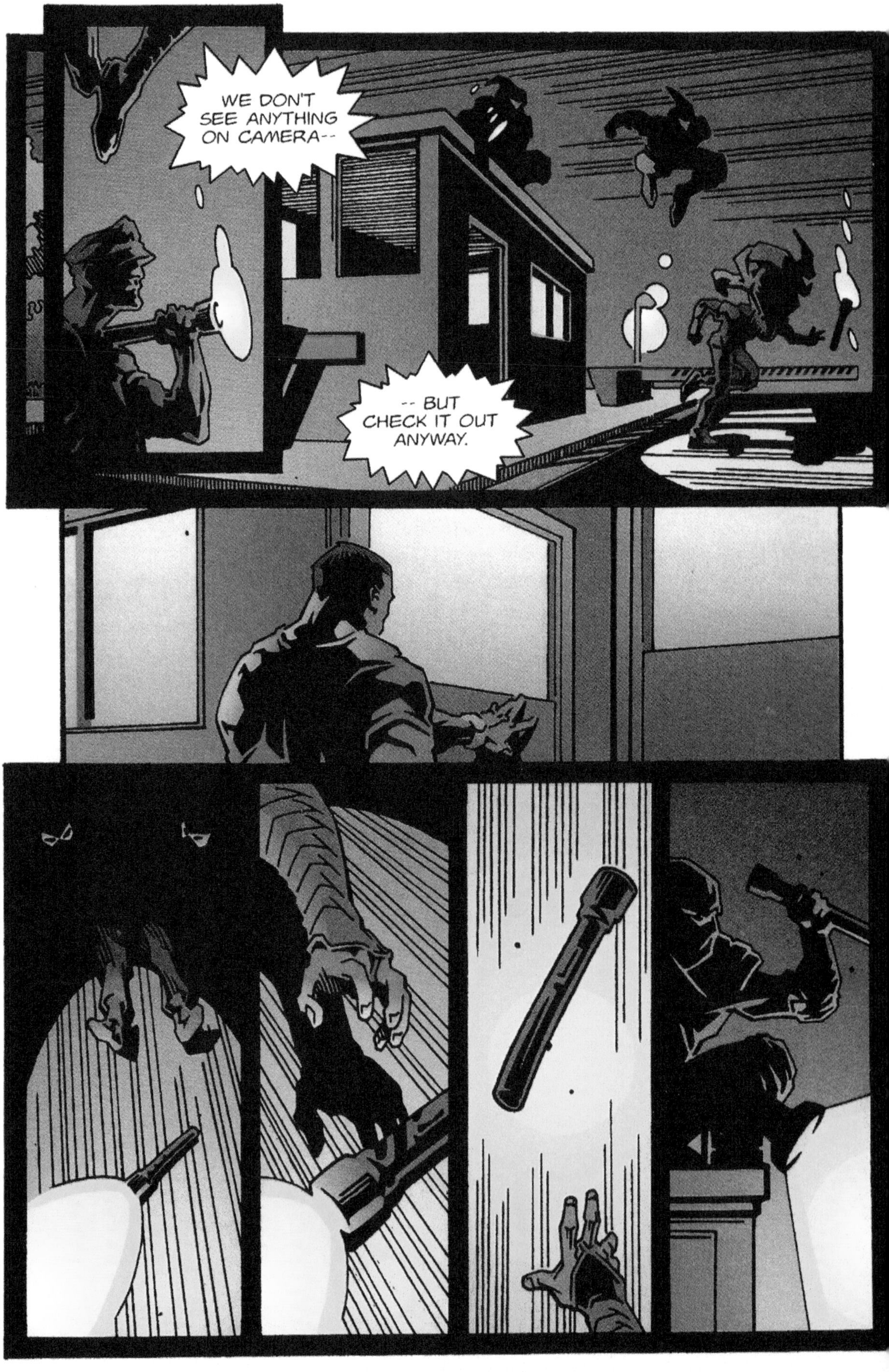

WE DON'T SEE ANYTHING ON CAMERA--
-- BUT CHECK IT OUT ANYWAY.

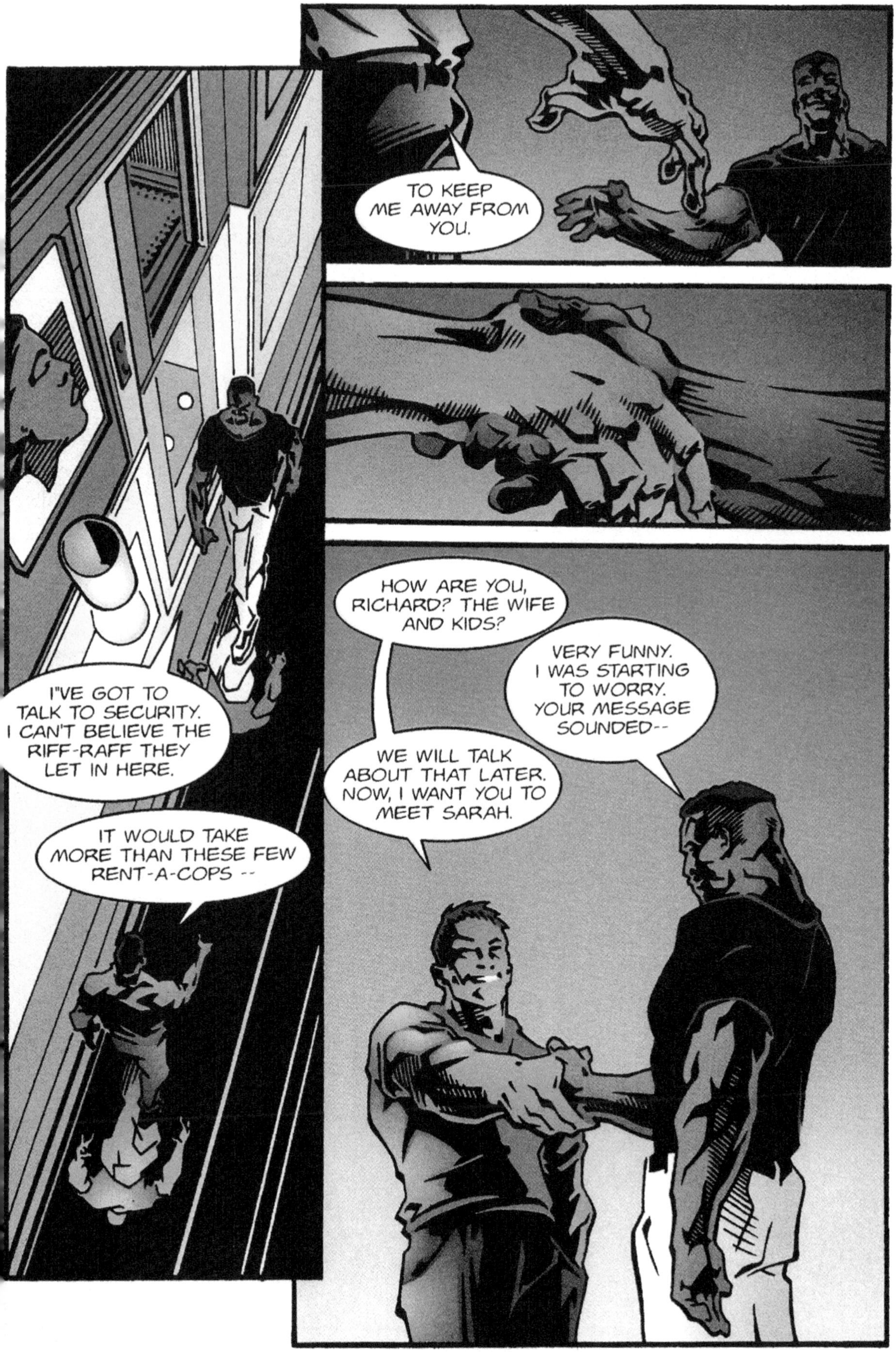

TO KEEP ME AWAY FROM YOU.
I'VE GOT TO TALK TO SECURITY. I CAN'T BELIEVE THE RIFF-RAFF THEY LET IN HERE.
IT WOULD TAKE MORE THAN THESE FEW RENT-A-COPS --
HOW ARE YOU, RICHARD? THE WIFE AND KIDS?
VERY FUNNY. I WAS STARTING TO WORRY. YOUR MESSAGE SOUNDED--
WE WILL TALK ABOUT THAT LATER. NOW, I WANT YOU TO MEET SARAH.

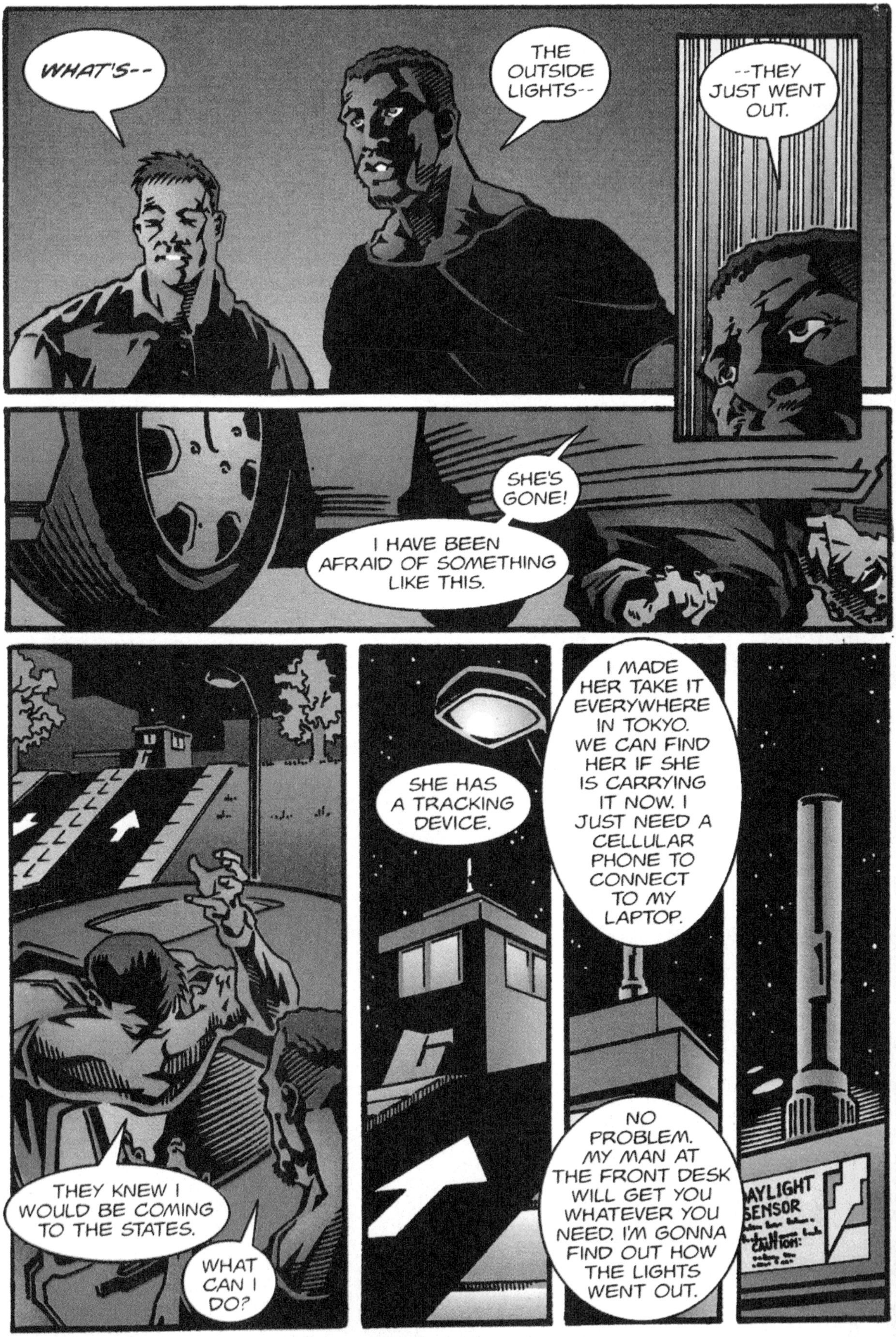
WHAT'S--
THE OUTSIDE LIGHTS--
--THEY JUST WENT OUT.
SHE'S GONE!
I HAVE BEEN AFRAID OF SOMETHING LIKE THIS.
THEY KNEW I WOULD BE COMING TO THE STATES.
WHAT CAN I DO?
SHE HAS A TRACKING DEVICE.
I MADE HER TAKE IT EVERYWHERE IN TOKYO. WE CAN FIND HER IF SHE IS CARRYING IT NOW. I JUST NEED A CELLULAR PHONE TO CONNECT TO MY LAPTOP.
NO PROBLEM. MY MAN AT THE FRONT DESK WILL GET YOU WHATEVER YOU NEED. I'M GONNA FIND OUT HOW THE LIGHTS WENT OUT.
AYLIGHT SENSOR

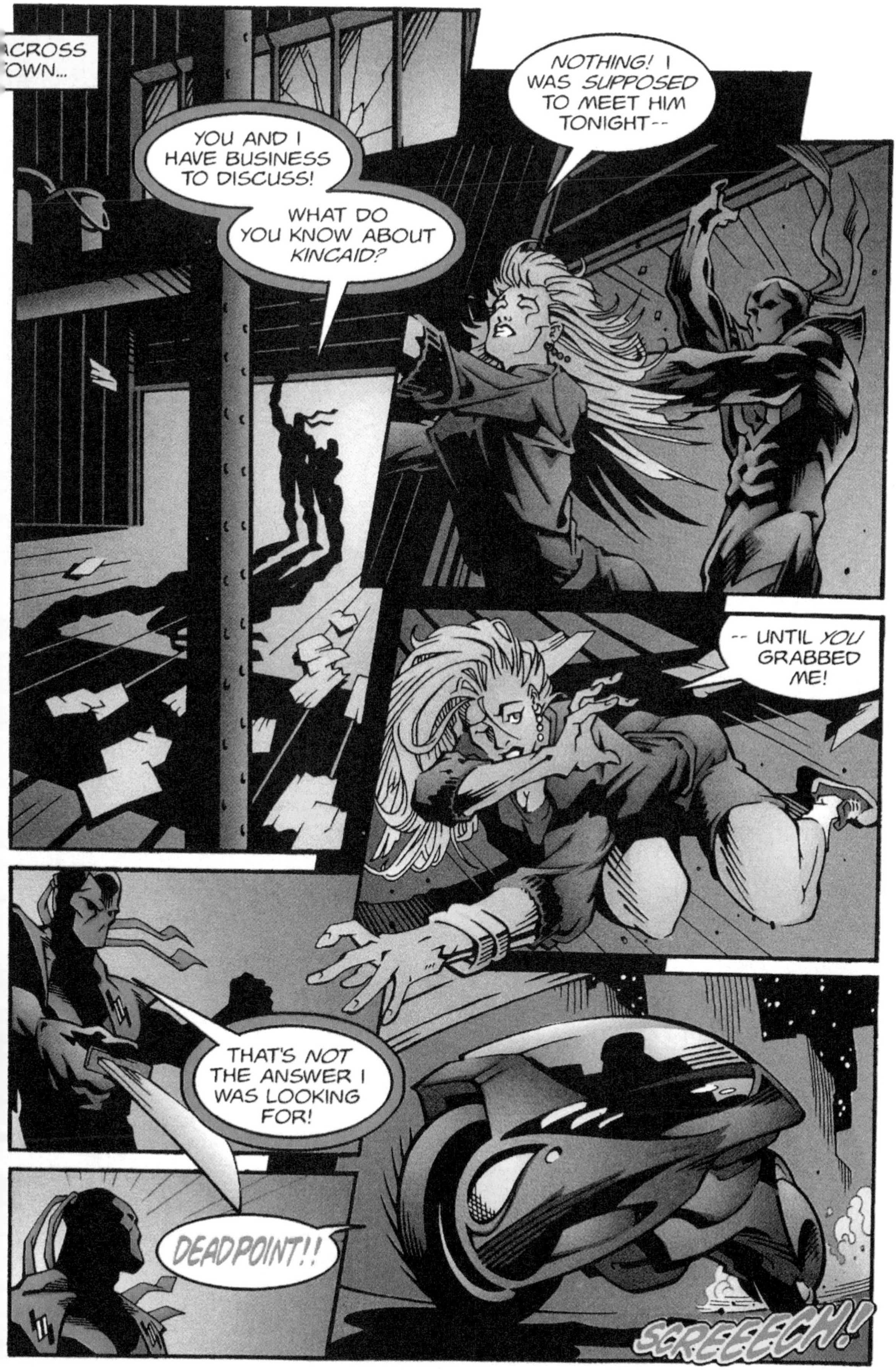
ACROSS TOWN...
YOU AND I HAVE BUSINESS TO DISCUSS!
WHAT DO YOU KNOW ABOUT KINCAID?
NOTHING! I WAS SUPPOSED TO MEET HIM TONIGHT--
-- UNTIL YOU GRABBED ME!
THAT'S NOT THE ANSWER I WAS LOOKING FOR!
DEADPOINT!!
SCREEEECH!

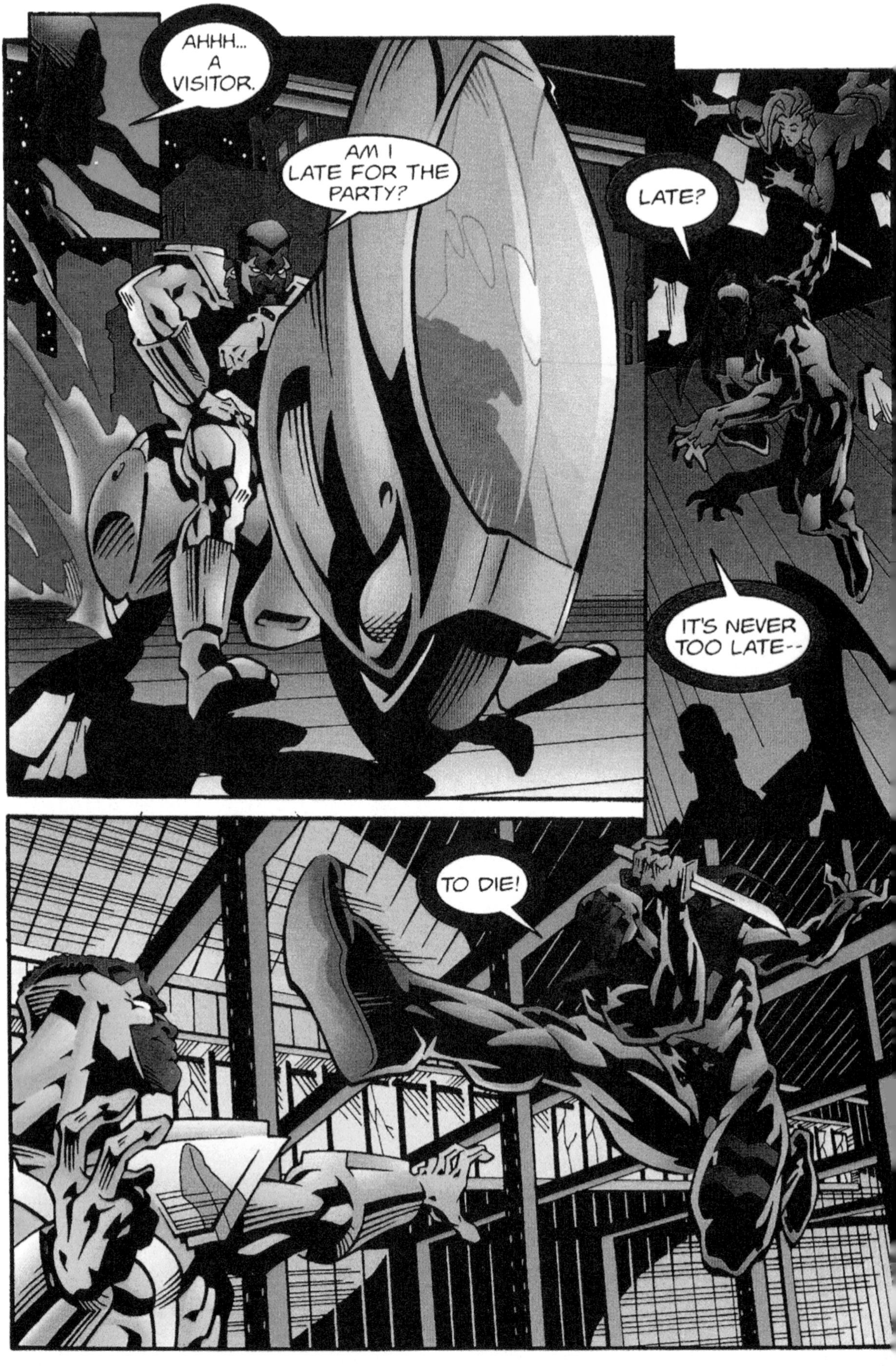
AHHH... A VISITOR.
AM I LATE FOR THE PARTY?
LATE?
IT'S NEVER TOO LATE--
TO DIE!

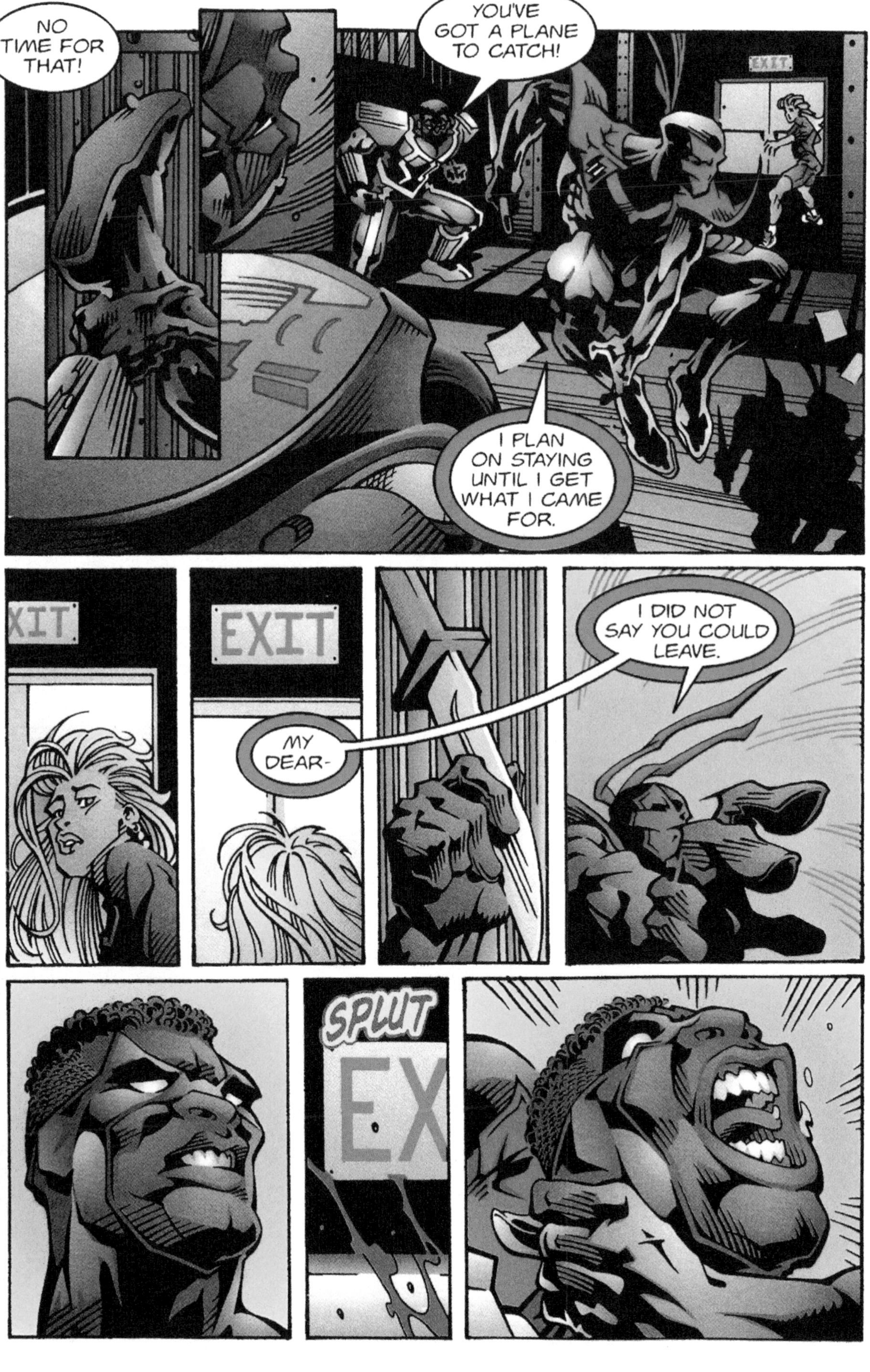
NO TIME FOR THAT!
YOU'VE GOT A PLANE TO CATCH!
EXIT
I PLAN ON STAYING UNTIL I GET WHAT I CAME FOR.
XIT
EXIT
MY DEAR-
I DID NOT SAY YOU COULD LEAVE.
SPLUT
EX

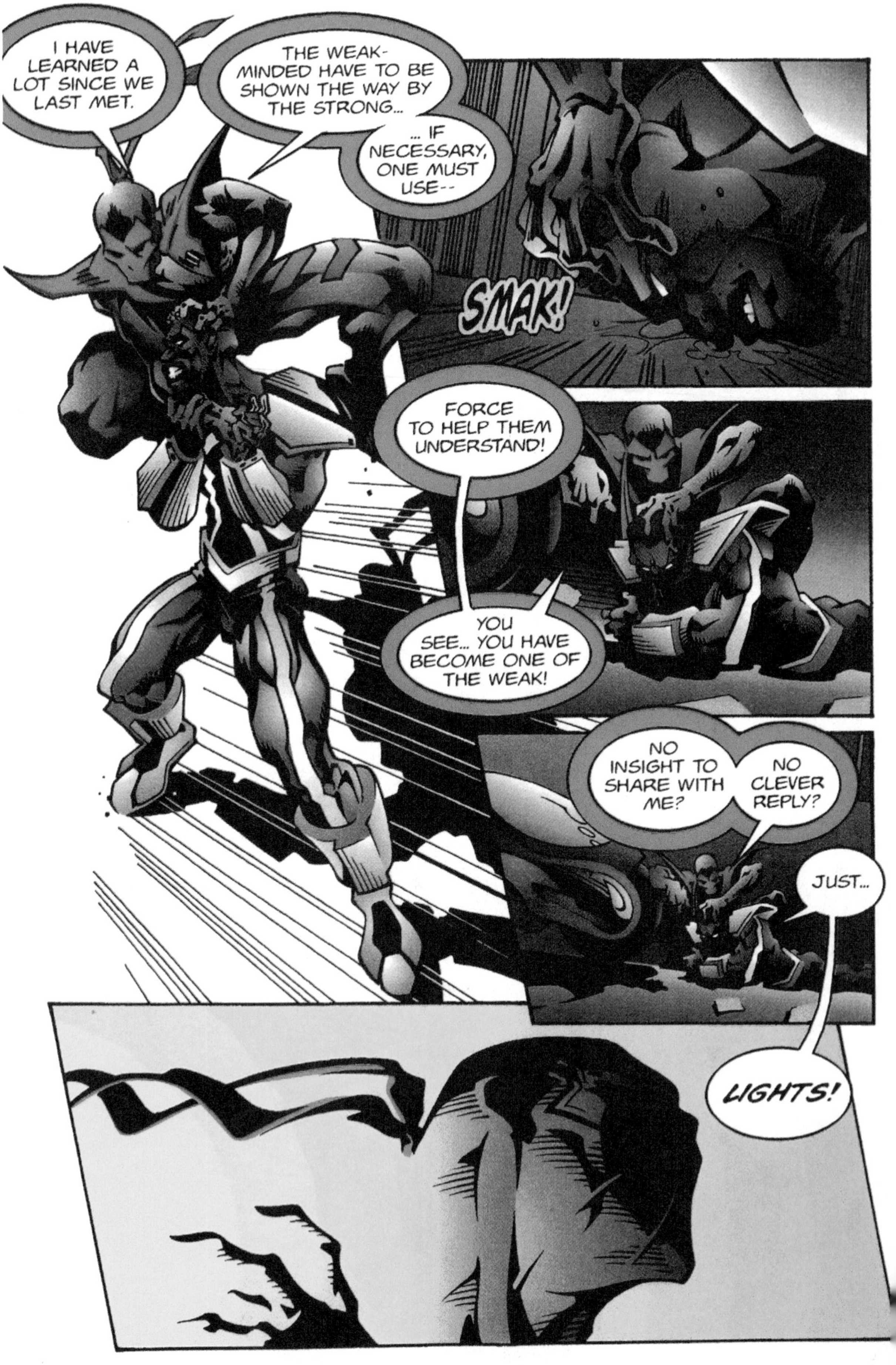
I HAVE LEARNED A LOT SINCE WE LAST MET.
THE WEAK-MINDED HAVE TO BE SHOWN THE WAY BY THE STRONG...
... IF NECESSARY, ONE MUST USE--
SMAK!
FORCE TO HELP THEM UNDERSTAND!
YOU SEE... YOU HAVE BECOME ONE OF THE WEAK!
NO INSIGHT TO SHARE WITH ME?
NO CLEVER REPLY?
JUST...
LIGHTS!

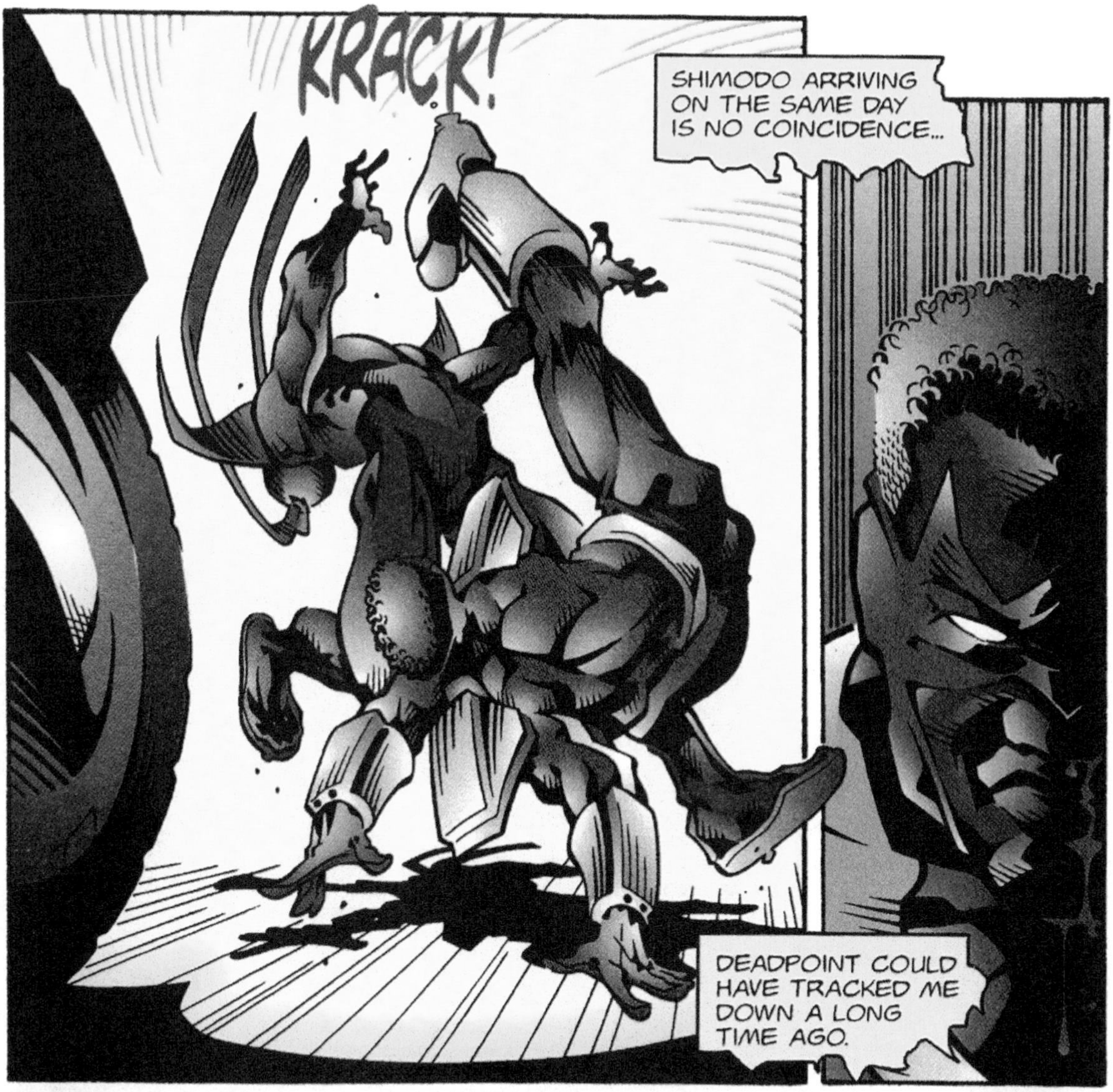
KRACK!
SHIMODO ARRIVING ON THE SAME DAY IS NO COINCIDENCE...
DEADPOINT COULD HAVE TRACKED ME DOWN A LONG TIME AGO.

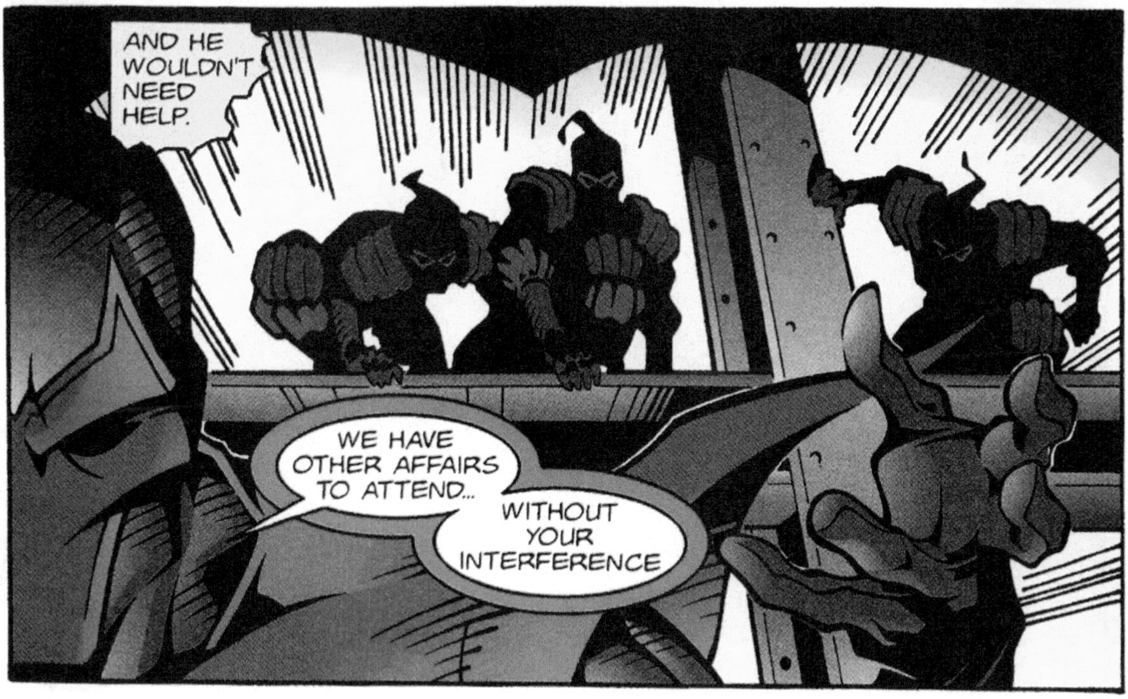
AND HE WOULDN'T NEED HELP.
WE HAVE OTHER AFFAIRS TO ATTEND...
WITHOUT YOUR INTERFERENCE

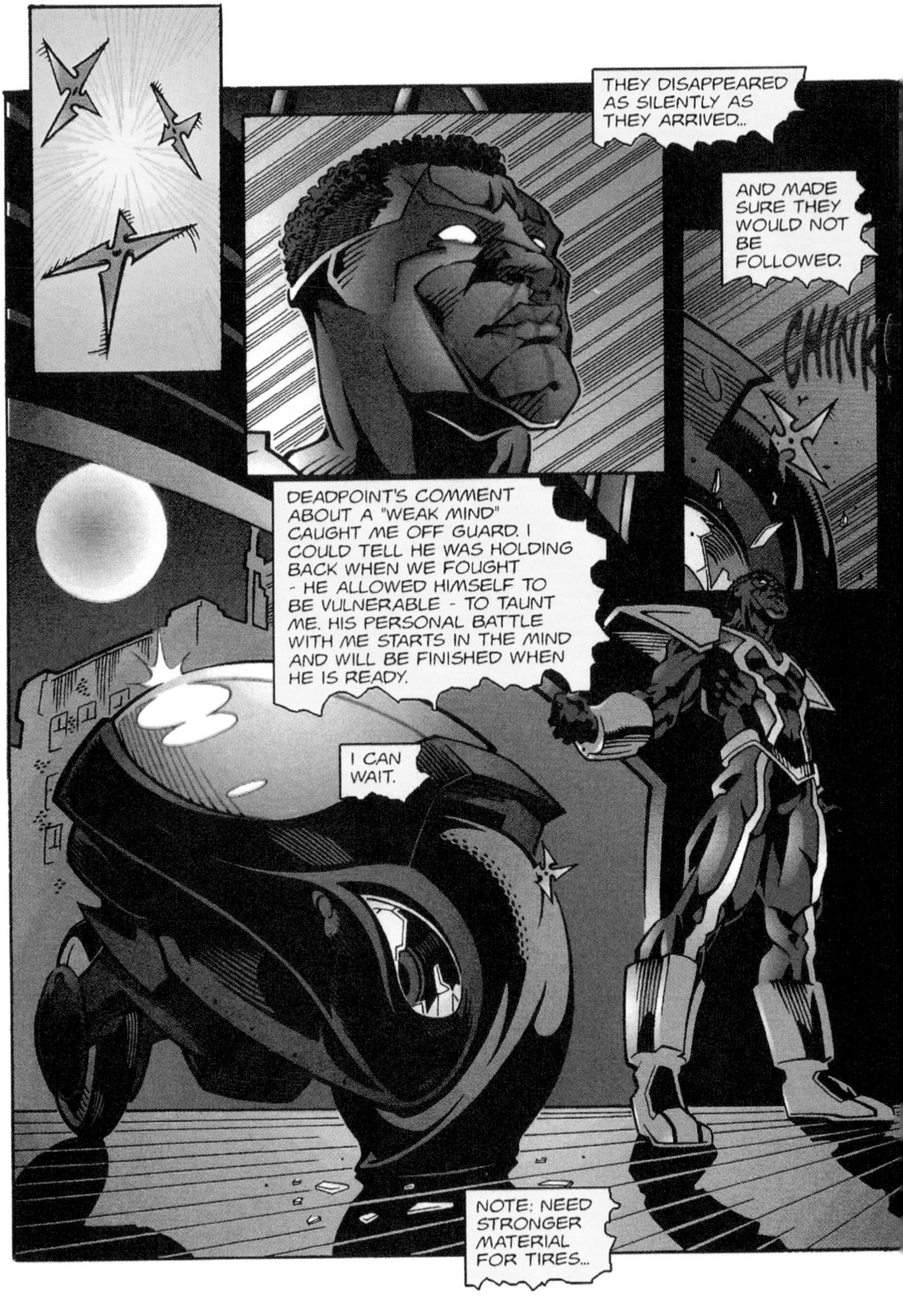
THEY DISAPPEARED AS SILENTLY AS THEY ARRIVED...
AND MADE SURE THEY WOULD NOT BE FOLLOWED.
CHINK
DEADPOINT'S COMMENT ABOUT A "WEAK MIND" CAUGHT ME OFF GUARD. I COULD TELL HE WAS HOLDING BACK WHEN WE FOUGHT - HE ALLOWED HIMSELF TO BE VULNERABLE - TO TAUNT ME. HIS PERSONAL BATTLE WITH ME STARTS IN THE MIND AND WILL BE FINISHED WHEN HE IS READY.
I CAN WAIT.
NOTE: NEED STRONGER MATERIAL FOR TIRES...

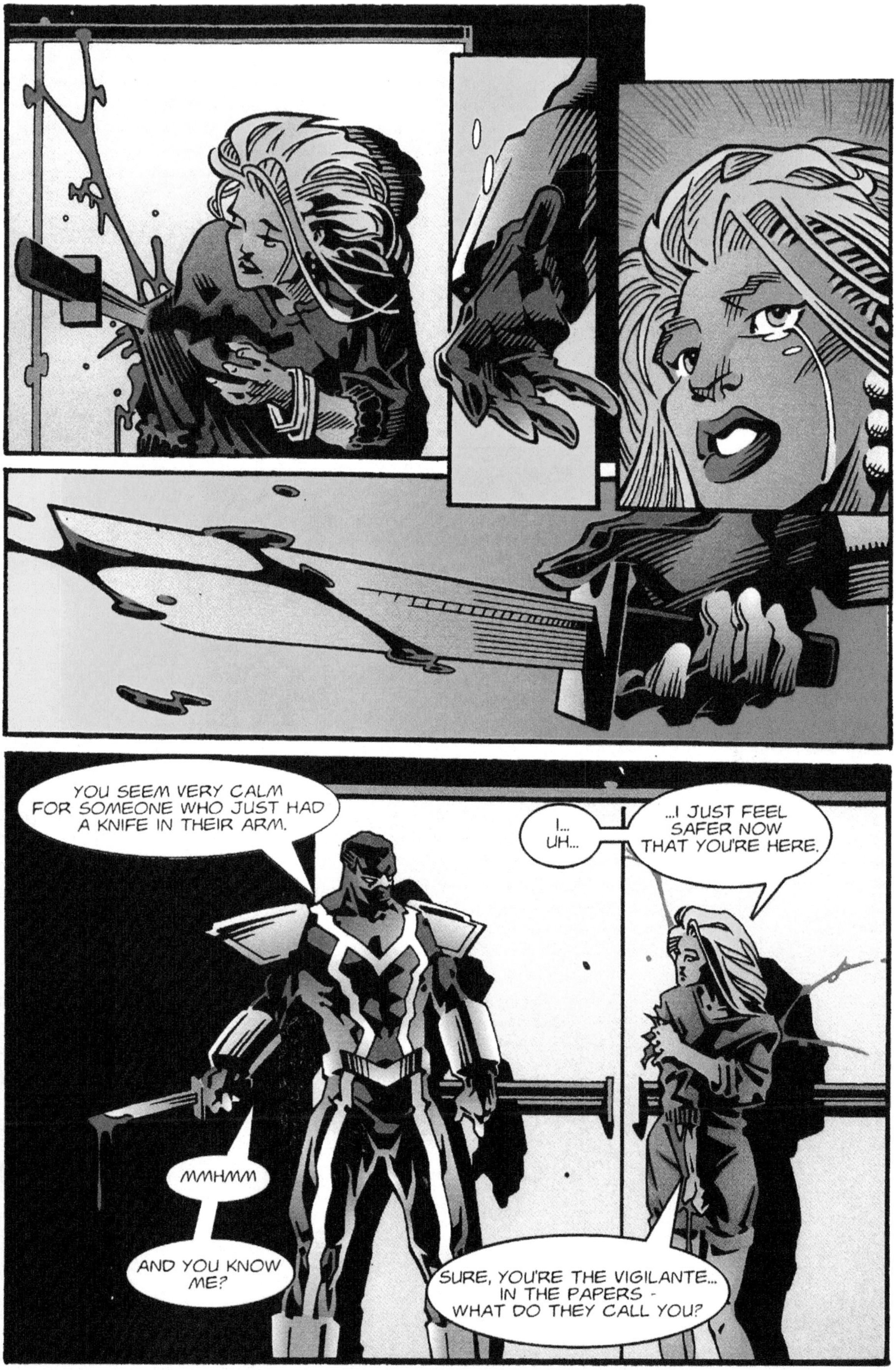
YOU SEEM VERY CALM FOR SOMEONE WHO JUST HAD A KNIFE IN THEIR ARM.
I... UH...
...I JUST FEEL SAFER NOW THAT YOU'RE HERE.
MMHMM
AND YOU KNOW ME?
SURE, YOU'RE THE VIGILANTE... IN THE PAPERS - WHAT DO THEY CALL YOU?

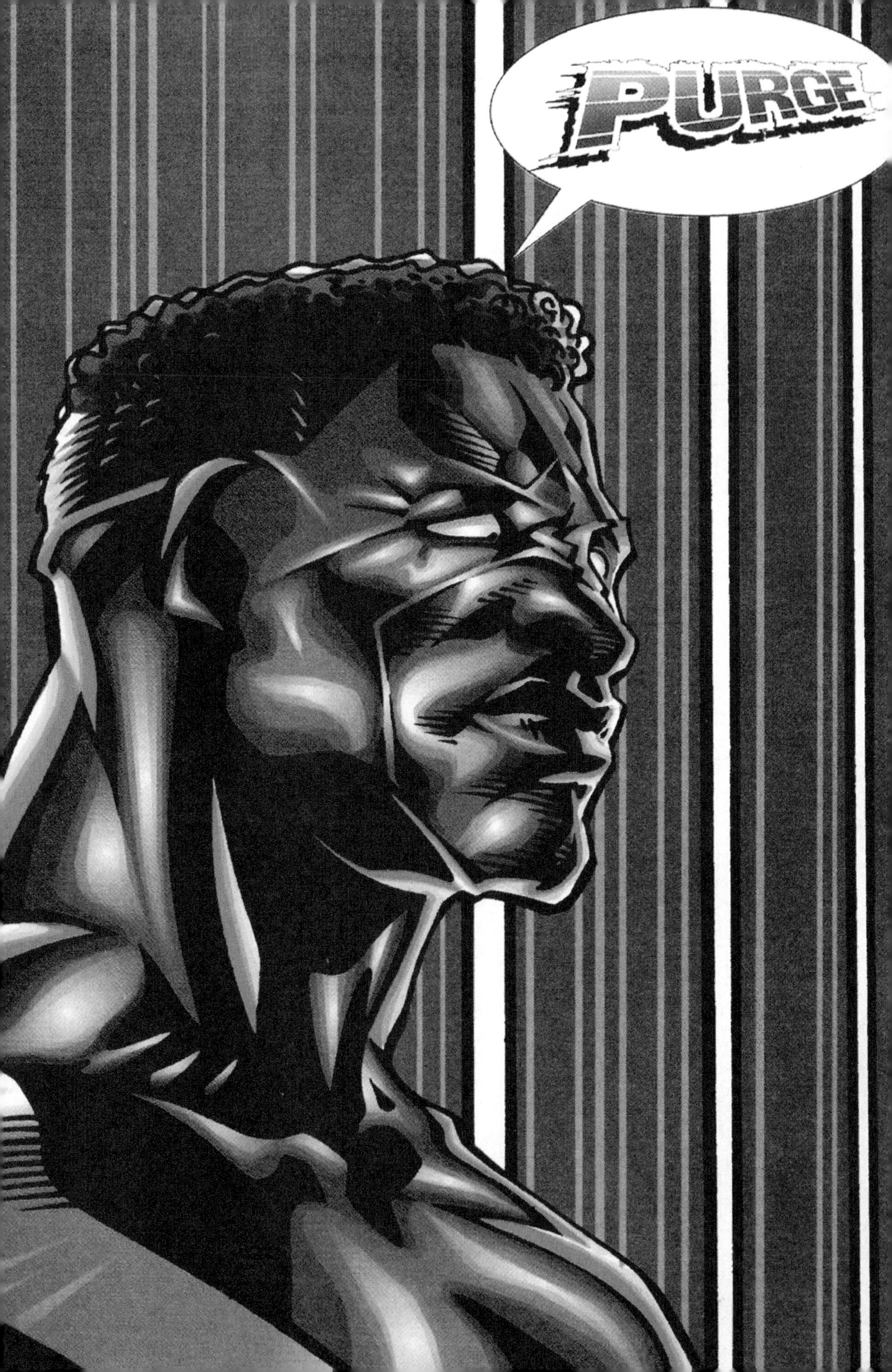
PURGE

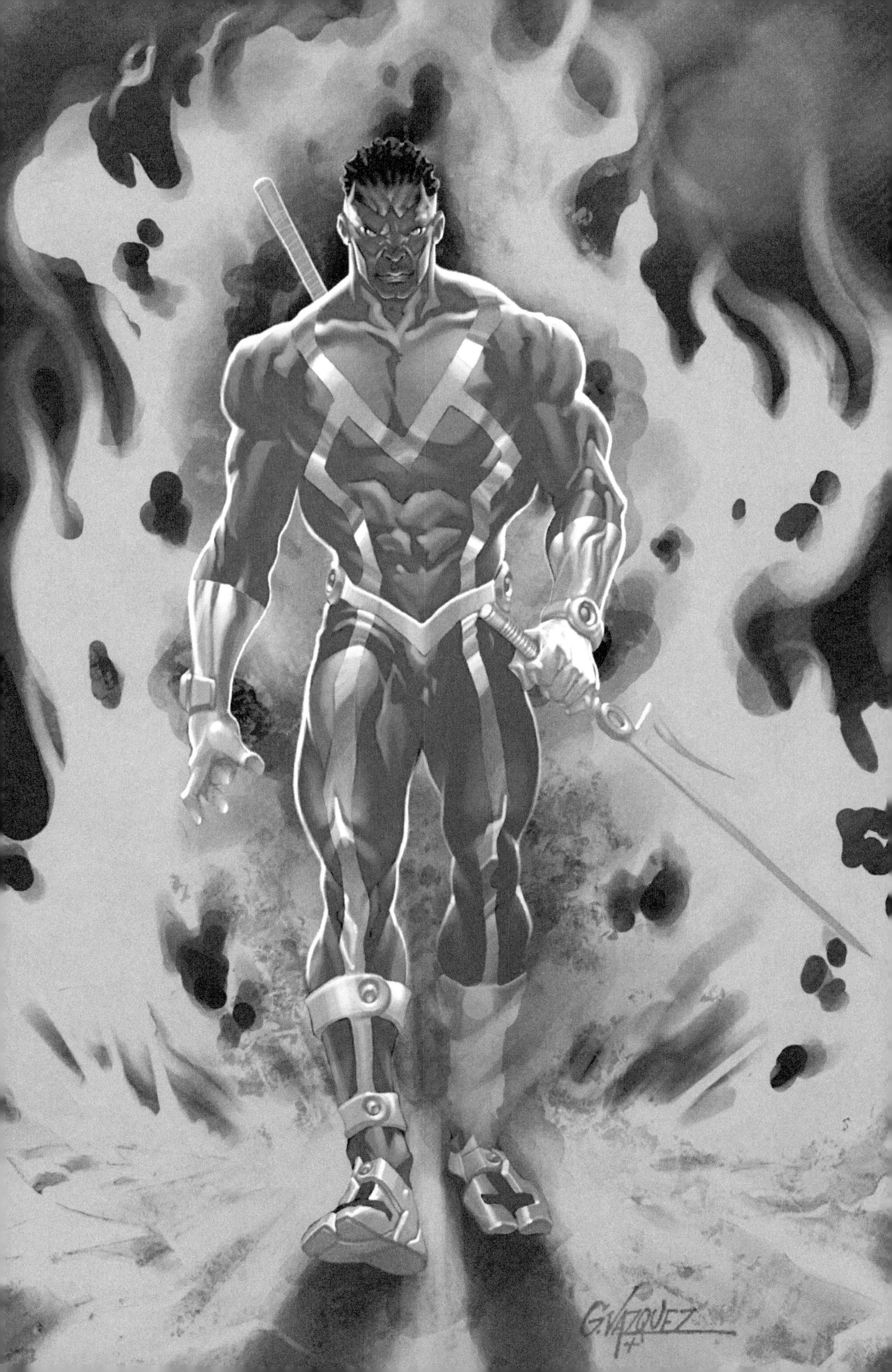
G.VAZQUEZ

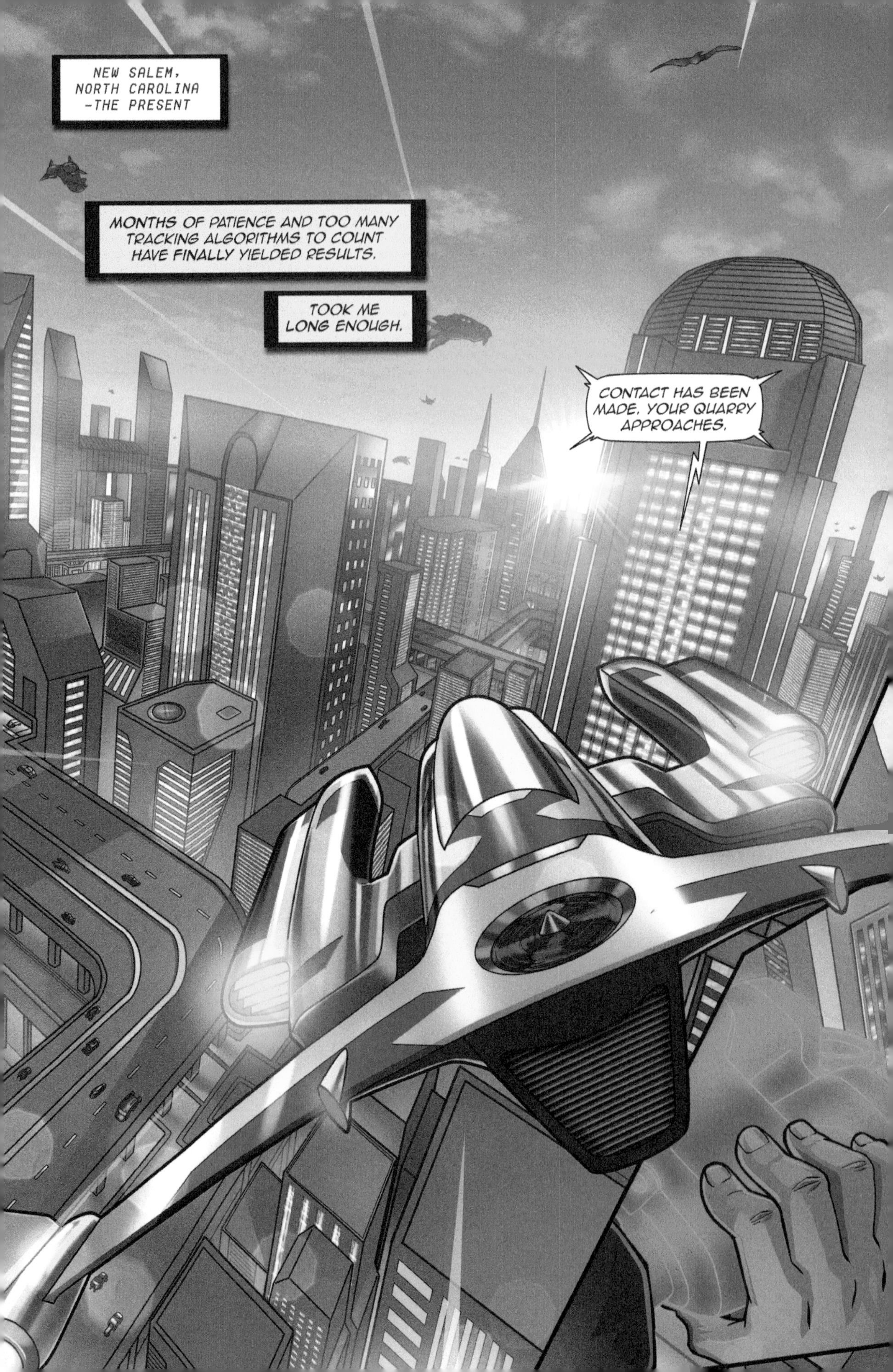
NEW SALEM,
NORTH CAROLINA
-THE PRESENT
MONTHS OF PATIENCE AND TOO MANY TRACKING ALGORITHMS TO COUNT HAVE FINALLY YIELDED RESULTS.
TOOK ME LONG ENOUGH.
CONTACT HAS BEEN MADE. YOUR QUARRY APPROACHES.

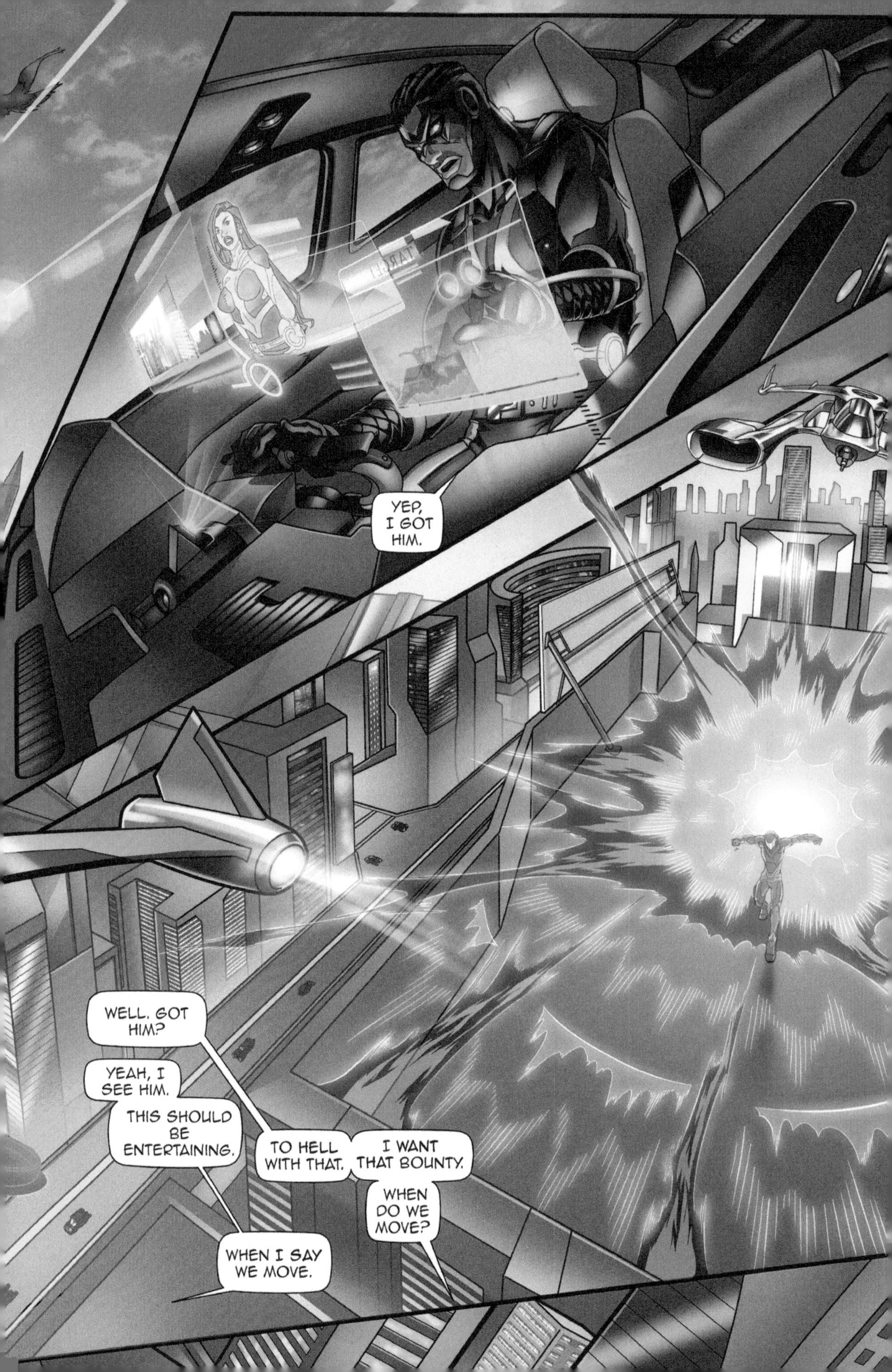
YEP, I GOT HIM.
WELL. GOT HIM?
YEAH, I SEE HIM.
THIS SHOULD BE ENTERTAINING.
TO HELL WITH THAT.
I WANT THAT BOUNTY.
WHEN DO WE MOVE?
WHEN I SAY WE MOVE.

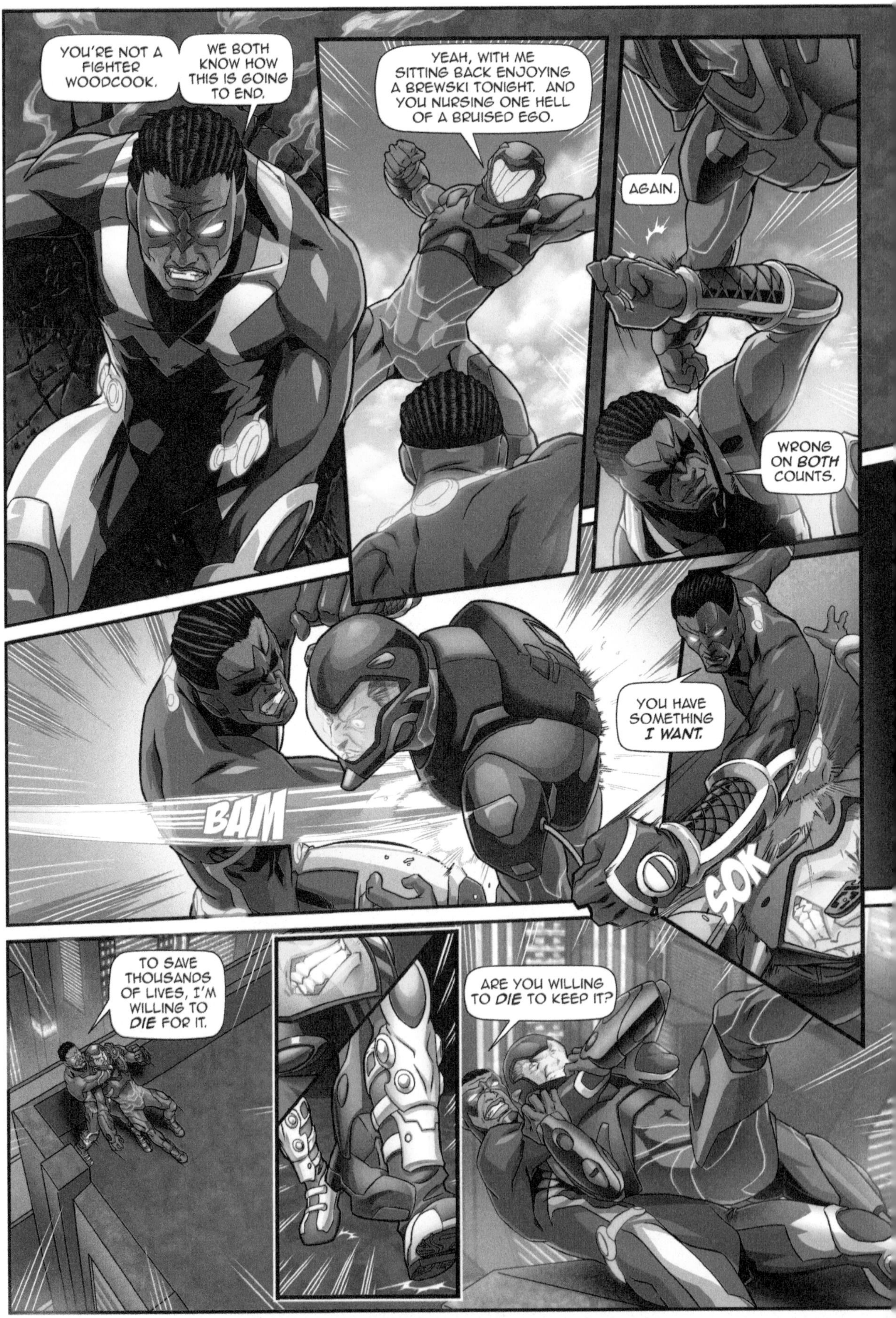
YOU'RE NOT A FIGHTER WOODCOOK.
WE BOTH KNOW HOW THIS IS GOING TO END.
YEAH, WITH ME SITTING BACK ENJOYING A BREWSKI TONIGHT. AND YOU NURSING ONE HELL OF A BRUISED EGO.
AGAIN.
WRONG ON BOTH COUNTS.
BAM
YOU HAVE SOMETHING I WANT.
SOK
TO SAVE THOUSANDS OF LIVES, I'M WILLING TO DIE FOR IT.
ARE YOU WILLING TO DIE TO KEEP IT?

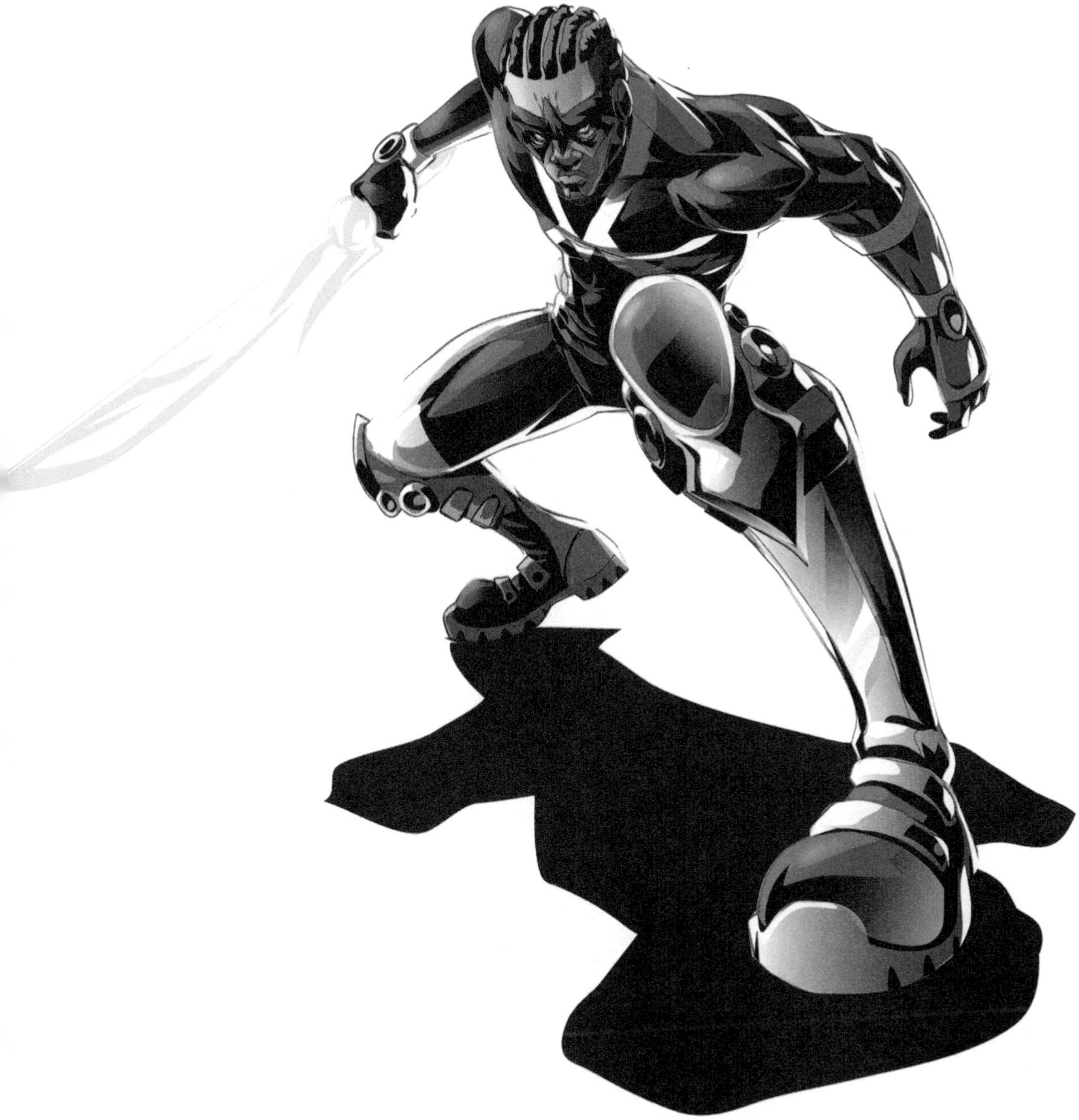

THE SOUNDTRACK OF BLACK SCI-FI

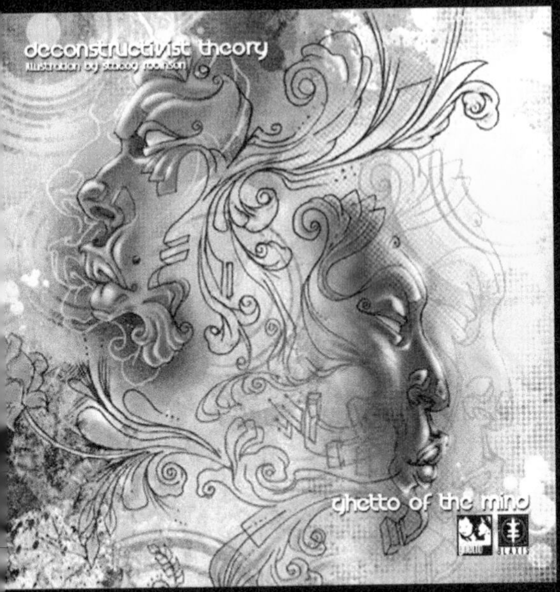
deconstructivist theory
ghetto of the mind

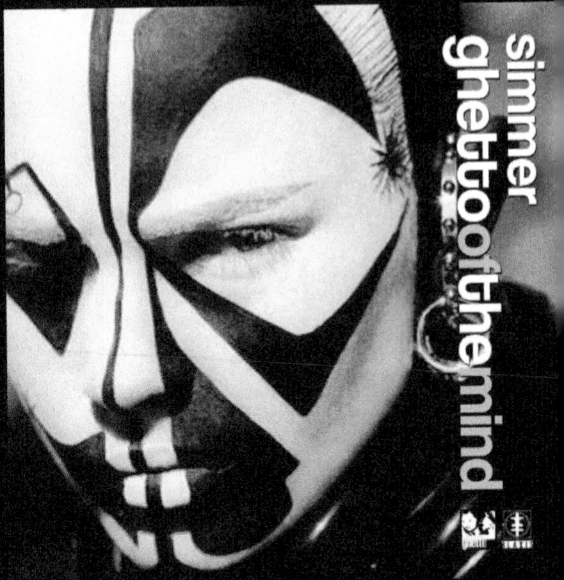
simmer
ghettoofthemind

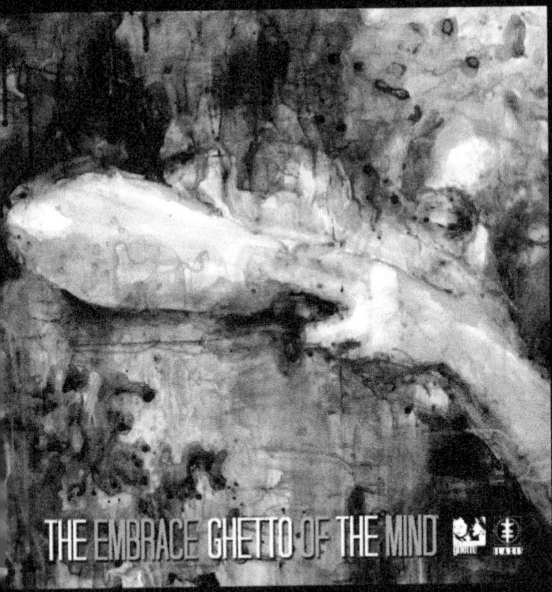
THE EMBRACE GHETTO OF THE MIND

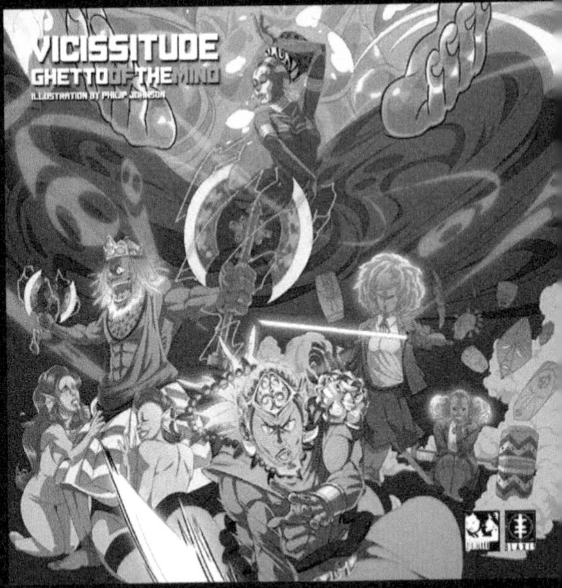
VICISSITUDE
GHETTO OF THE MIND
ILLUSTRATION BY PHILIP JOHNSON

I battle the forces of mediocrity on a daily basis.

I walk the Eightfold Path of righteousness seeking the Universal Truth.

I stand on the rooftop with my barbaric yawp calling to the tribe.

I scream at the top of my lungs to the heavens letting them know that warriors have entered the celestial plane.

I change the world in my own way, with passion, with panache, and with style...

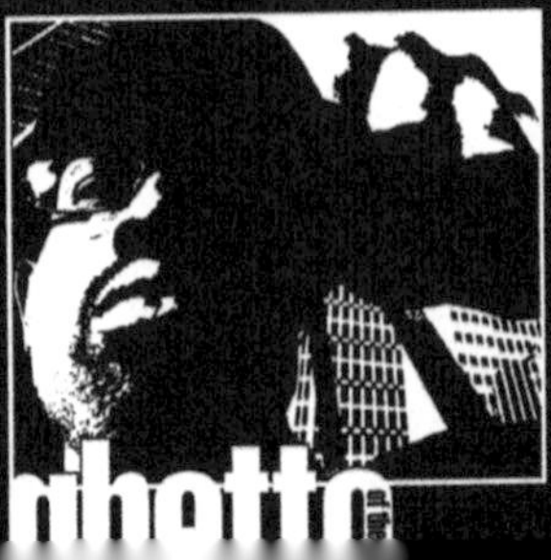

Episodes available now on Itunes

Project: WILDFIRE

IT'S NOT LOST ON ME. WHEN I WAS A KID, I DIDN'T HAVE A LOT OF HEROES THAT LOOKED LIKE ME...

I KNOW THAT FOR A KID JUST LIKE ME, I CAN REPRESENT HOPE.

I CAN MAKE AN IMPACT...

GOTTA GO.

THAT'S NOT LOST ON ME.

PEOPLE NEED HOPE.

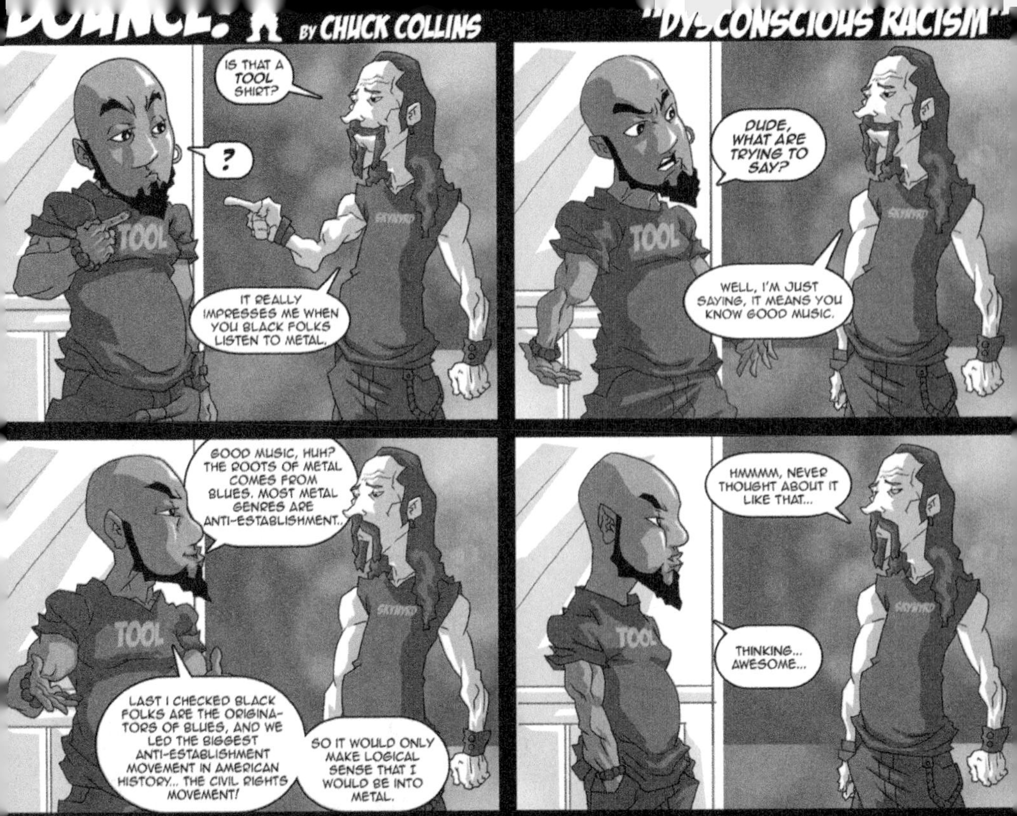
BOUNCE! BY CHUCK COLLINS
"DYSCONSCIOUS RACISM"
IS THAT A TOOL SHIRT?
?
IT REALLY IMPRESSES ME WHEN YOU BLACK FOLKS LISTEN TO METAL.
TOOL
SKYNYRD
DUDE, WHAT ARE TRYING TO SAY?
WELL, I'M JUST SAYING, IT MEANS YOU KNOW GOOD MUSIC.
GOOD MUSIC, HUH? THE ROOTS OF METAL COMES FROM BLUES. MOST METAL GENRES ARE ANTI-ESTABLISHMENT...
LAST I CHECKED BLACK FOLKS ARE THE ORIGINATORS OF BLUES, AND WE LED THE BIGGEST ANTI-ESTABLISHMENT MOVEMENT IN AMERICAN HISTORY... THE CIVIL RIGHTS MOVEMENT!
SO IT WOULD ONLY MAKE LOGICAL SENSE THAT I WOULD BE INTO METAL.
HMMMM, NEVER THOUGHT ABOUT IT LIKE THAT...
THINKING... AWESOME...

08222014CC

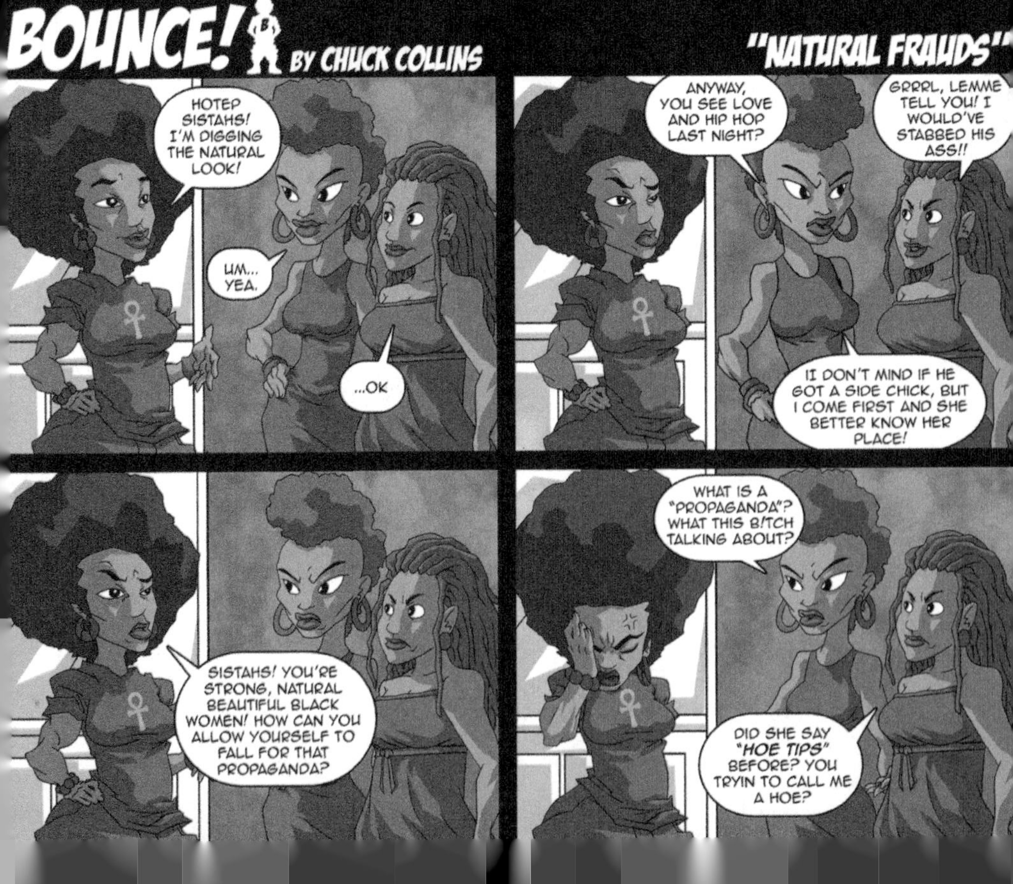
BOUNCE! BY CHUCK COLLINS
"NATURAL FRAUDS"
HOTEP SISTAHS! I'M DIGGING THE NATURAL LOOK!
UM... YEA.
...OK
ANYWAY, YOU SEE LOVE AND HIP HOP LAST NIGHT?
GRRRL, LEMME TELL YOU! I WOULD'VE STABBED HIS ASS!!
I DON'T MIND IF HE GOT A SIDE CHICK, BUT I COME FIRST AND SHE BETTER KNOW HER PLACE!
SISTAHS! YOU'RE STRONG, NATURAL BEAUTIFUL BLACK WOMEN! HOW CAN YOU ALLOW YOURSELF TO FALL FOR THAT PROPAGANDA?
WHAT IS A "PROPAGANDA"? WHAT THIS B!TCH TALKING ABOUT?
DID SHE SAY "HOE TIPS" BEFORE? YOU TRYIN TO CALL ME A HOE?

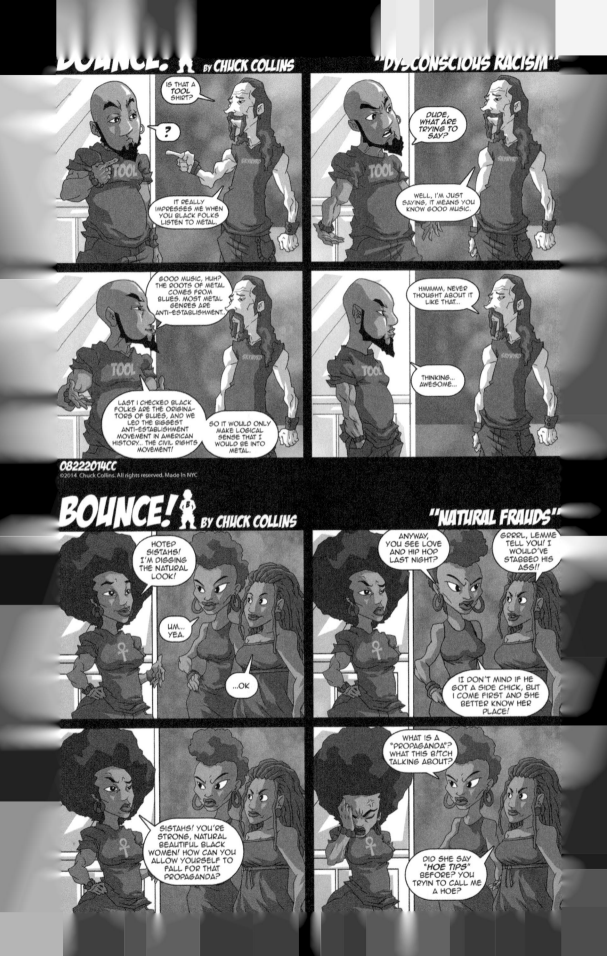

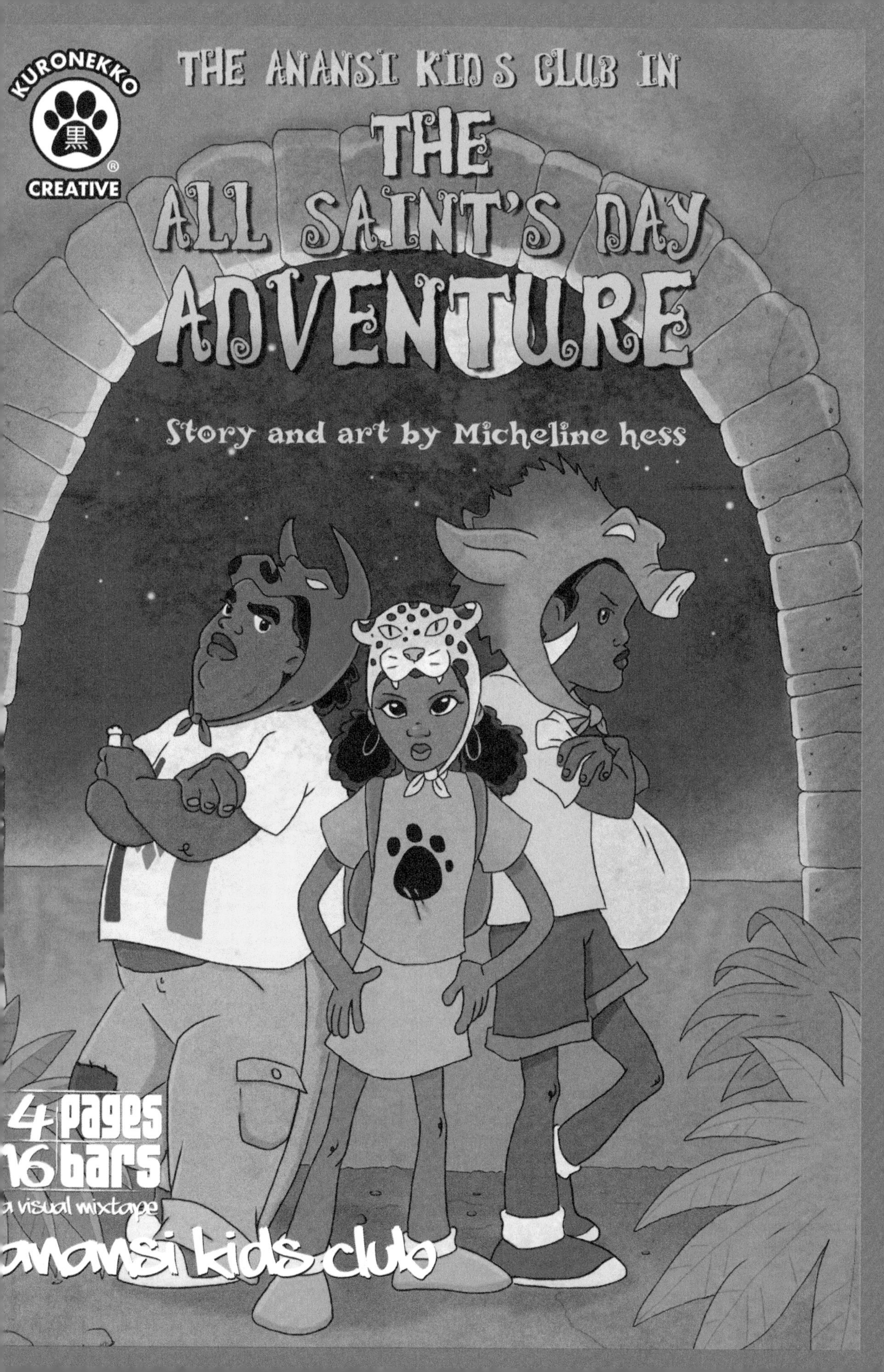
KURONEKKO
CREATIVE
THE ANANSI KID'S CLUB IN
THE ALL SAINT'S DAY ADVENTURE
Story and art by Micheline hess
4 pages 16 bars
a visual mixtape
anansi kids club

Born and raised in NYC, **Micheline Hess** does design at a prominent ad agency in Chelsea and spends her spare time developing graphic novels, short stories, and interactive iBooks for kids. She has always been fascinated by the visual narrative in books and film and is constantly endeavoring to weave her own sense of humorous story-telling into both her personal and sometimes professional work.

Micheline is most adept at creating characters and stories that provide a safe and fun way to inspire young children. Through colorful flights of fun and fancy, she hopes to encourage a stronger sense of self-love, friendship, and a hunger to embrace all things new and different in the world around them which is evident in her creation for *The Anansi Kids Club*.

website: about.me/kuronekko

THE ANANSI KID S CLUB IN

THE ALL SAINT'S DAY ADVENTURE

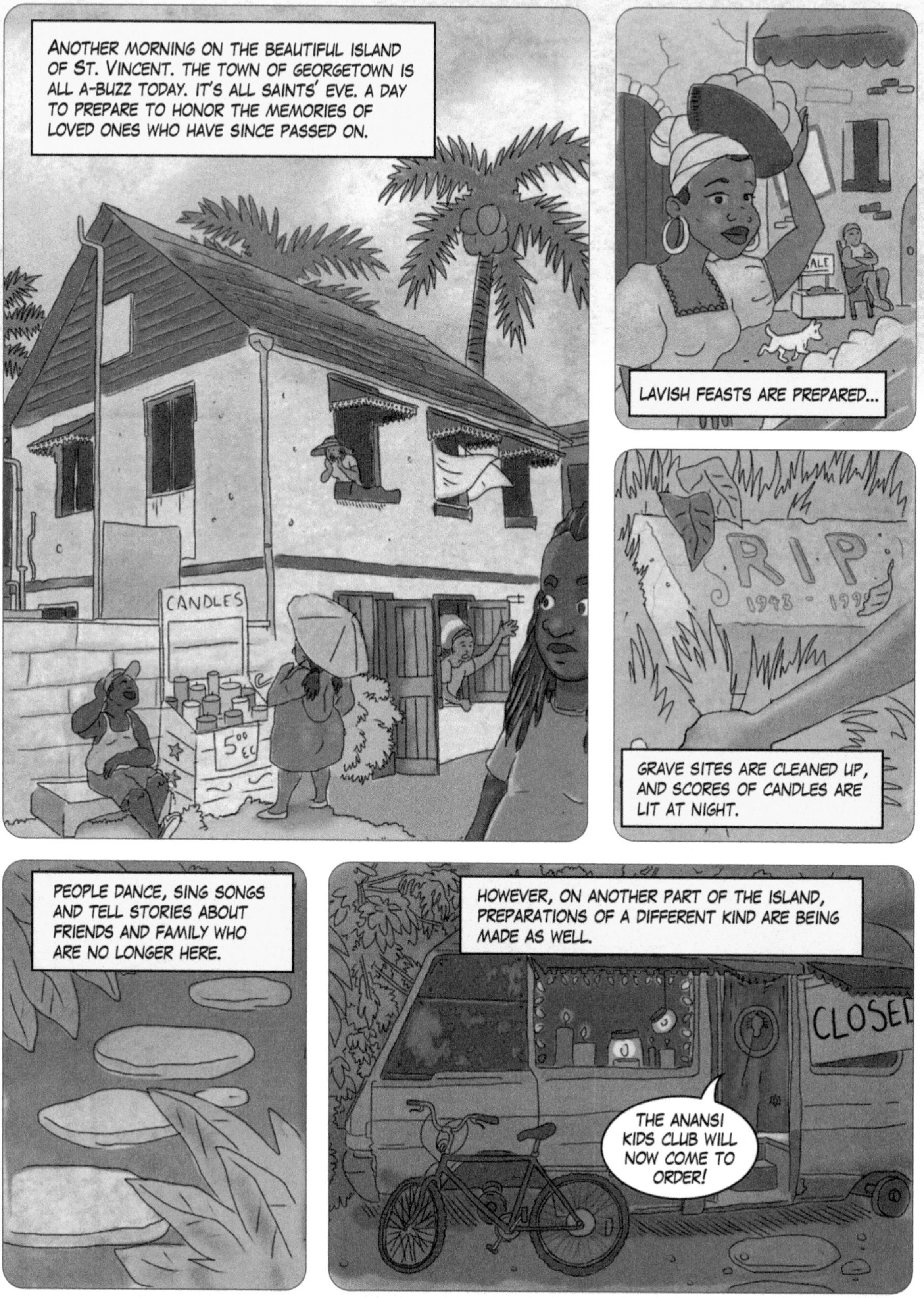
ANOTHER MORNING ON THE BEAUTIFUL ISLAND OF ST. VINCENT. THE TOWN OF GEORGETOWN IS ALL A-BUZZ TODAY. IT'S ALL SAINTS' EVE. A DAY TO PREPARE TO HONOR THE MEMORIES OF LOVED ONES WHO HAVE SINCE PASSED ON.
CANDLES
LAVISH FEASTS ARE PREPARED...
RIP
GRAVE SITES ARE CLEANED UP, AND SCORES OF CANDLES ARE LIT AT NIGHT.
PEOPLE DANCE, SING SONGS AND TELL STORIES ABOUT FRIENDS AND FAMILY WHO ARE NO LONGER HERE.
HOWEVER, ON ANOTHER PART OF THE ISLAND, PREPARATIONS OF A DIFFERENT KIND ARE BEING MADE AS WELL.
CLOSED
THE ANANSI KIDS CLUB WILL NOW COME TO ORDER!

THE ANANSI KID S CLUB IN

THE ALL SAINT'S DAY ADVENTURE

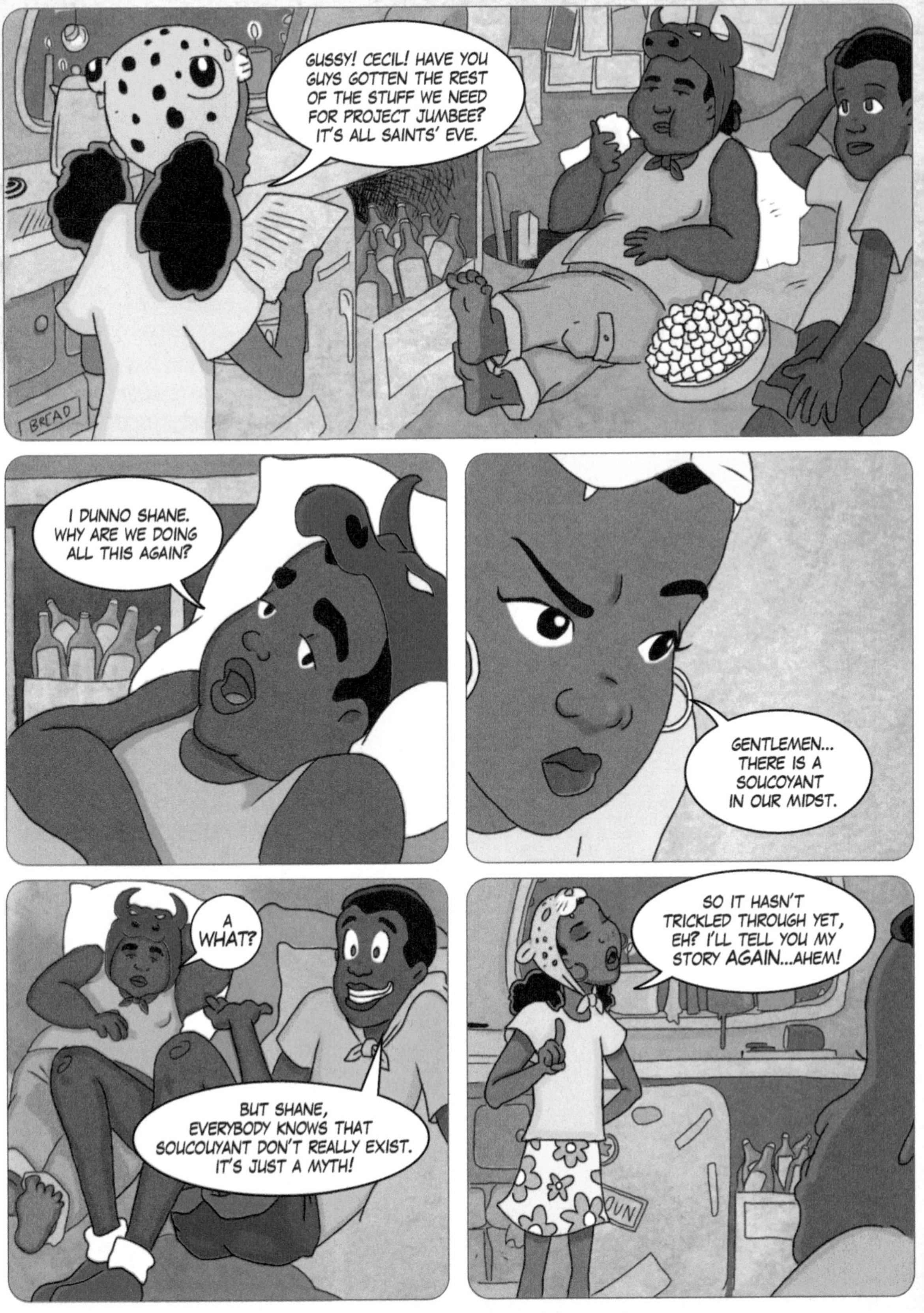

GUSSY! CECIL! HAVE YOU GUYS GOTTEN THE REST OF THE STUFF WE NEED FOR PROJECT JUMBEE? IT'S ALL SAINTS' EVE.
BREAD
I DUNNO SHANE. WHY ARE WE DOING ALL THIS AGAIN?
GENTLEMEN... THERE IS A SOUCOYANT IN OUR MIDST.
A WHAT?
BUT SHANE, EVERYBODY KNOWS THAT SOUCOUYANT DON'T REALLY EXIST. IT'S JUST A MYTH!
SO IT HASN'T TRICKLED THROUGH YET, EH? I'LL TELL YOU MY STORY AGAIN...AHEM!

THE ANANSI KIDS CLUB IN

THE ALL SAINT'S DAY ADVENTURE

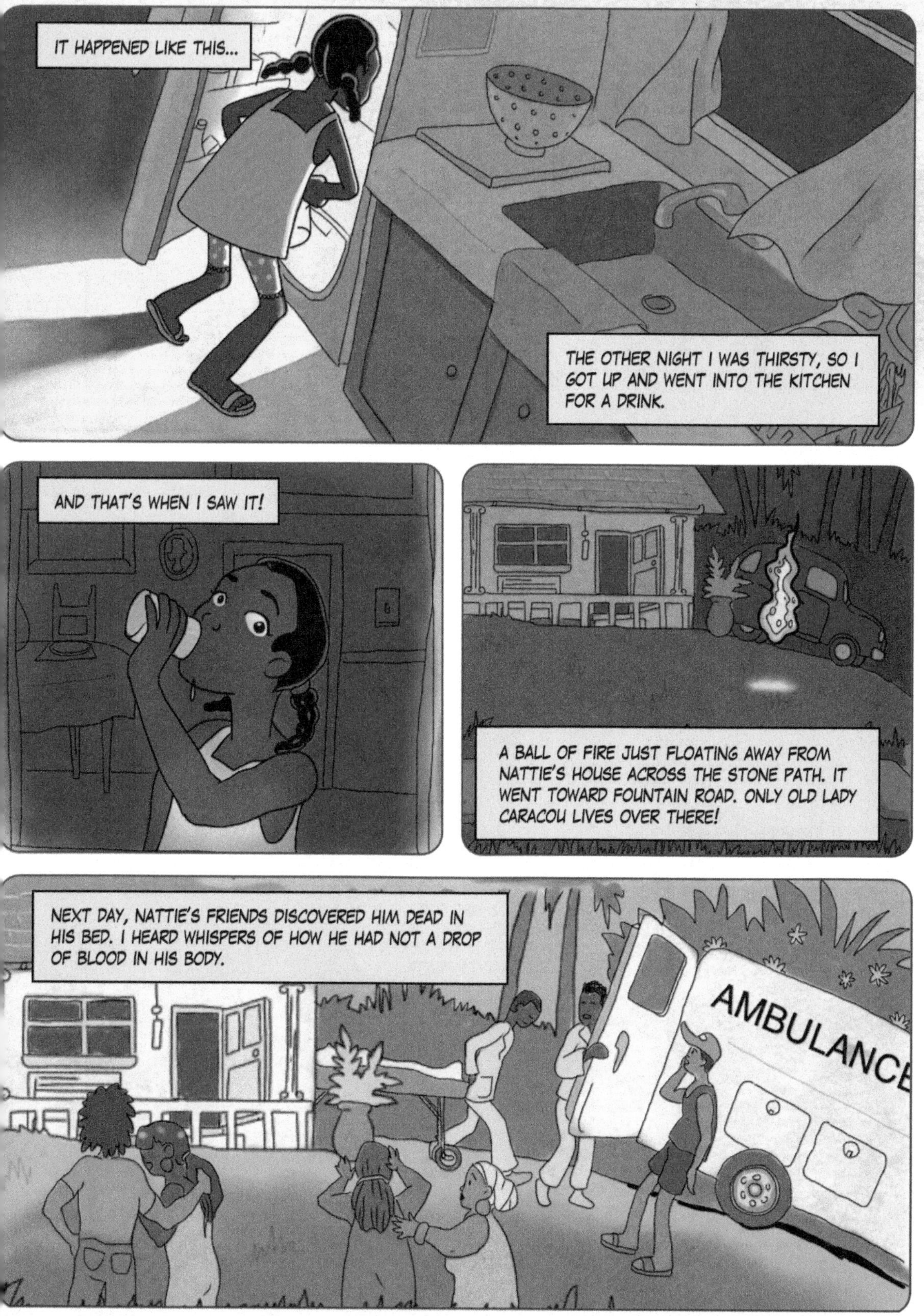

IT HAPPENED LIKE THIS...
THE OTHER NIGHT I WAS THIRSTY, SO I GOT UP AND WENT INTO THE KITCHEN FOR A DRINK.
AND THAT'S WHEN I SAW IT!
A BALL OF FIRE JUST FLOATING AWAY FROM NATTIE'S HOUSE ACROSS THE STONE PATH. IT WENT TOWARD FOUNTAIN ROAD. ONLY OLD LADY CARACOU LIVES OVER THERE!
NEXT DAY, NATTIE'S FRIENDS DISCOVERED HIM DEAD IN HIS BED. I HEARD WHISPERS OF HOW HE HAD NOT A DROP OF BLOOD IN HIS BODY.
AMBULANCE

THE ANANSI KIDS CLUB IN

THE ALL SAINT'S DAY ADVENTURE

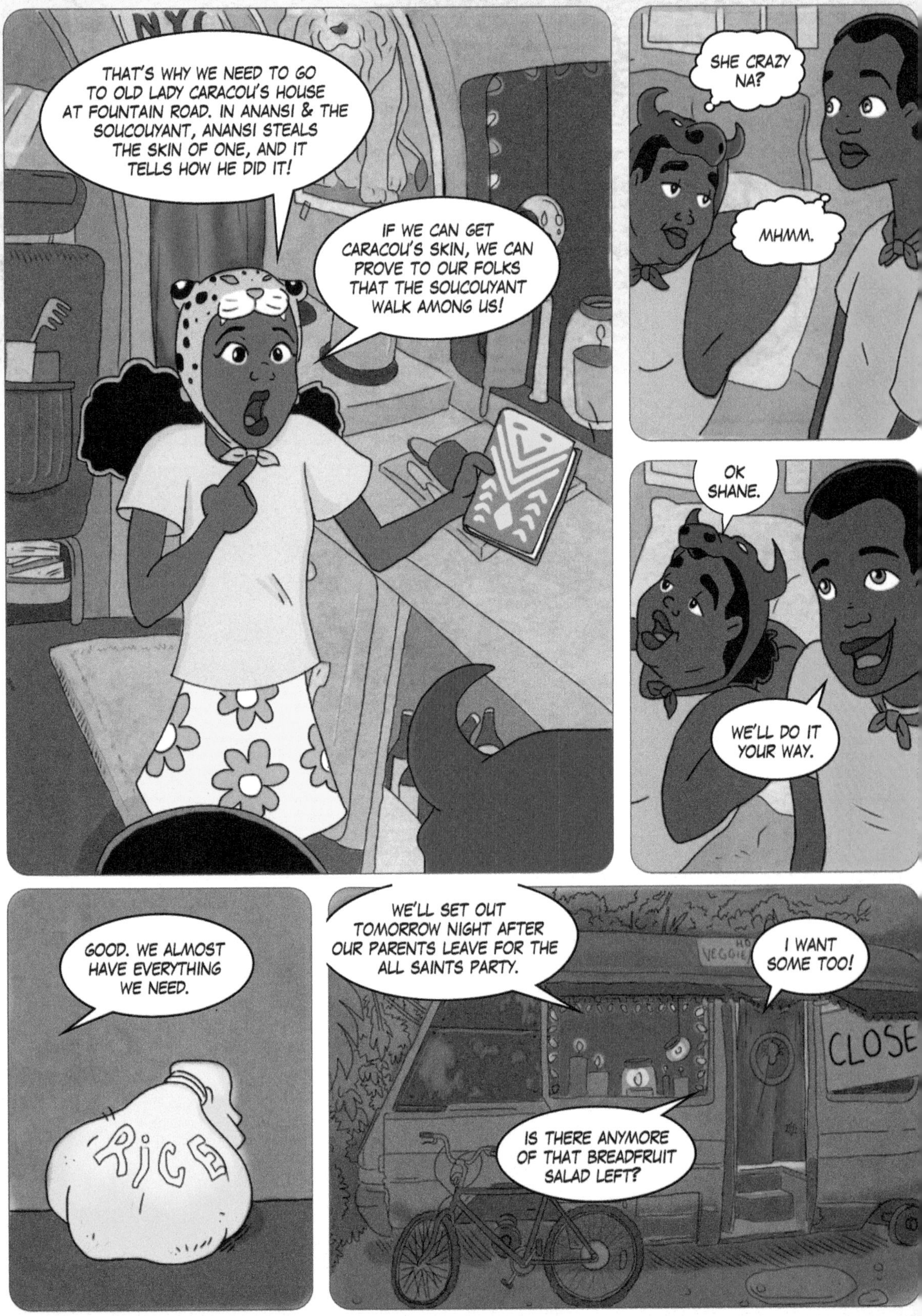
NYC
THAT'S WHY WE NEED TO GO TO OLD LADY CARACOU'S HOUSE AT FOUNTAIN ROAD. IN ANANSI & THE SOUCOUYANT, ANANSI STEALS THE SKIN OF ONE, AND IT TELLS HOW HE DID IT!
IF WE CAN GET CARACOU'S SKIN, WE CAN PROVE TO OUR FOLKS THAT THE SOUCOUYANT WALK AMONG US!
SHE CRAZY NA?
MHMM.
OK SHANE.
WE'LL DO IT YOUR WAY.
GOOD. WE ALMOST HAVE EVERYTHING WE NEED.
RICE
WE'LL SET OUT TOMORROW NIGHT AFTER OUR PARENTS LEAVE FOR THE ALL SAINTS PARTY.
I WANT SOME TOO!
VEGGIE
CLOSE
IS THERE ANYMORE OF THAT BREADFRUIT SALAD LEFT?

THE ANANSI KID'S CLUB IN

THE ALL SAINT'S DAY ADVENTURE

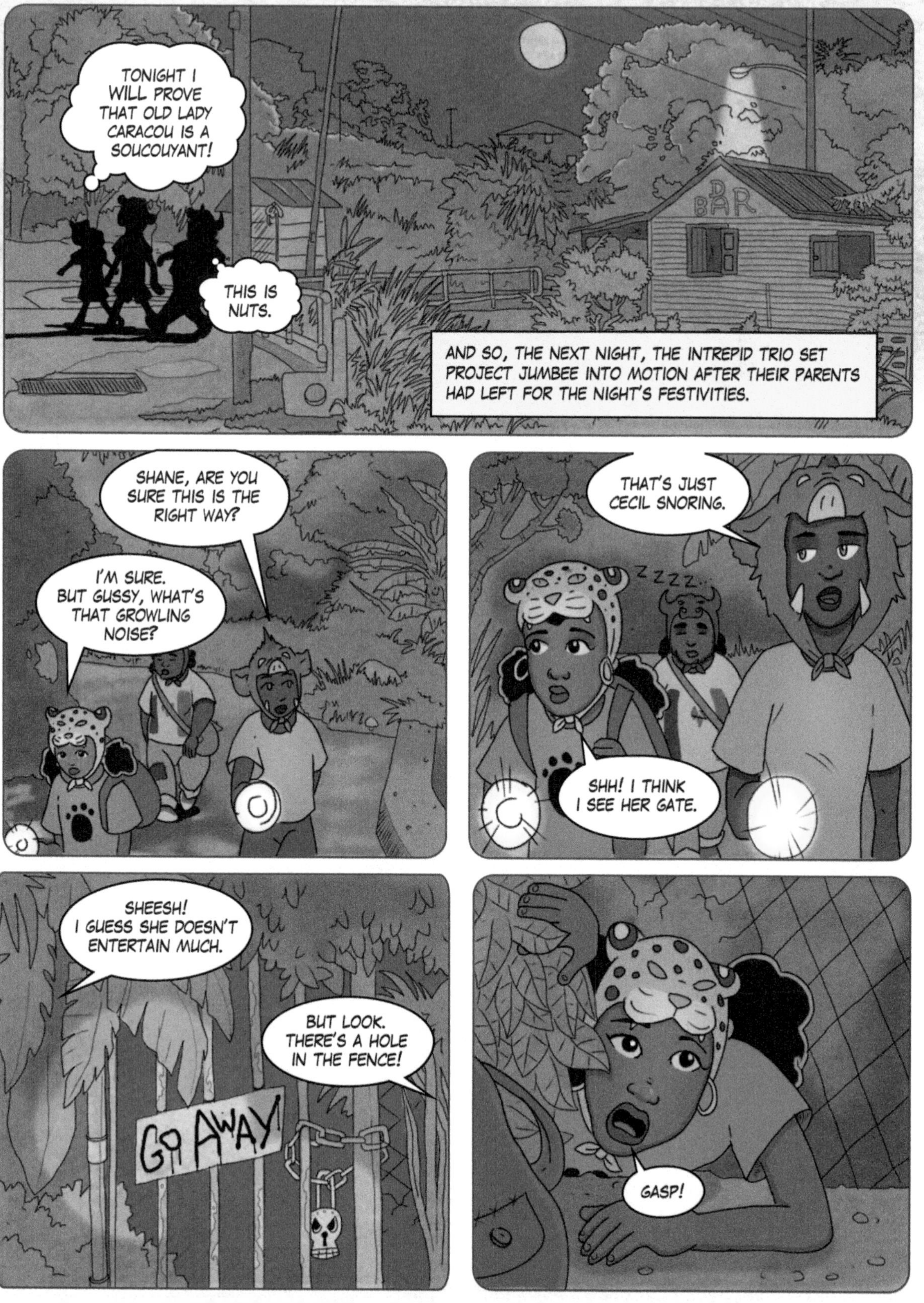

TONIGHT I WILL PROVE THAT OLD LADY CARACOU IS A SOUCOUYANT!
THIS IS NUTS.
BAR
AND SO, THE NEXT NIGHT, THE INTREPID TRIO SET PROJECT JUMBEE INTO MOTION AFTER THEIR PARENTS HAD LEFT FOR THE NIGHT'S FESTIVITIES.
SHANE, ARE YOU SURE THIS IS THE RIGHT WAY?
I'M SURE. BUT GUSSY, WHAT'S THAT GROWLING NOISE?
THAT'S JUST CECIL SNORING.
ZZZZ
SHH! I THINK I SEE HER GATE.
SHEESH! I GUESS SHE DOESN'T ENTERTAIN MUCH.
BUT LOOK. THERE'S A HOLE IN THE FENCE!
GO AWAY
GASP!

THE ANANSI KID'S CLUB IN

THE ALL SAINT'S DAY ADVENTURE

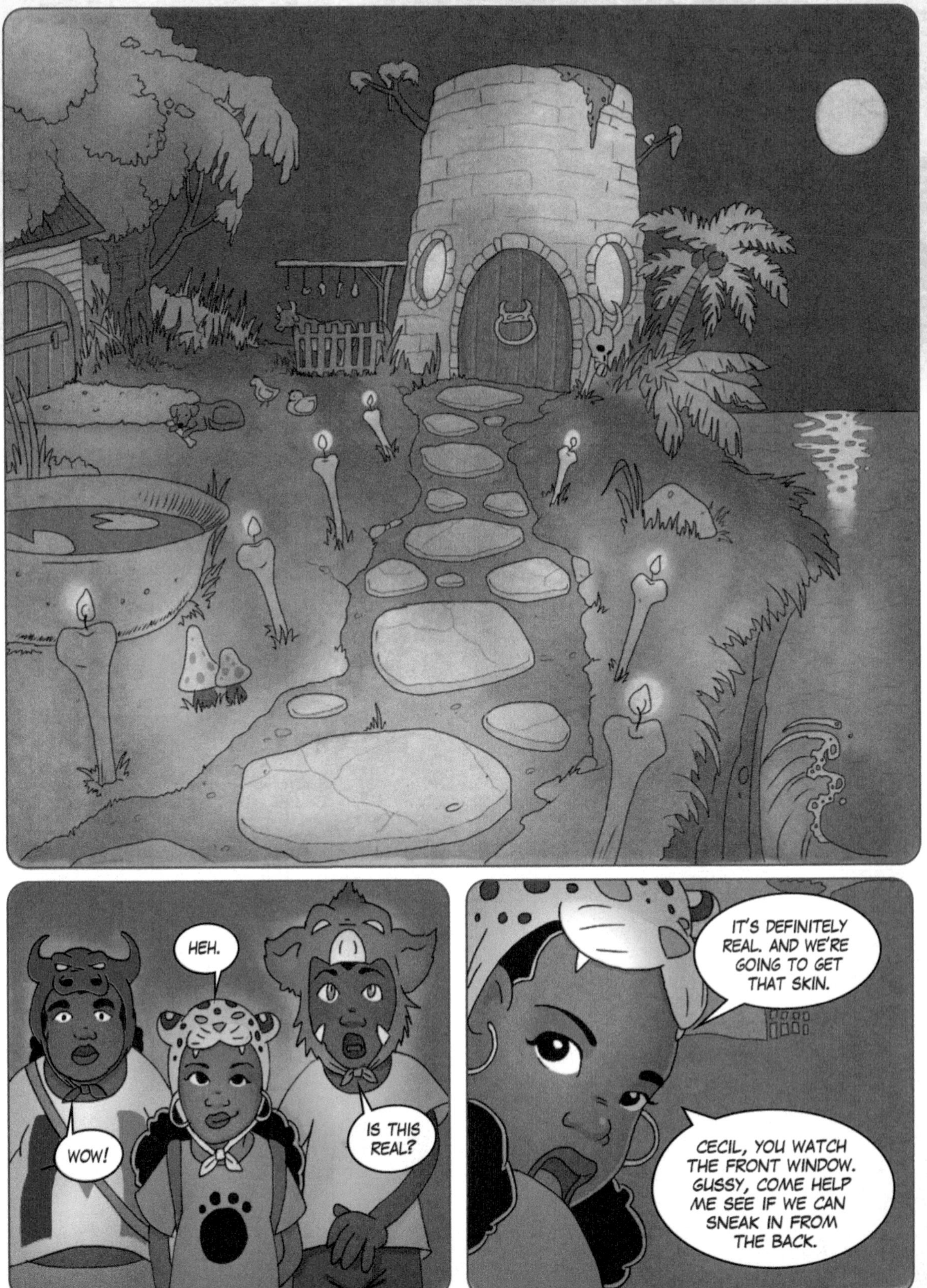
HEH.
WOW!
IS THIS REAL?
IT'S DEFINITELY REAL. AND WE'RE GOING TO GET THAT SKIN.
CECIL, YOU WATCH THE FRONT WINDOW. GUSSY, COME HELP ME SEE IF WE CAN SNEAK IN FROM THE BACK.

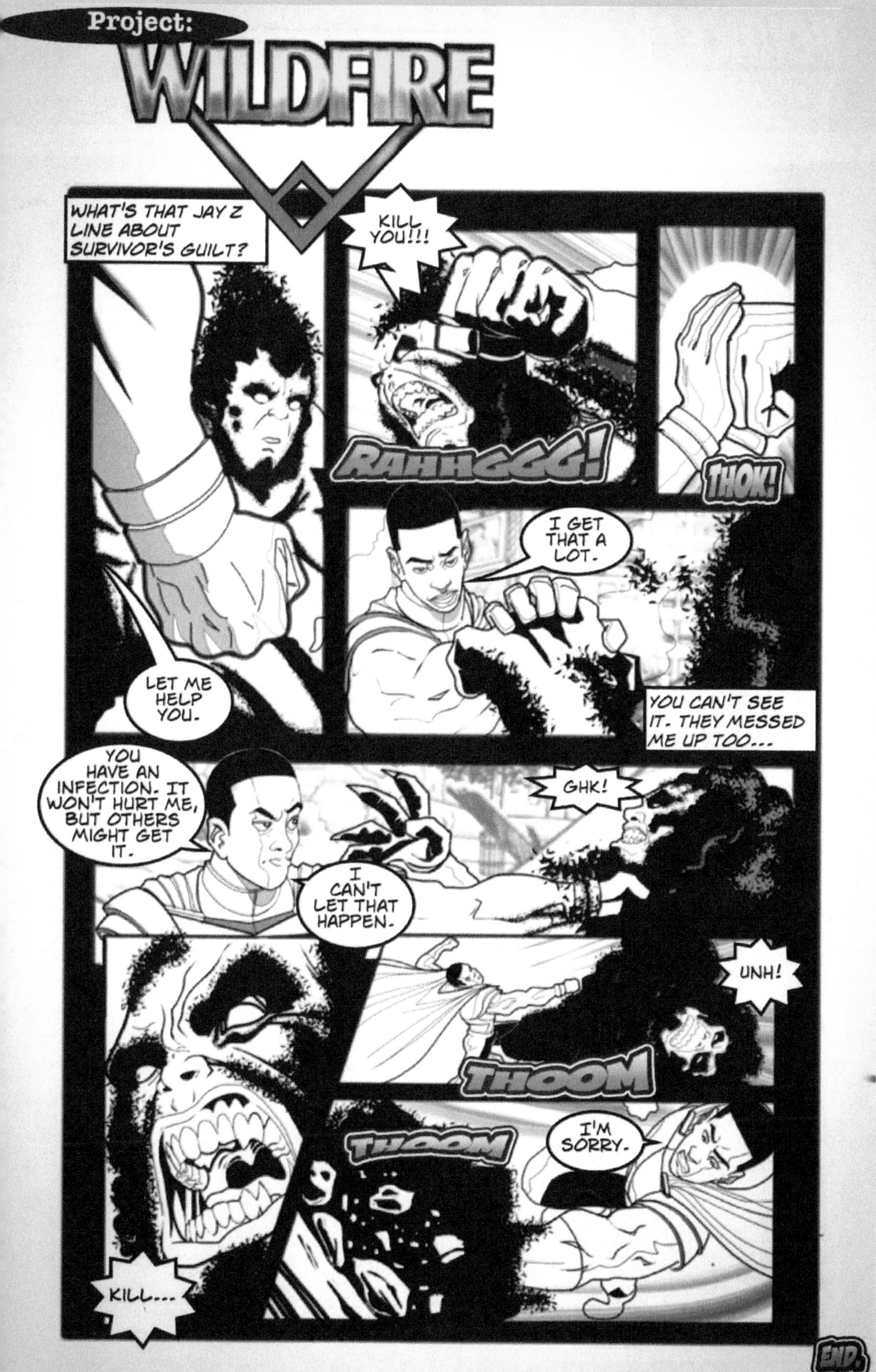
Project:
WILDFIRE
WHAT'S THAT JAY Z LINE ABOUT SURVIVOR'S GUILT?
KILL YOU!!!
RAHHGGG!
THOK!
I GET THAT A LOT.
LET ME HELP YOU.
YOU CAN'T SEE IT. THEY MESSED ME UP TOO...
YOU HAVE AN INFECTION. IT WON'T HURT ME, BUT OTHERS MIGHT GET IT.
GHK!
I CAN'T LET THAT HAPPEN.
UNH!
THOOM
THOOM
I'M SORRY.
KILL...
END.

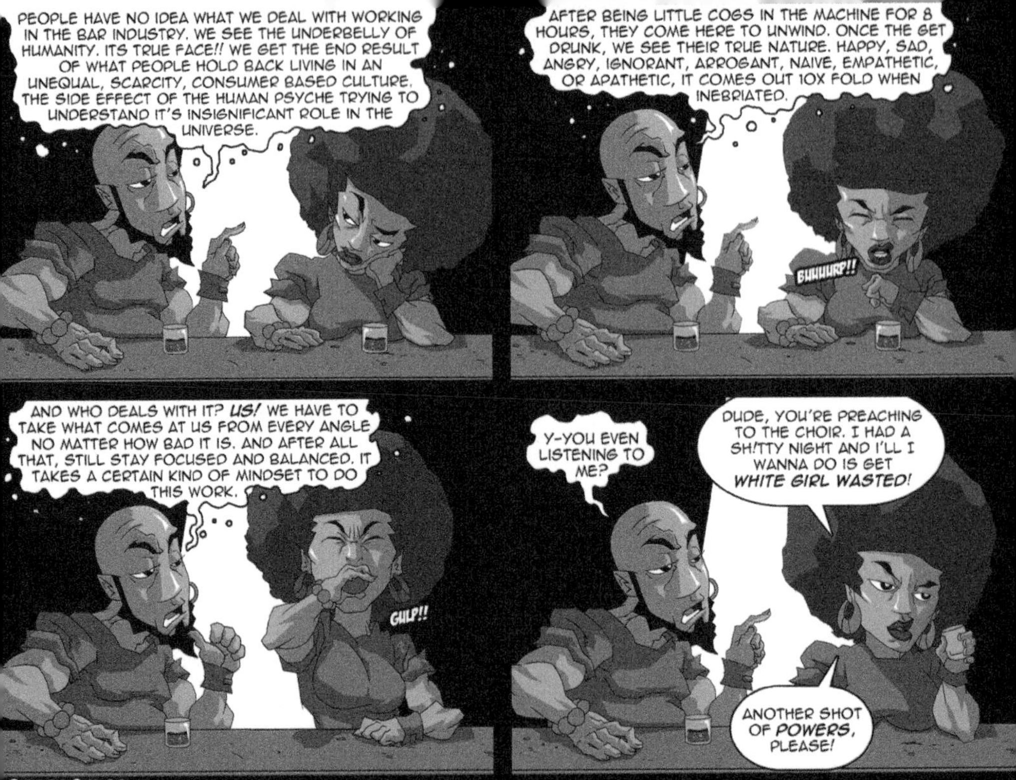
PEOPLE HAVE NO IDEA WHAT WE DEAL WITH WORKING IN THE BAR INDUSTRY. WE SEE THE UNDERBELLY OF HUMANITY. ITS TRUE FACE!! WE GET THE END RESULT OF WHAT PEOPLE HOLD BACK LIVING IN AN UNEQUAL, SCARCITY, CONSUMER BASED CULTURE. THE SIDE EFFECT OF THE HUMAN PSYCHE TRYING TO UNDERSTAND IT'S INSIGNIFICANT ROLE IN THE UNIVERSE.
AFTER BEING LITTLE COGS IN THE MACHINE FOR 8 HOURS, THEY COME HERE TO UNWIND. ONCE THE GET DRUNK, WE SEE THEIR TRUE NATURE. HAPPY, SAD, ANGRY, IGNORANT, ARROGANT, NAIVE, EMPATHETIC, OR APATHETIC, IT COMES OUT 10X FOLD WHEN INEBRIATED.
BUHHURP!!
AND WHO DEALS WITH IT? US! WE HAVE TO TAKE WHAT COMES AT US FROM EVERY ANGLE NO MATTER HOW BAD IT IS. AND AFTER ALL THAT, STILL STAY FOCUSED AND BALANCED. IT TAKES A CERTAIN KIND OF MINDSET TO DO THIS WORK.
GULP!!
Y-YOU EVEN LISTENING TO ME?
DUDE, YOU'RE PREACHING TO THE CHOIR. I HAD A SH!TTY NIGHT AND I'LL I WANNA DO IS GET WHITE GIRL WASTED!
ANOTHER SHOT OF POWERS, PLEASE!

09192014CC

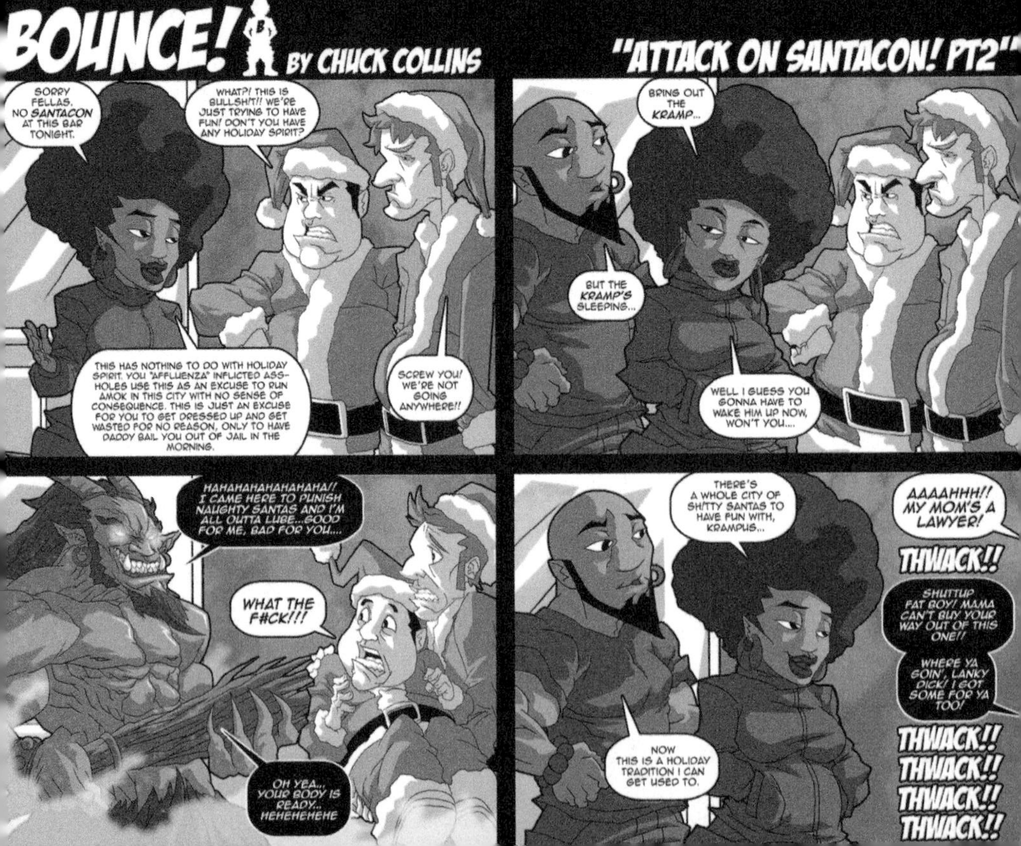
BOUNCE! BY CHUCK COLLINS
"ATTACK ON SANTACON! PT2"
SORRY FELLAS. NO SANTACON AT THIS BAR TONIGHT.
WHAT?! THIS IS BULLSH!T!! WE'RE JUST TRYING TO HAVE FUN! DON'T YOU HAVE ANY HOLIDAY SPIRIT?
THIS HAS NOTHING TO DO WITH HOLIDAY SPIRIT. YOU "AFFLUENZA" INFLICTED ASS-HOLES USE THIS AS AN EXCUSE TO RUN AMOK IN THIS CITY WITH NO SENSE OF CONSEQUENCE. THIS IS JUST AN EXCUSE FOR YOU TO GET DRESSED UP AND GET WASTED FOR NO REASON, ONLY TO HAVE DADDY BAIL YOU OUT OF JAIL IN THE MORNING.
SCREW YOU! WE'RE NOT GOING ANYWHERE!!
BRING OUT THE KRAMP...
BUT THE KRAMP'S SLEEPING...
WELL I GUESS YOU GONNA HAVE TO WAKE HIM UP NOW, WON'T YOU....
HAHAHAHAHAHAHAHAHA!! I CAME HERE TO PUNISH NAUGHTY SANTAS AND I'M ALL OUTTA LUBE...GOOD FOR ME, BAD FOR YOU....
WHAT THE F#CK!!!
OH YEA... YOUR BODY IS READY... HEHEHEHEHE
THERE'S A WHOLE CITY OF SH!TTY SANTAS TO HAVE FUN WITH, KRAMPUS...
NOW THIS IS A HOLIDAY TRADITION I CAN GET USED TO.
AAAAHHH!! MY MOM'S A LAWYER!
THWACK!!
SHUTTUP FAT BOY! MAMA CAN'T BUY YOUR WAY OUT OF THIS ONE!!
WHERE YA GOIN', LANKY DICK! I GOT SOME FOR YA TOO!
THWACK!!
THWACK!!
THWACK!!
THWACK!!

from the throne

BY MAIA "CROWN" WILLIAMS

Peace, everyone. My name is **Maia "Crown" Williams**. I have been organizing comic book conventions, give or take, for 5 years in the city of Detroit. I first started out by working with a smaller local Convention in the area, before finally having the courage to branch off in 2013 with organizing my very own, **Midwest Ethnic Convention for Comics and Arts**, aka **MECCA Con**.

Through these years, I have worked side by side with some of the most amazing writers, artists, publishers, organizers, and collectors. More importantly, I have given back to the children of my community. It can be a struggle, yes. It is also a huge blessing. There is nothing better than seeing the smiles on children who experience holding a comic book with characters that look like them for the first time in their lives. It is one of the most empowering feelings one could ever have.

More often than not, the subject of diversity in comics has been the talk of the town as of late. At first, I was one of the main ones going all extra, lol. It moved me to see so many in the industry are so passionate about being included. I felt that specifically my **Black** people deserve to be seen **and** heard, read **and** watched, writing **and** owning.

I soon learned how quickly that high could come down. It was such a subconscious high, that it almost seemed artificial. More *ecstasy* than *kush*, if one must be figurative. I started to pay **closer** attention to what many in the industry were actually saying, and slowly began to detest what I was hearing. I started to realize that people were complaining more about not having enough "people of color" in Marvel or DC, and I found that to be a tad bit puerile.

My main problem with this subject is the fact that instead of people focusing on why this can't be this and that, why can't those same people focus on creating our **own**? There is absolutely nothing wrong with supporting or working with mainstream companies. I have many comrades that do it, and do it successfully. I even support a few, especially **David Walker**, **Khary Randolph**, and **Sanford Greene**. If *Shaft* were on Marvel, I'd be the biggest Marvel fan out here, **trust** me, lol. I support independent comics first and foremost, but I have never been silly enough to completely shut down the mainstream.

ILLUSTRATIONS BY JASON REEVES

So many times I see people saying what we need, when in actuality, we already *have*. Facebook group pages like **Comic Nerds Of Color**, **LeSean Thomas**, **Black Science Fiction Society**, **State Of Black Science Fiction**, **Tribble Nation**, and **Geek Mode** will prove that there is an abundance of POC comic books, artists, and writers out here. Just because you don't know about them, it doesn't mean they do not exist.

POC comic cons are also necessary in getting our work out there to the public. While I enjoy mainstream conventions, we are always far and few between, especially with the local cons. If I'm looking for something specific, I am going to go somewhere it specializes in just that. That goes for life in general. I'm not going to go to a Chinese restaurant and be upset that their collard greens don't taste right. So why be upset that Marvel doesn't represent POCs right? Do you go to **Olive Garden** and ask for tacos? Are you going to **Walmart** in search for a bottle of **Trèsor**? So why be upset that DC doesn't have enough POC creators?

Want POC books, art, etc? There are an abundance of creators who have work ready to be supported and purchased. **Peep Game Comix** is a black-owned and operated medium that you can order digital downloads from. There are also a lot of comics from POC creators on **IndyPlanet**, as well as quite a few on **Comixology**. Indie is just that: **Indie**. Their money is gained and spent, all at once. They don't have the luxury of having a big name publicist to pay for everything. They instead are paying for everything themselves.

They don't get to have their books placed in stores automatically every Wednesday.

They have to network and do product placement themselves. Not to mention, they have to prove to that store that their book that no one has ever even heard of is worthy of that store shelving it. Many times with indie comics, the writer **and** the artists are funding the project, and **no one** gets profit for a hot minute.

These are just a few of the reasons that the indie community needs your support. It also is important to promote them. Just like many of you are unaware that black Indie exists, your friends and family might be unaware as well. Not all of you can throw conventions, but you **can** share a link or five on your social media. The creators more than appreciate it. Just make sure that when you share artwork, you give credit to the artist. **please** give credit always in all ways. I will go deeper about that topic in **Volume Two**, for that subject bothers me more than I am ready to express right now.

4 Pages | 16 Bars is a wonderful project that my fellow Detroit native, Jiba Molei Anderson has initiated. I am more than honored to have been asked to be a part of it. I see a lot of greatness in the art community, and it gives me pleasure know that I am contributing to just that. In this book, as well as Volume 2, you will find outstanding artists, writers, and publishers, all here to further build their future as well as yours.

It's **nation** time.... Protect ya neck.

Maia "Crown" Williams
Midwest Ethnic Convention For Comics and Arts,
CEO and Founder
All Detroit Everything

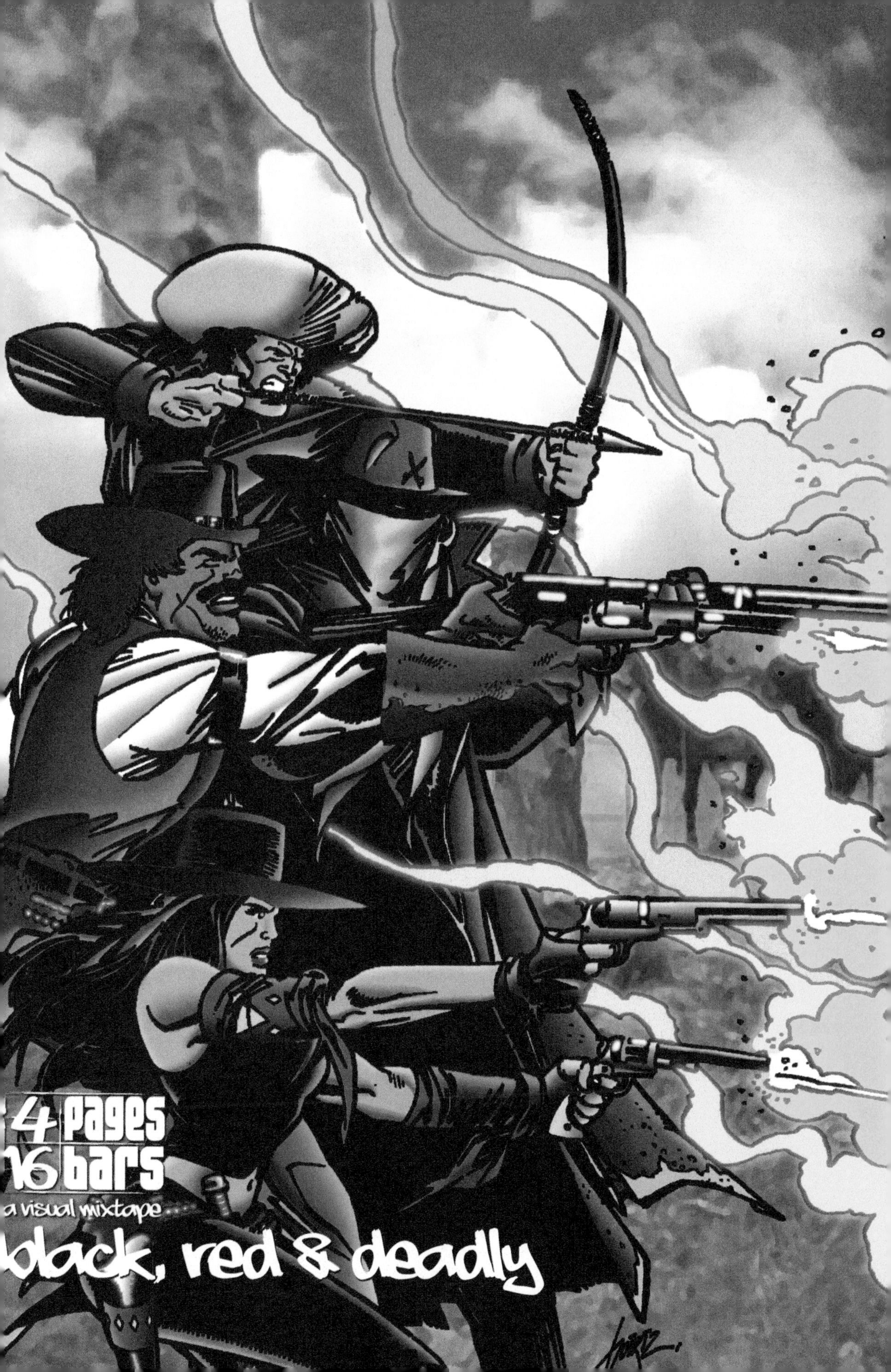
4 pages
16 bars
a visual mixtape...
black, red & deadly

COVER ILLUSTRATION BY
ROBERTO GORIZ

INTERIOR ART BY
ROBERTO GORIZ

La Morris Richmond first broke onto the comics scene with
the *Real Ghostbusters* published by NOW Comics in 1988.
From there he went on to create horror stories for Northstar's *Splatter*,
including *12 Gauge Solution* and the controversial slasher comic book
Boots Of The Oppressor. La Morris spent the next several years working
as City Editor and columnist at The Chicago Defender newspaper before
returning to his first love in life — comics.

After a brief stint as interim Editor-In-Chief of **Griot Enterprises**,
he founded B.L.A.M. Comics! self-publishing the Kung Fu comedy
Canton Kid, and the blood and guts western **Purge: Black, Red & Deadly**.
Excited by his return to Griot Enterprises La Morris shares
the vision of creating a thriving intellectual property company
for the 21st century and beyond.

website: biglamorriscomics.com

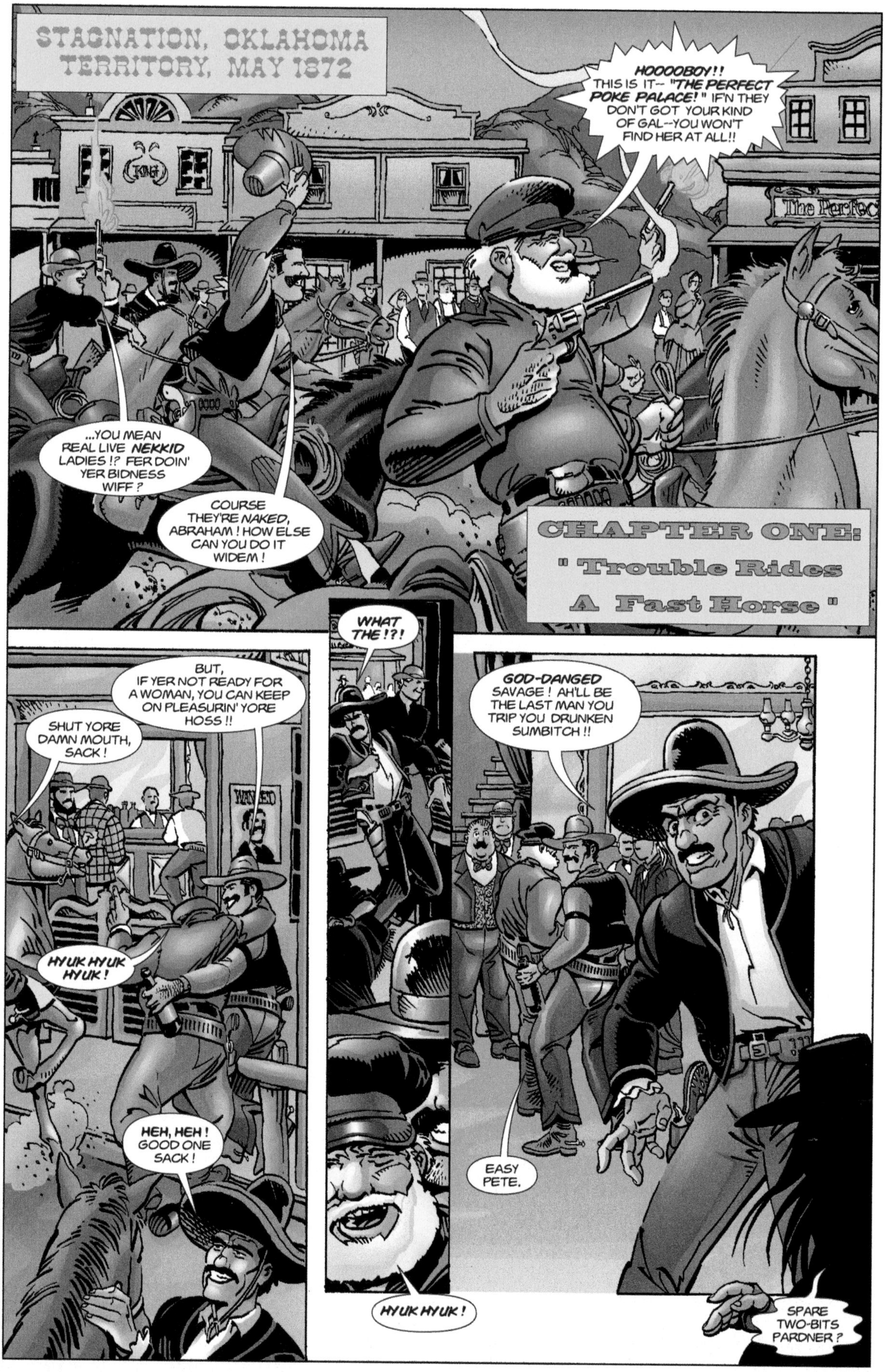
STAGNATION, OKLAHOMA TERRITORY, MAY 1872
HOOOOBOY!! THIS IS IT-- "THE PERFECT POKE PALACE!" IF'N THEY DON'T GOT YOUR KIND OF GAL--YOU WON'T FIND HER AT ALL!!
The Perfec
...YOU MEAN REAL LIVE NEKKID LADIES !? FER DOIN' YER BIDNESS WIFF ?
COURSE THEY'RE NAKED, ABRAHAM ! HOW ELSE CAN YOU DO IT WIDEM !
CHAPTER ONE: " Trouble Rides A Fast Horse "
BUT, IF YER NOT READY FOR A WOMAN, YOU CAN KEEP ON PLEASURIN' YORE HOSS !!
SHUT YORE DAMN MOUTH, SACK !
HYUK HYUK HYUK !
HEH, HEH ! GOOD ONE SACK !
WHAT THE !?!
HYUK HYUK !
GOD-DANGED SAVAGE ! AH'LL BE THE LAST MAN YOU TRIP YOU DRUNKEN SUMBITCH !!
EASY PETE.
SPARE TWO-BITS PARDNER ?

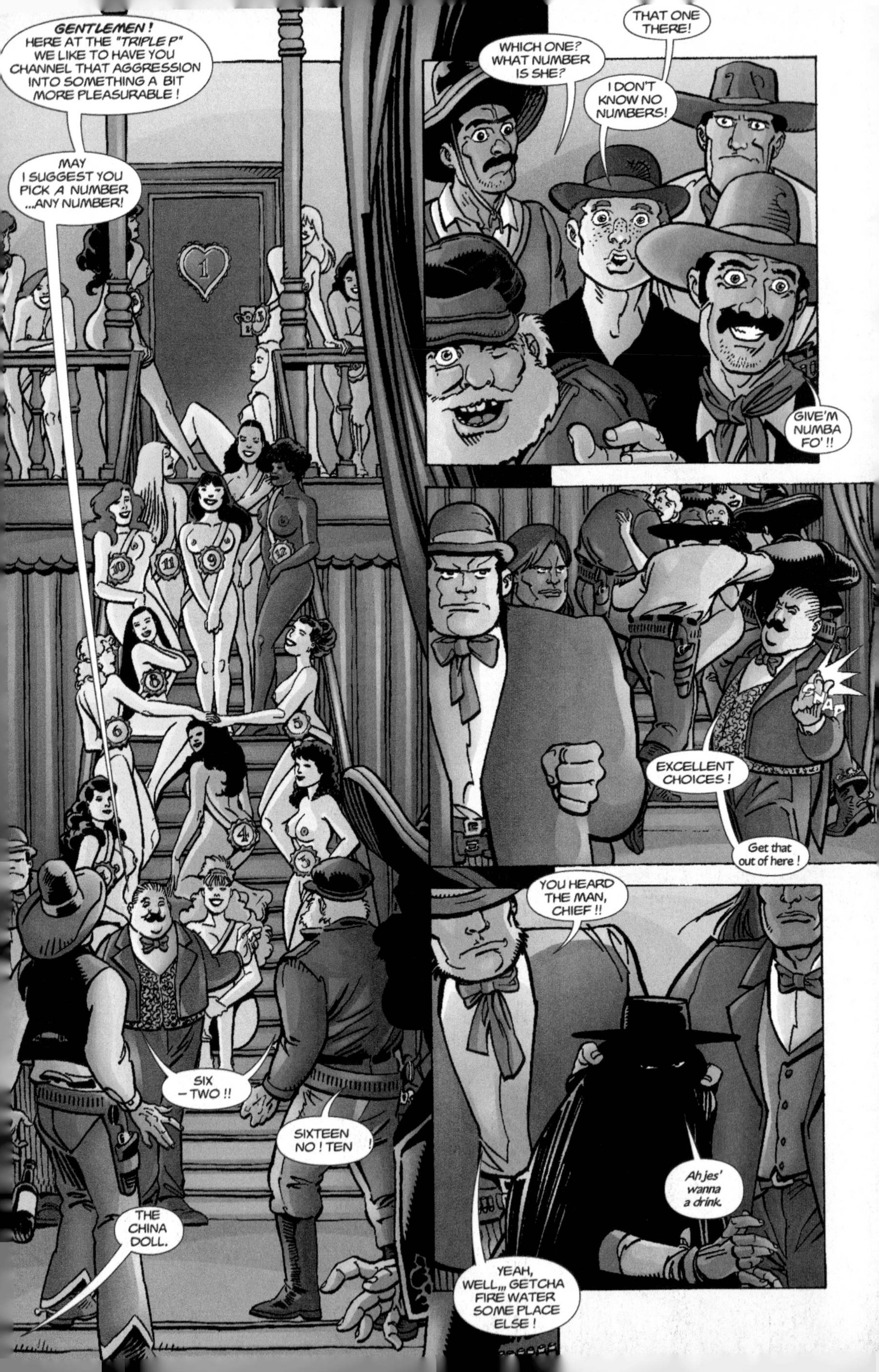
GENTLEMEN! HERE AT THE "TRIPLE P" WE LIKE TO HAVE YOU CHANNEL THAT AGGRESSION INTO SOMETHING A BIT MORE PLEASURABLE!
MAY I SUGGEST YOU PICK A NUMBER ...ANY NUMBER!
SIX – TWO !!
SIXTEEN NO ! TEN !
THE CHINA DOLL.
WHICH ONE? WHAT NUMBER IS SHE?
THAT ONE THERE!
I DON'T KNOW NO NUMBERS!
GIVE'M NUMBA FO' !!
SNAP
EXCELLENT CHOICES !
Get that out of here !
YOU HEARD THE MAN, CHIEF !!
Ah jes' wanna a drink.
YEAH, WELL,,, GETCHA FIRE WATER SOME PLACE ELSE !

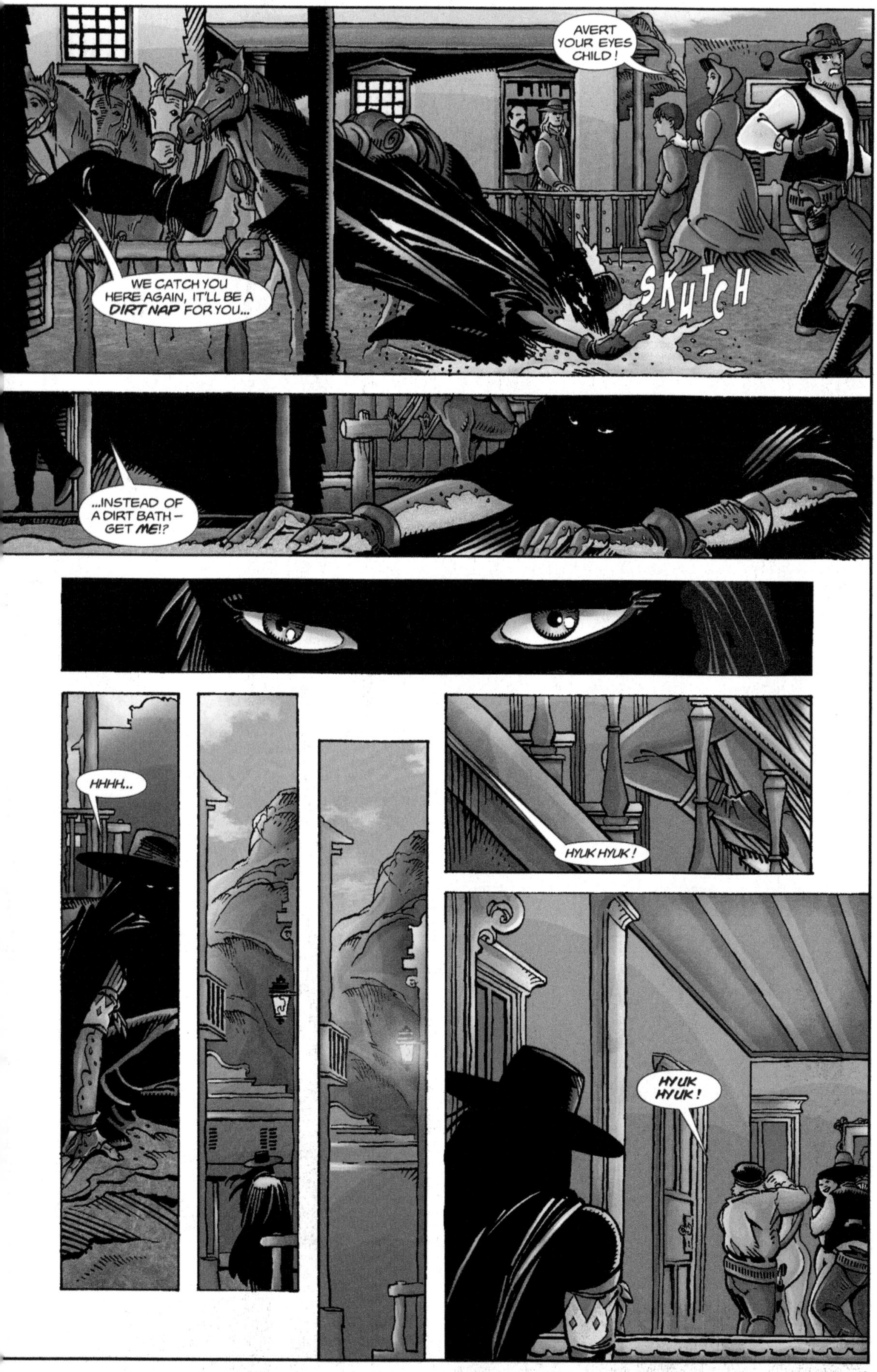
AVERT YOUR EYES CHILD!
WE CATCH YOU HERE AGAIN, IT'LL BE A DIRT NAP FOR YOU...
SKUTCH
...INSTEAD OF A DIRT BATH – GET ME!?
HHHH...
HYUK HYUK!
HYUK HYUK!

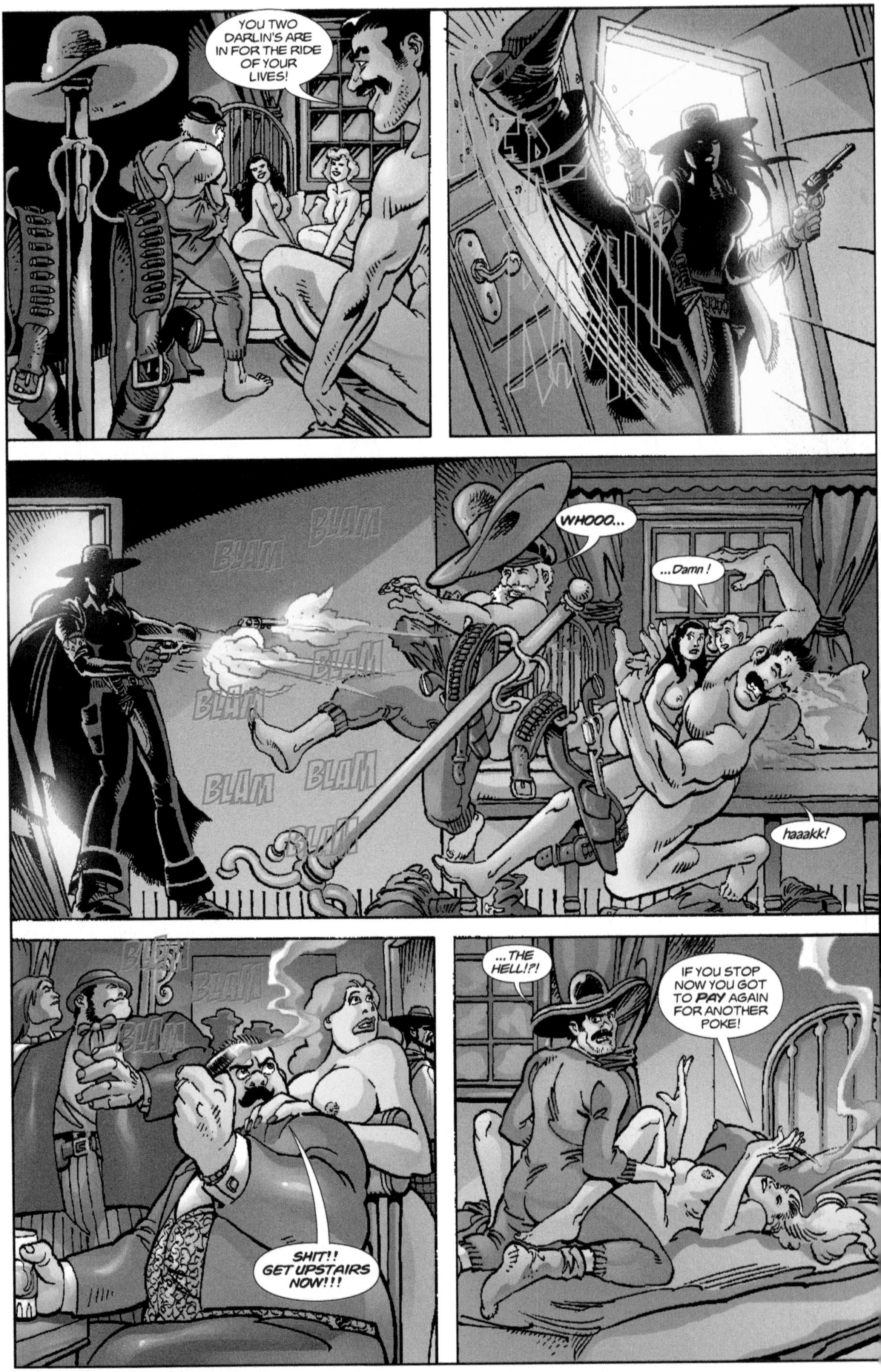
YOU TWO DARLIN'S ARE IN FOR THE RIDE OF YOUR LIVES!
BLAM
BLAM
WHOOO...
...Damn!
BLAM
BLAM
BLAM
BLAM
BLAM
haaakk!
BLAM
BLAM
BLAM
SHIT!! GET UPSTAIRS NOW!!!
...THE HELL!?!
IF YOU STOP NOW YOU GOT TO *PAY* AGAIN FOR ANOTHER POKE!

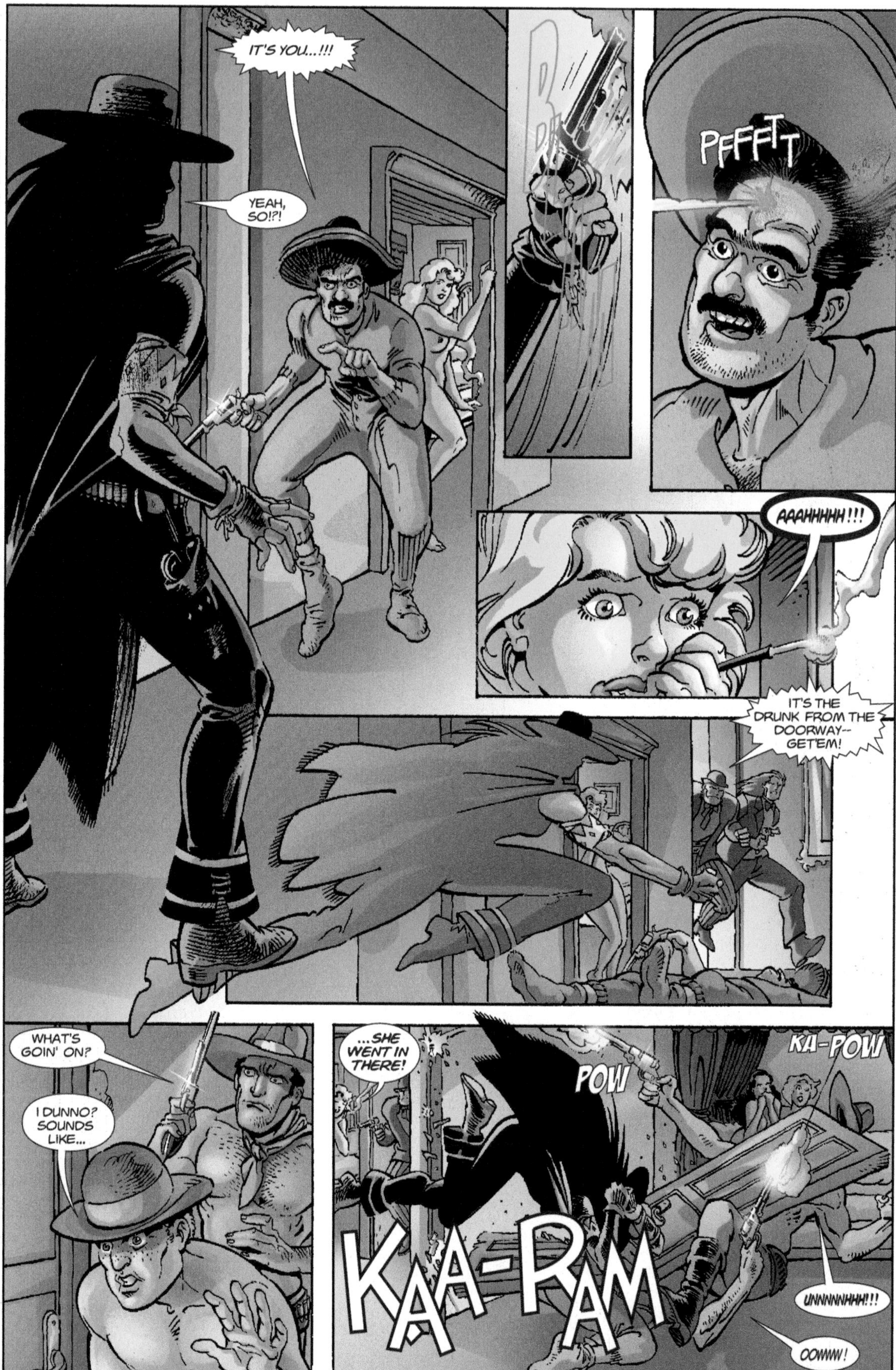
IT'S YOU...!!!
YEAH, SO!?!
PFFFTT
AAAHHHHH!!!
IT'S THE DRUNK FROM THE DOORWAY-- GET'EM!
WHAT'S GOIN' ON?
I DUNNO? SOUNDS LIKE...
...SHE WENT IN THERE!
POW
KA-POW
KAA-RAM
UNNNNNHHH!!!
OOWW!

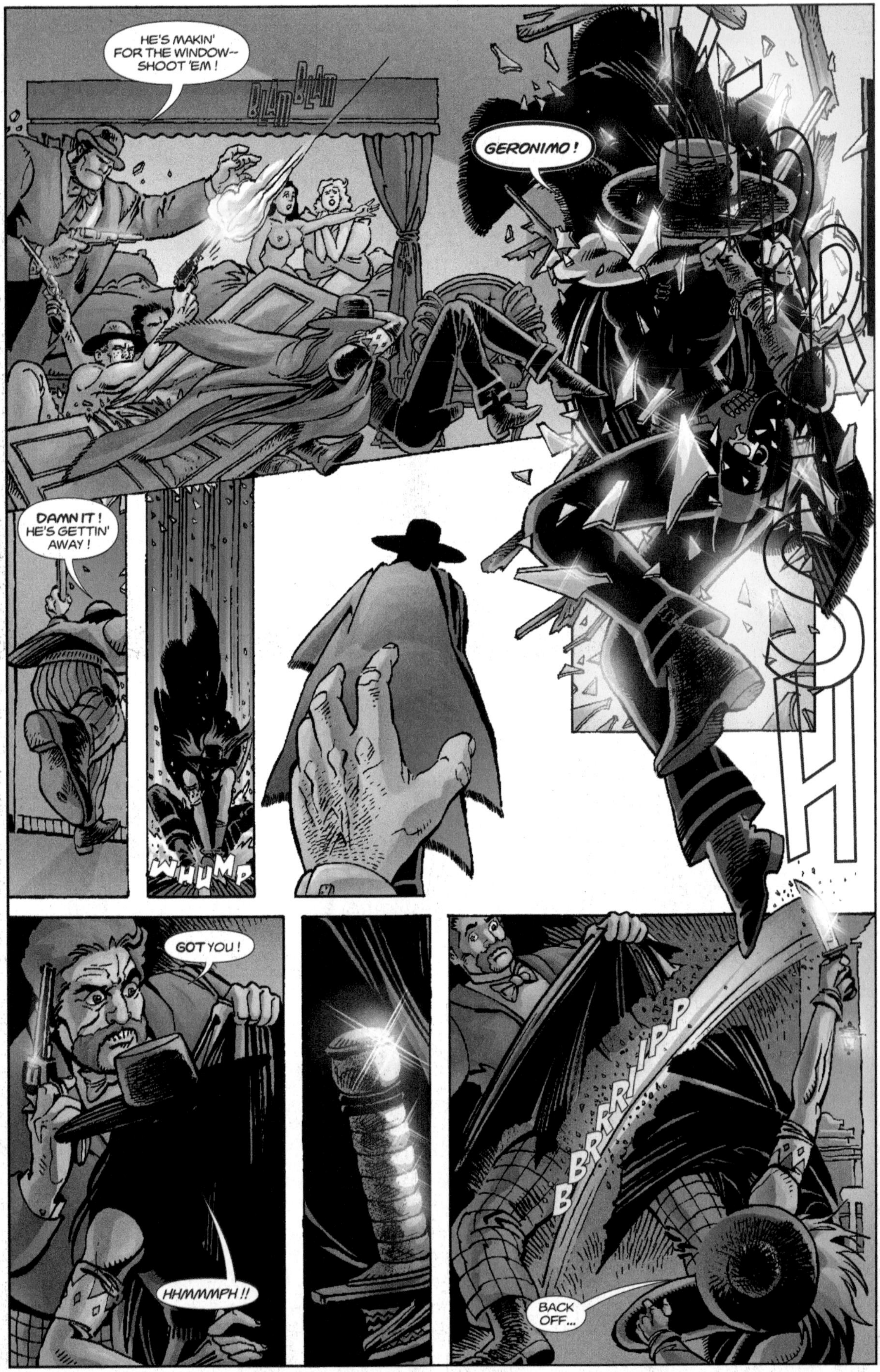

HE'S MAKIN' FOR THE WINDOW-- SHOOT 'EM !
BLAM BLAM
GERONIMO !
DAMN IT ! HE'S GETTIN' AWAY !
WHUMP
GOT YOU !
HHMMMPH !!
BBRRRIIPP
BACK OFF...

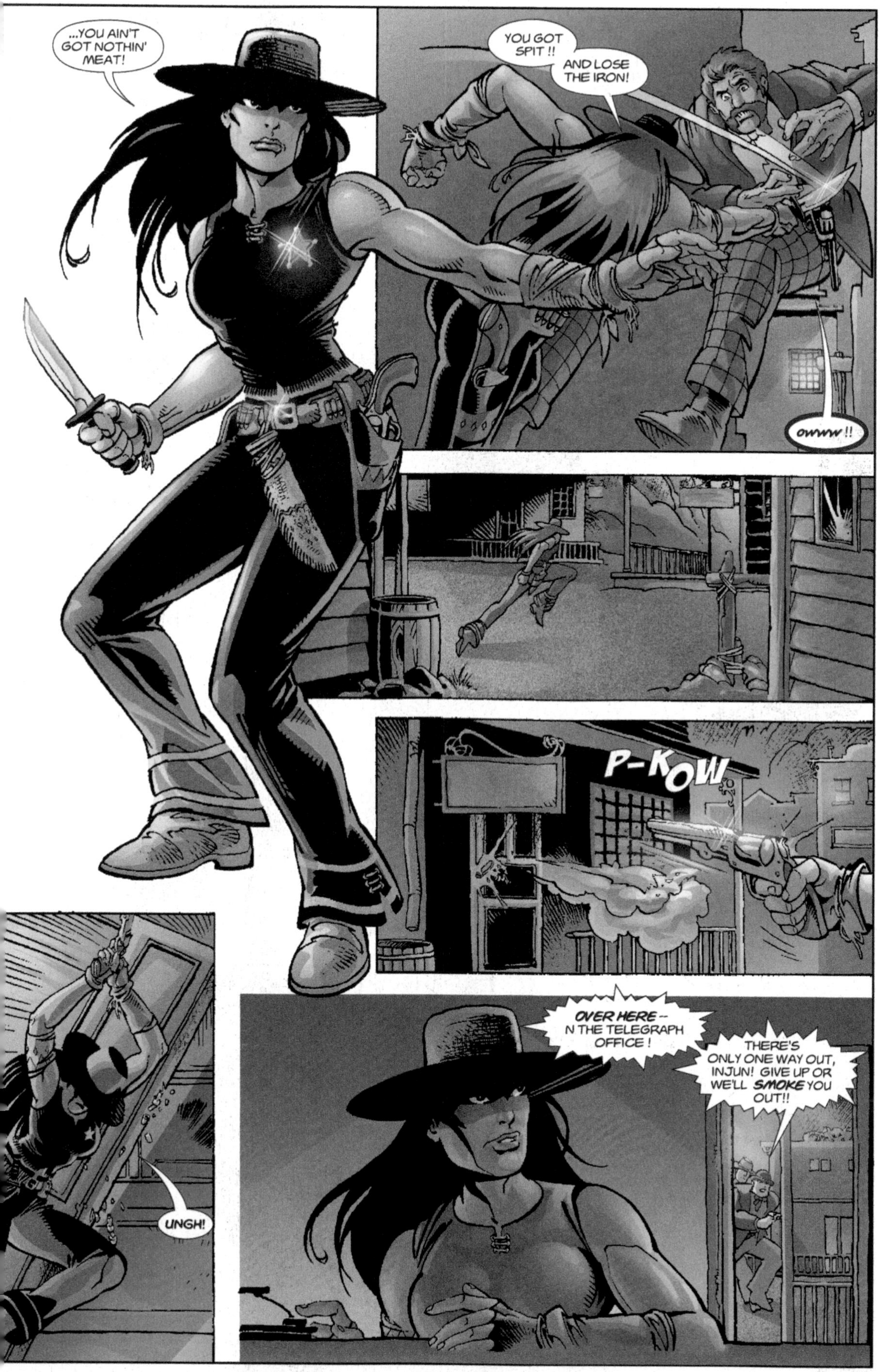
...YOU AIN'T GOT NOTHIN' MEAT!
YOU GOT SPIT !!
AND LOSE THE IRON!
OWWW !!
P-KOW
UNGH!
OVER HERE -- N THE TELEGRAPH OFFICE !
THERE'S ONLY ONE WAY OUT, INJUN! GIVE UP OR WE'LL SMOKE YOU OUT!!

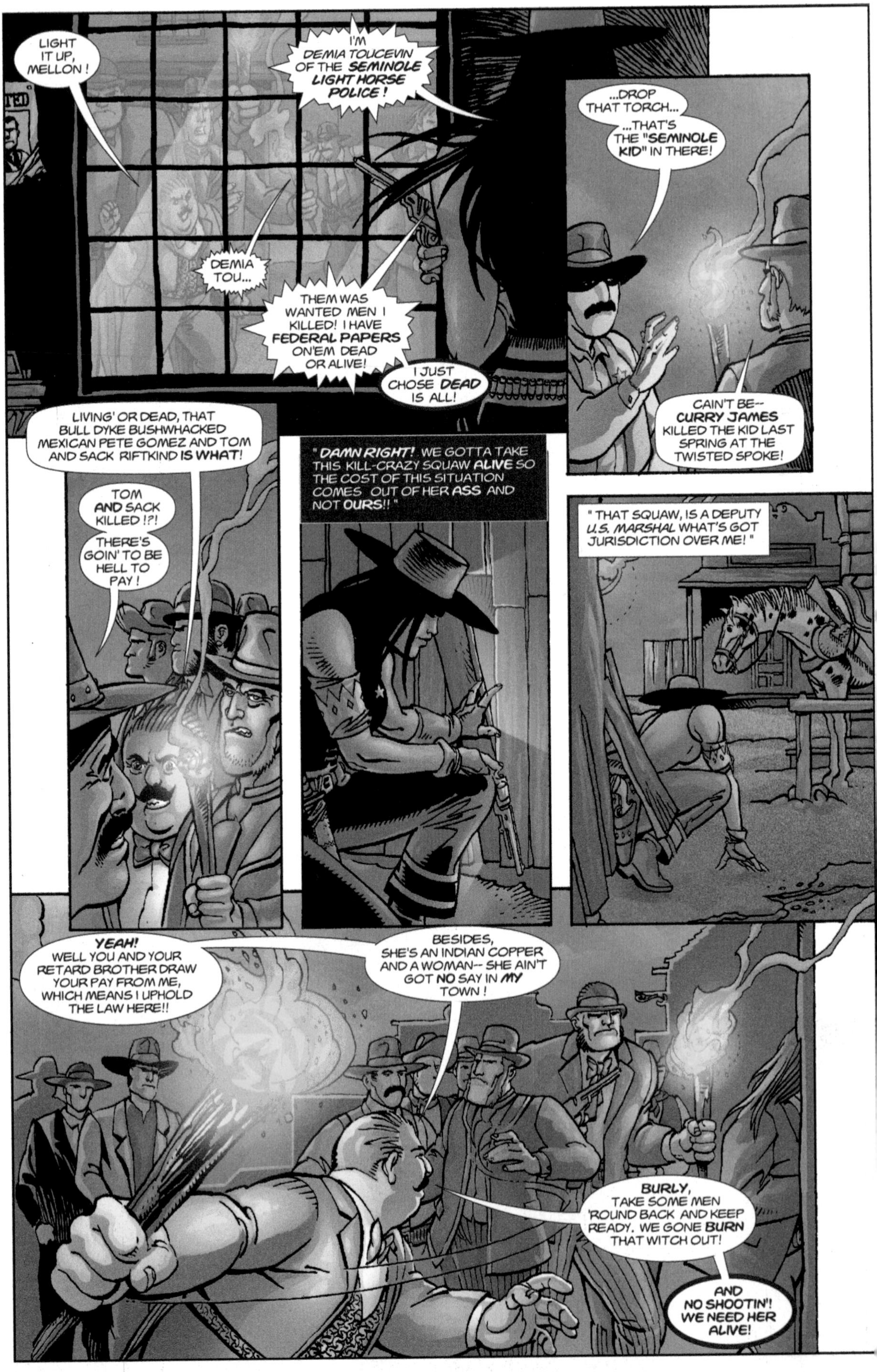
LIGHT IT UP, MELLON!
I'M DEMIA TOUCEVIN OF THE SEMINOLE LIGHT HORSE POLICE!
DEMIA TOU...
THEM WAS WANTED MEN I KILLED! I HAVE FEDERAL PAPERS ON'EM DEAD OR ALIVE!
I JUST CHOSE DEAD IS ALL!
...DROP THAT TORCH...
...THAT'S THE "SEMINOLE KID" IN THERE!
CAIN'T BE-- CURRY JAMES KILLED THE KID LAST SPRING AT THE TWISTED SPOKE!
LIVING' OR DEAD, THAT BULL DYKE BUSHWHACKED MEXICAN PETE GOMEZ AND TOM AND SACK RIFTKIND IS WHAT!
TOM AND SACK KILLED !?!
THERE'S GOIN' TO BE HELL TO PAY!
"DAMN RIGHT! WE GOTTA TAKE THIS KILL-CRAZY SQUAW ALIVE SO THE COST OF THIS SITUATION COMES OUT OF HER ASS AND NOT OURS!!"
" THAT SQUAW, IS A DEPUTY U.S. MARSHAL WHAT'S GOT JURISDICTION OVER ME! "
YEAH! WELL YOU AND YOUR RETARD BROTHER DRAW YOUR PAY FROM ME, WHICH MEANS I UPHOLD THE LAW HERE!!
BESIDES, SHE'S AN INDIAN COPPER AND A WOMAN-- SHE AIN'T GOT NO SAY IN MY TOWN!
BURLY, TAKE SOME MEN 'ROUND BACK AND KEEP READY. WE GONE BURN THAT WITCH OUT!
AND NO SHOOTIN'! WE NEED HER ALIVE!

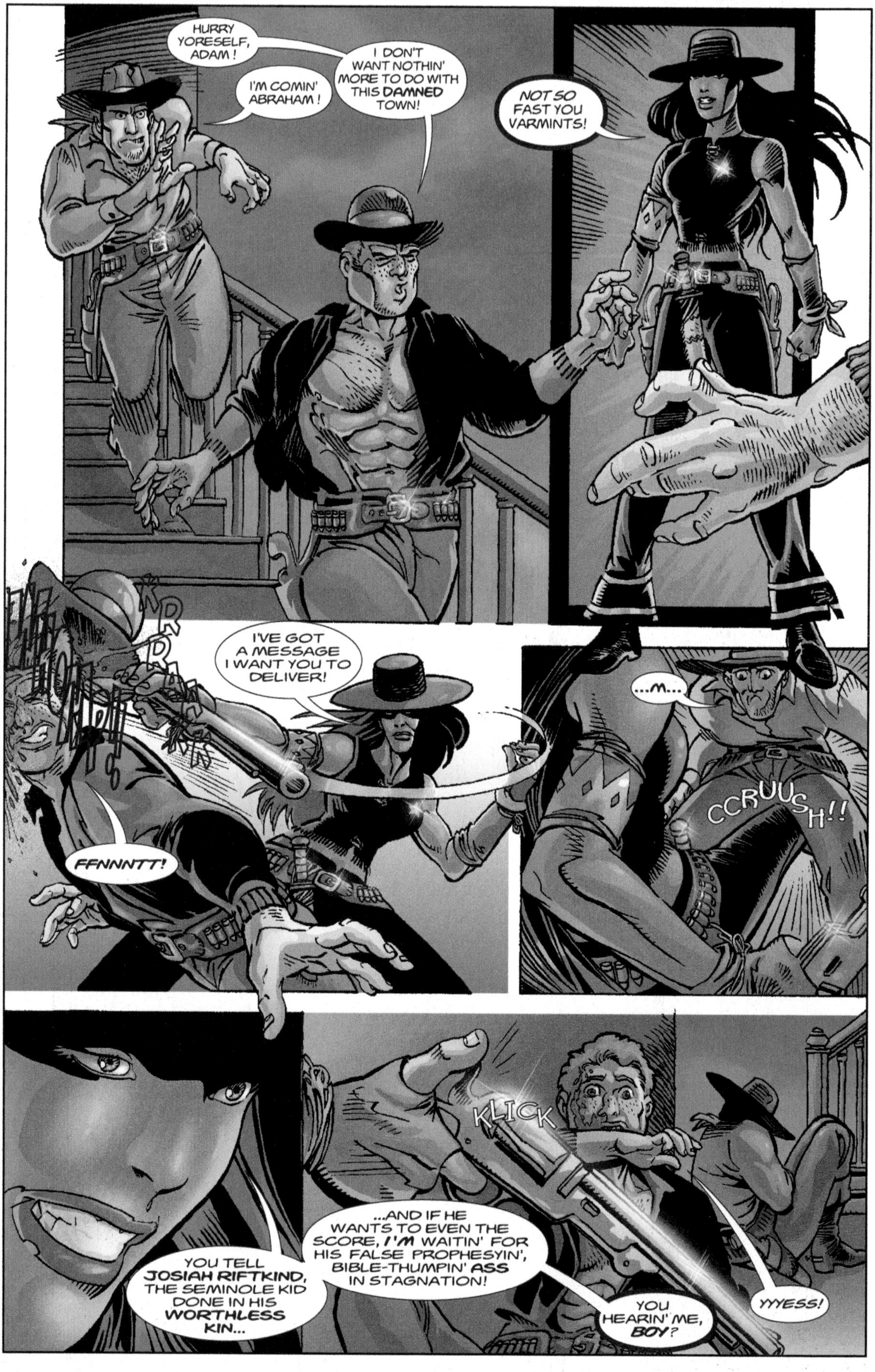

HURRY YORESELF, ADAM!
I'M COMIN' ABRAHAM!
I DON'T WANT NOTHIN' MORE TO DO WITH THIS **DAMNED** TOWN!
NOT SO FAST YOU VARMINTS!
I'VE GOT A MESSAGE I WANT YOU TO DELIVER!
FFNNNTT!
...M...
CCRUUSH!!
KLICK
YOU TELL **JOSIAH RIFTKIND**, THE SEMINOLE KID DONE IN HIS **WORTHLESS** KIN...
...AND IF HE WANTS TO EVEN THE SCORE, ***I'M*** WAITIN' FOR HIS FALSE PROPHESYIN', BIBLE-THUMPIN' **ASS** IN STAGNATION!
YOU HEARIN' ME, ***BOY***?
YYYESS!

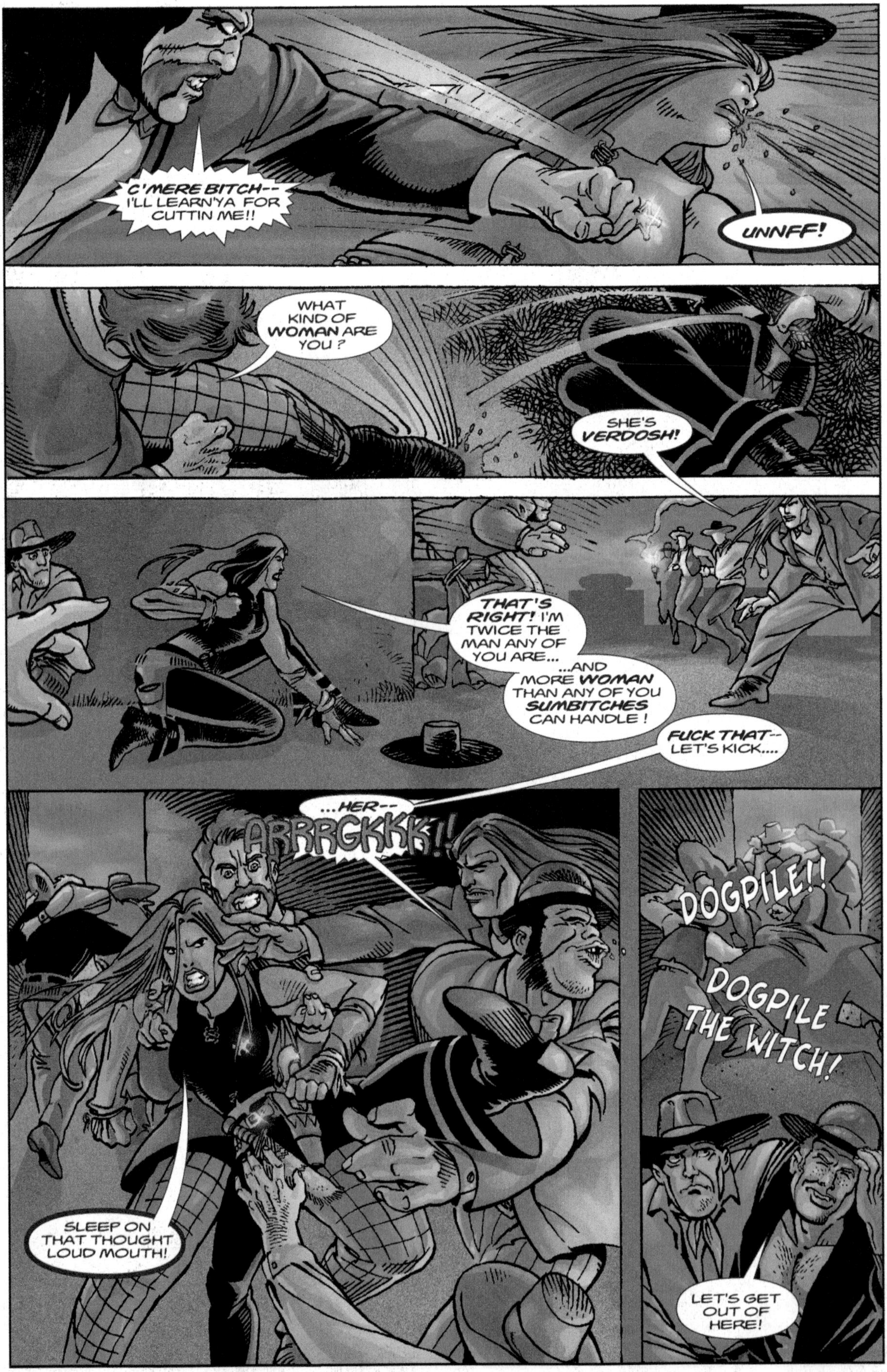
C'MERE BITCH--
I'LL LEARN'YA FOR
CUTTIN ME!!
UNNFF!
WHAT
KIND OF
WOMAN ARE
YOU ?
SHE'S
VERDOSH!
THAT'S
RIGHT! I'M
TWICE THE
MAN ANY OF
YOU ARE...
...AND
MORE WOMAN
THAN ANY OF YOU
SUMBITCHES
CAN HANDLE !
FUCK THAT--
LET'S KICK....
...HER--
ARRRGKKK!!
SLEEP ON
THAT THOUGHT
LOUD MOUTH!
DOGPILE!!
DOGPILE
THE WITCH!
LET'S GET
OUT OF
HERE!

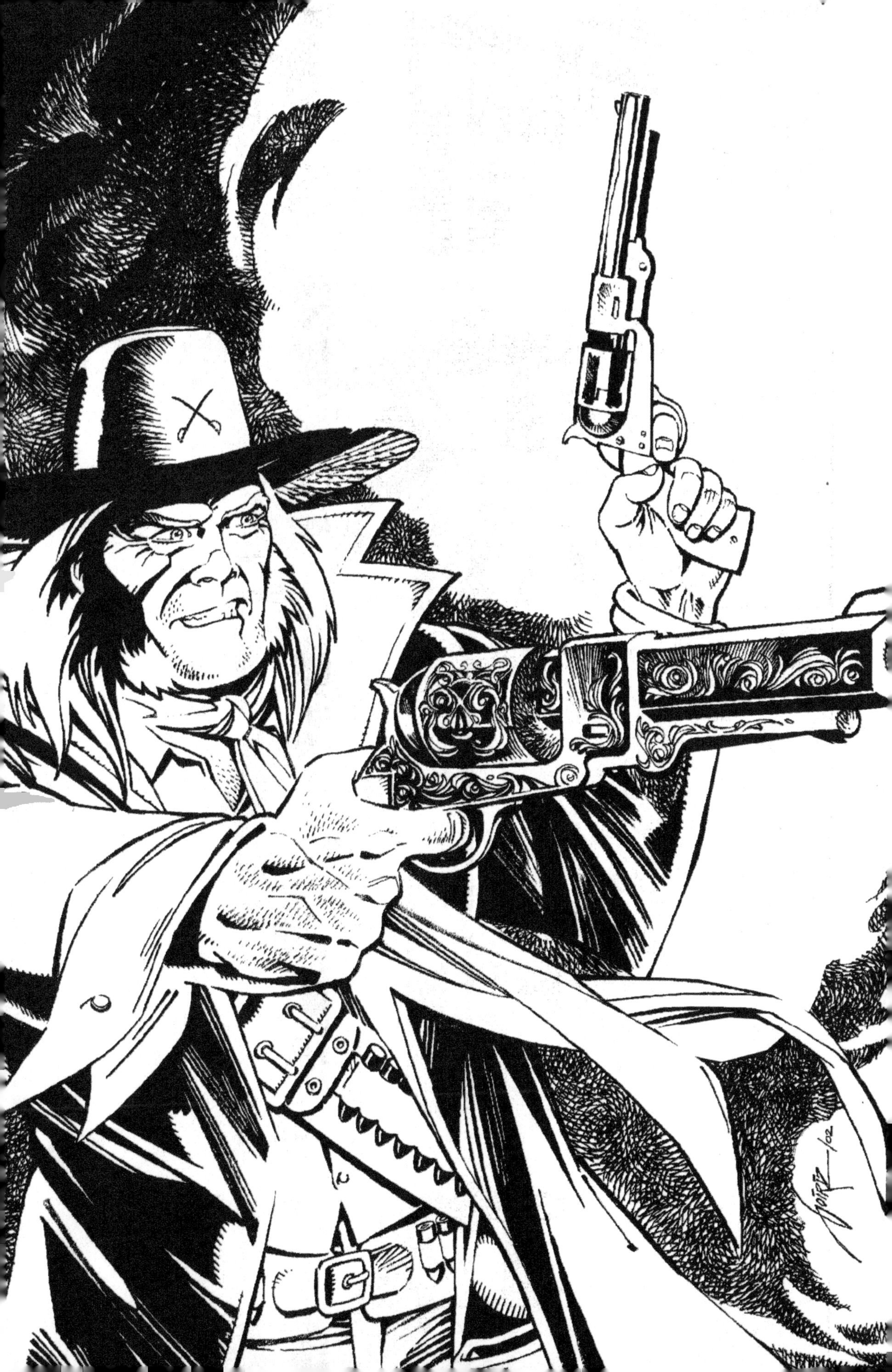

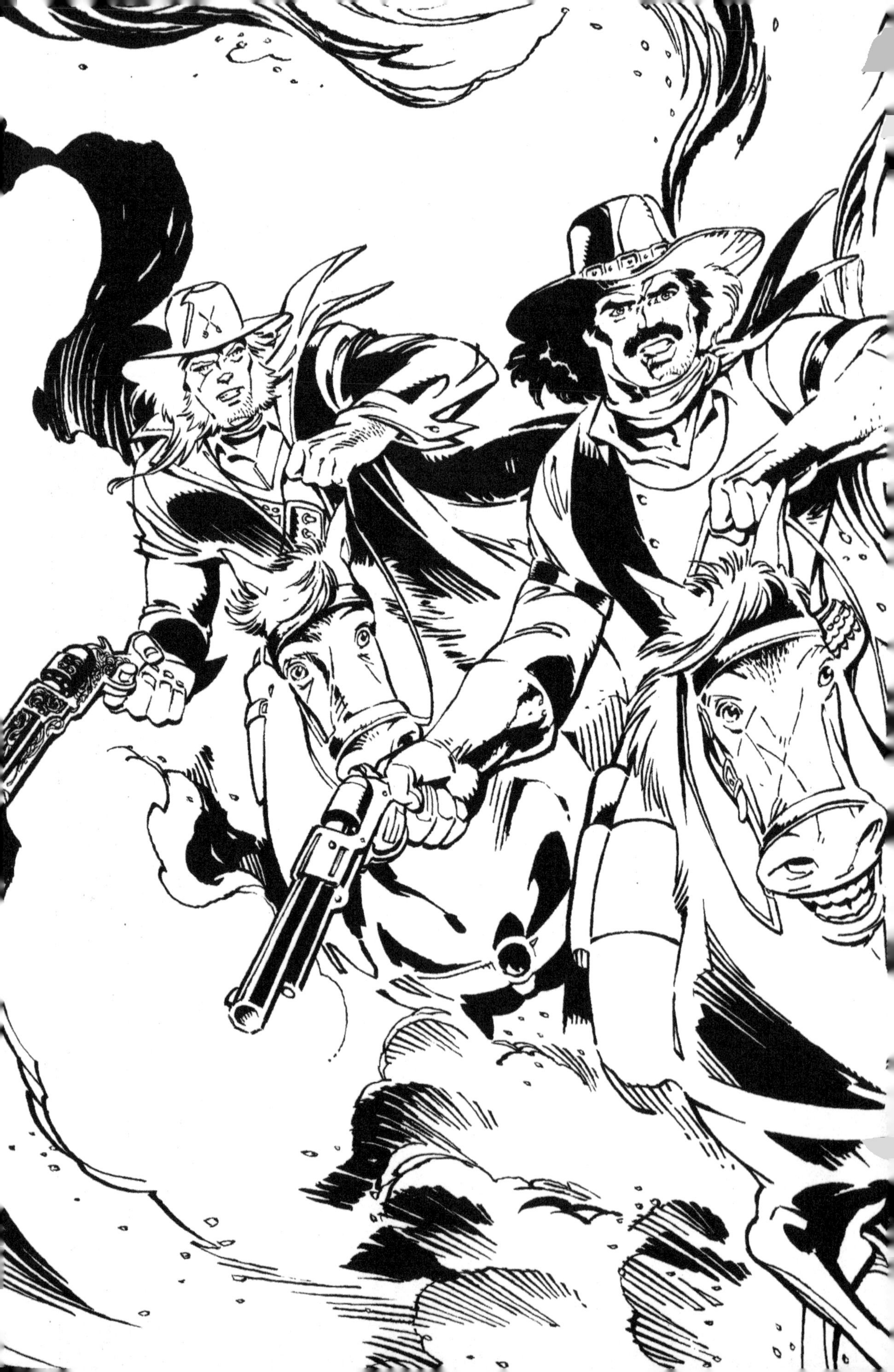

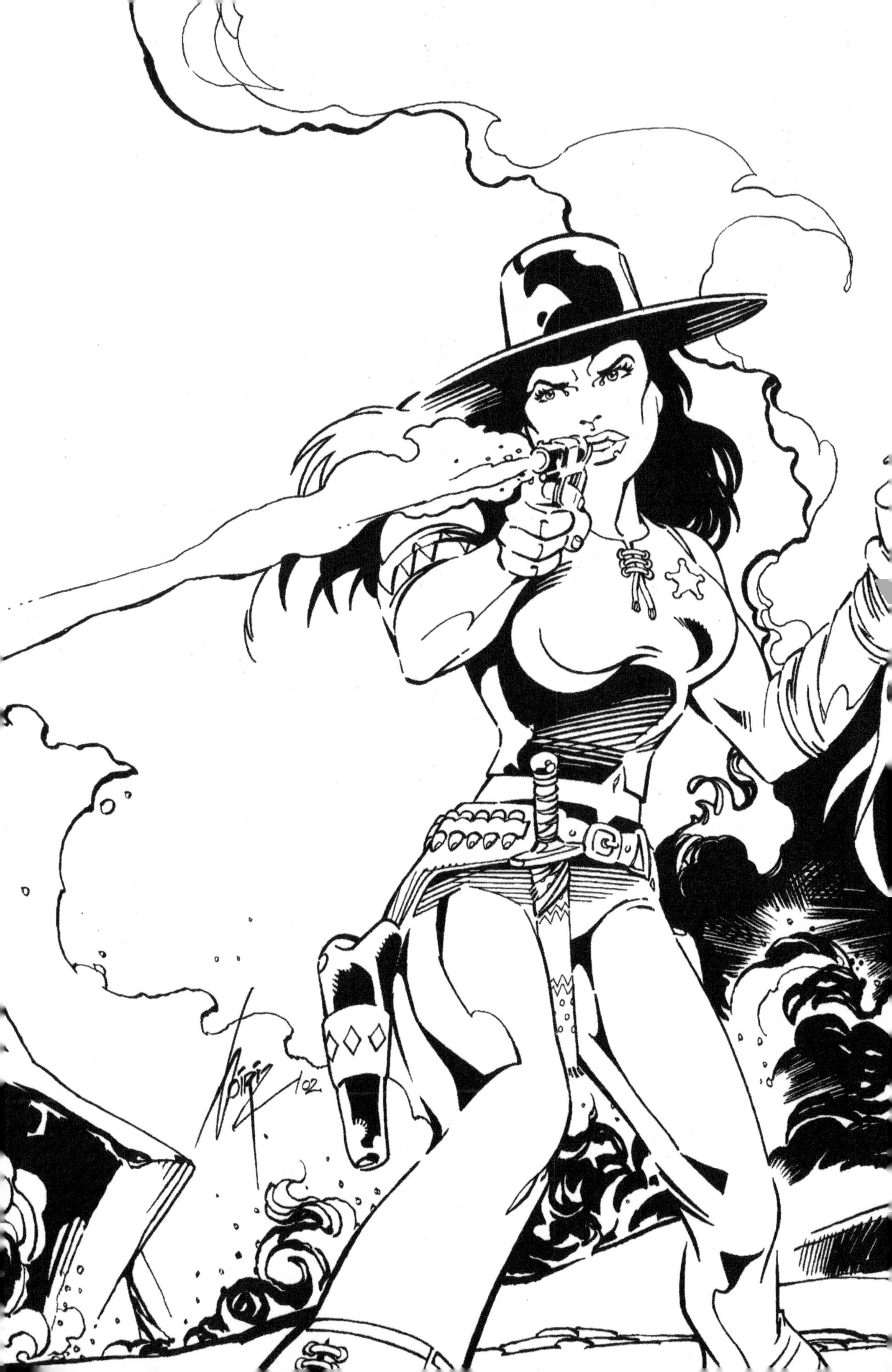

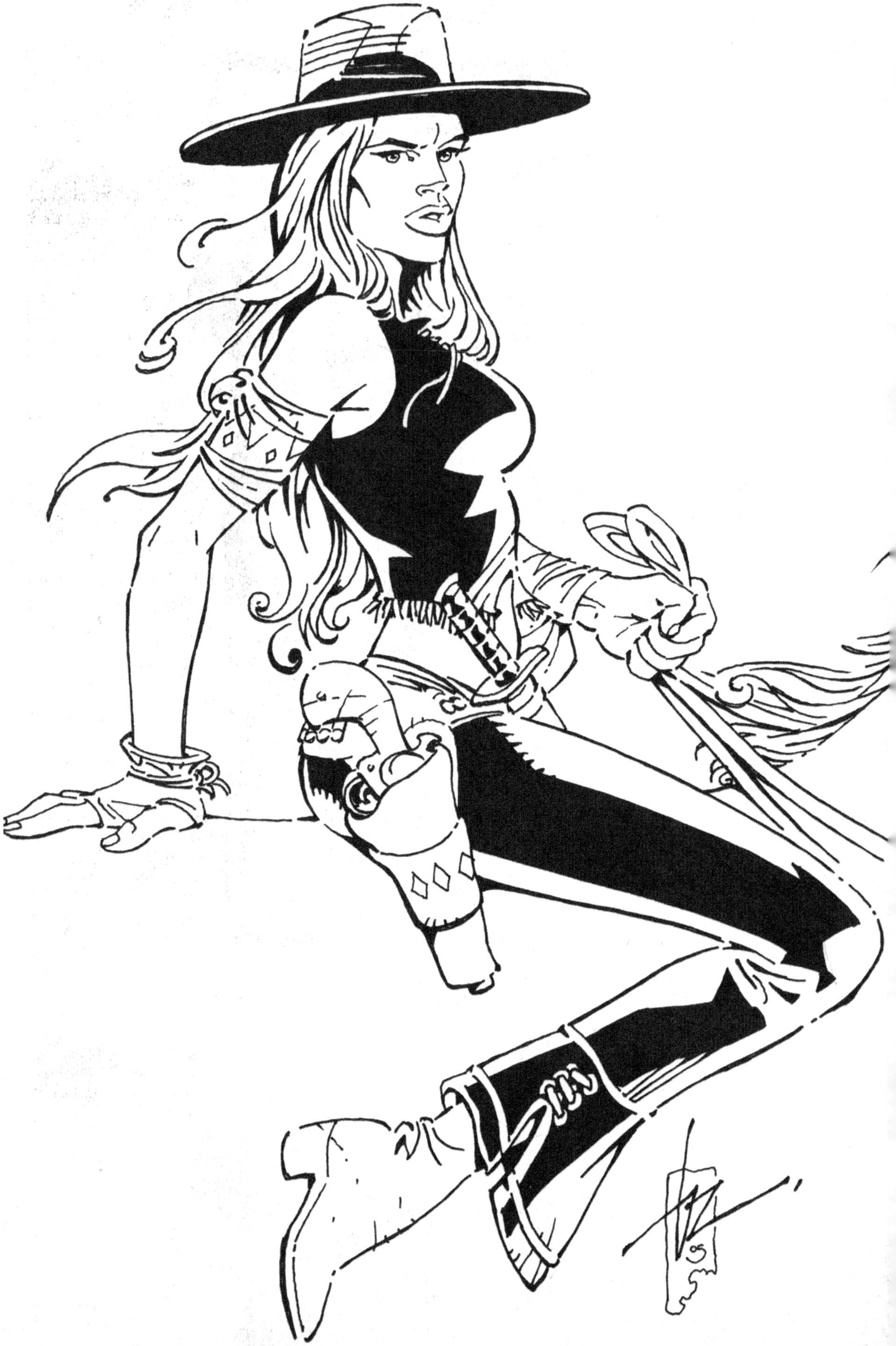

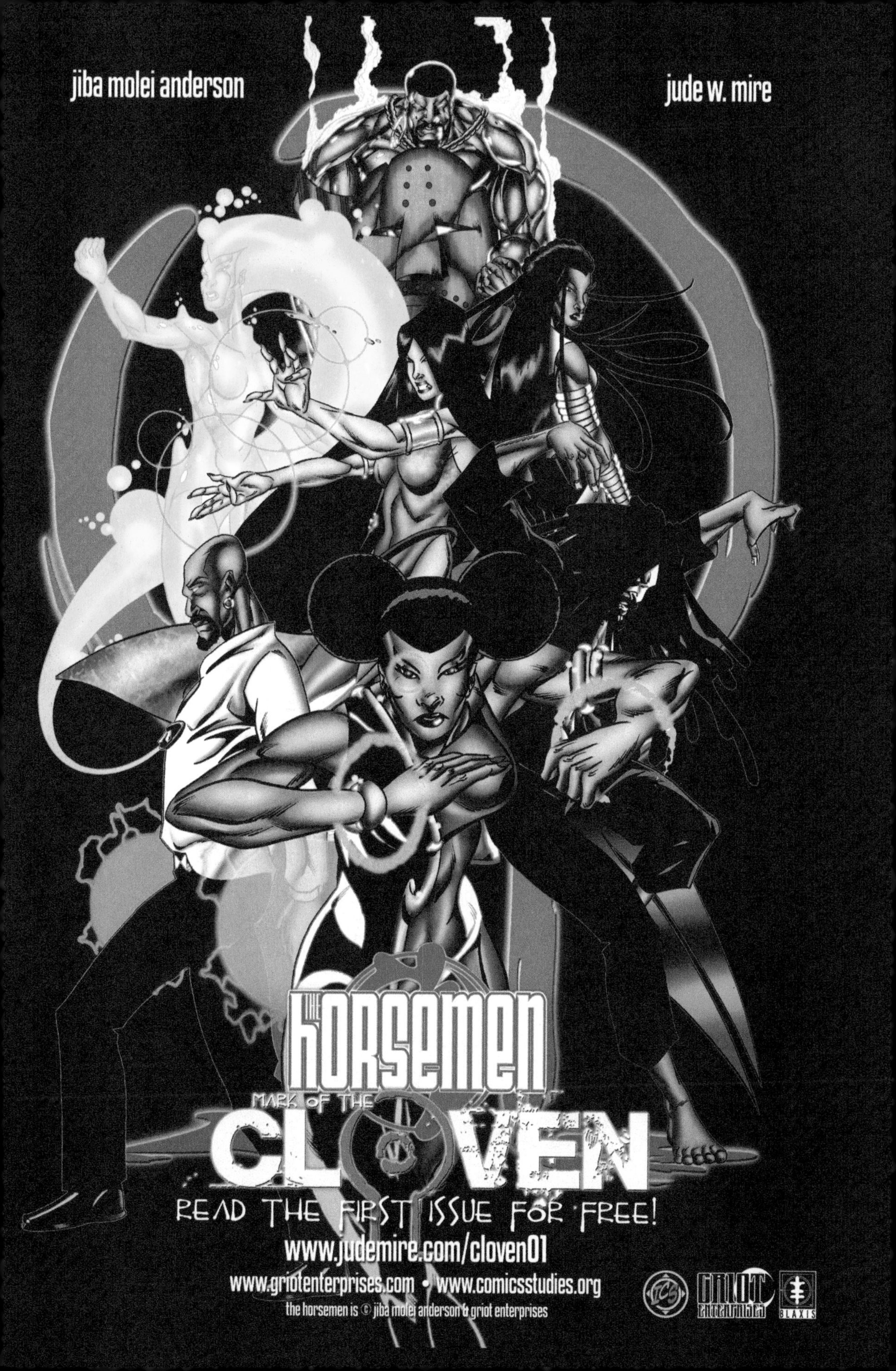
jiba molei anderson
jude w. mire
THE hORSEMEN
MARK OF THE
CLOVEN
READ THE FIRST ISSUE FOR FREE!
www.judemire.com/cloven01
www.griotenterprises.com • www.comicsstudies.org
the horsemen is © jiba molei anderson & griot enterprises
GRIOT ENTERPRISES
BLAXIS

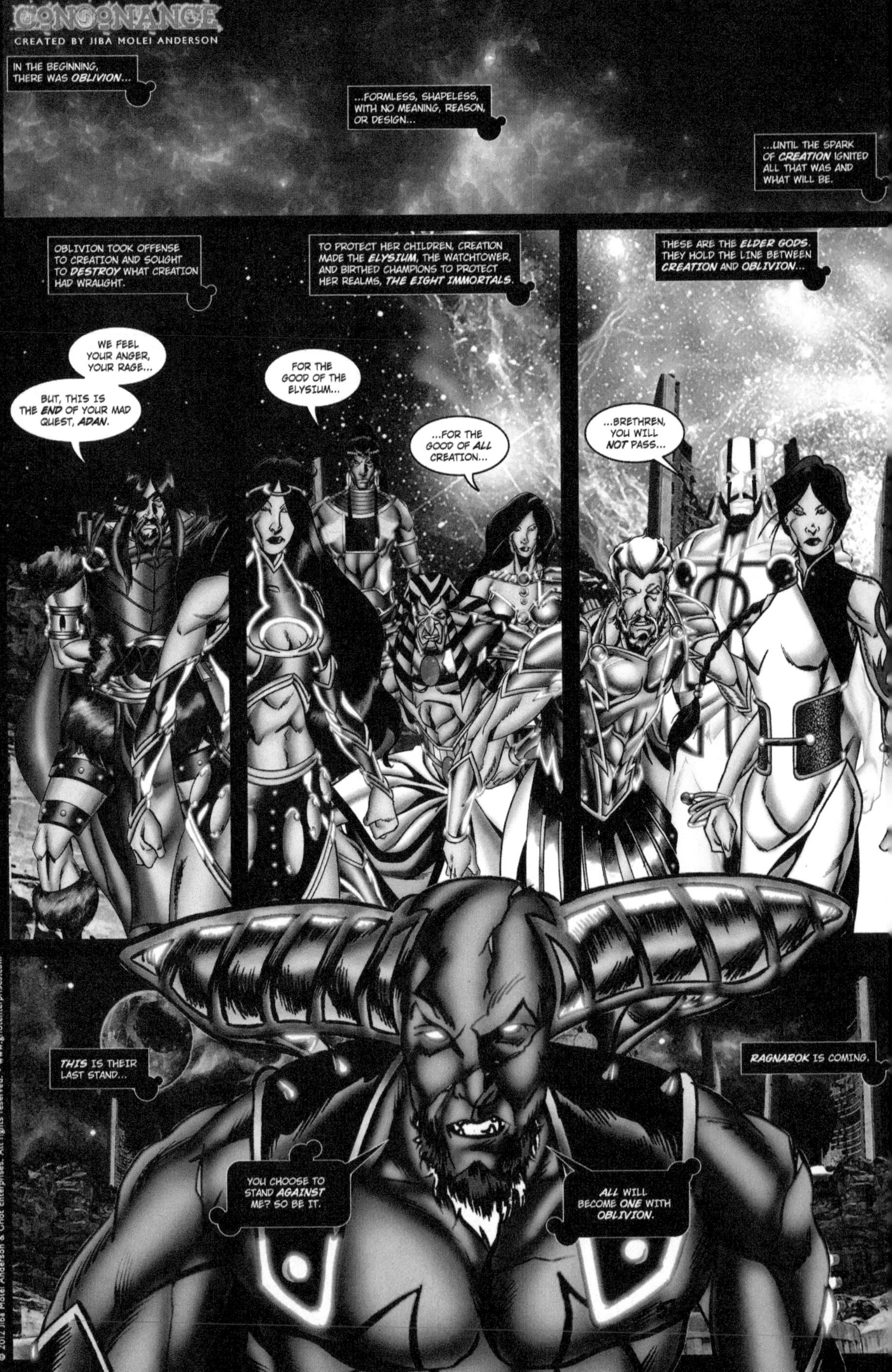
CONSONANCE
CREATED BY JIBA MOLEI ANDERSON
IN THE BEGINNING, THERE WAS OBLIVION...
...FORMLESS, SHAPELESS, WITH NO MEANING, REASON, OR DESIGN...
...UNTIL THE SPARK OF CREATION IGNITED ALL THAT WAS AND WHAT WILL BE.
OBLIVION TOOK OFFENSE TO CREATION AND SOUGHT TO DESTROY WHAT CREATION HAD WRAUGHT.
WE FEEL YOUR ANGER, YOUR RAGE...
BUT, THIS IS THE END OF YOUR MAD QUEST, ADAN.
TO PROTECT HER CHILDREN, CREATION MADE THE ELYSIUM, THE WATCHTOWER, AND BIRTHED CHAMPIONS TO PROTECT HER REALMS, THE EIGHT IMMORTALS.
FOR THE GOOD OF THE ELYSIUM...
...FOR THE GOOD OF ALL CREATION...
THESE ARE THE ELDER GODS. THEY HOLD THE LINE BETWEEN CREATION AND OBLIVION...
...BRETHREN, YOU WILL NOT PASS...
THIS IS THEIR LAST STAND...
RAGNAROK IS COMING.
YOU CHOOSE TO STAND AGAINST ME? SO BE IT.
ALL WILL BECOME ONE WITH OBLIVION.

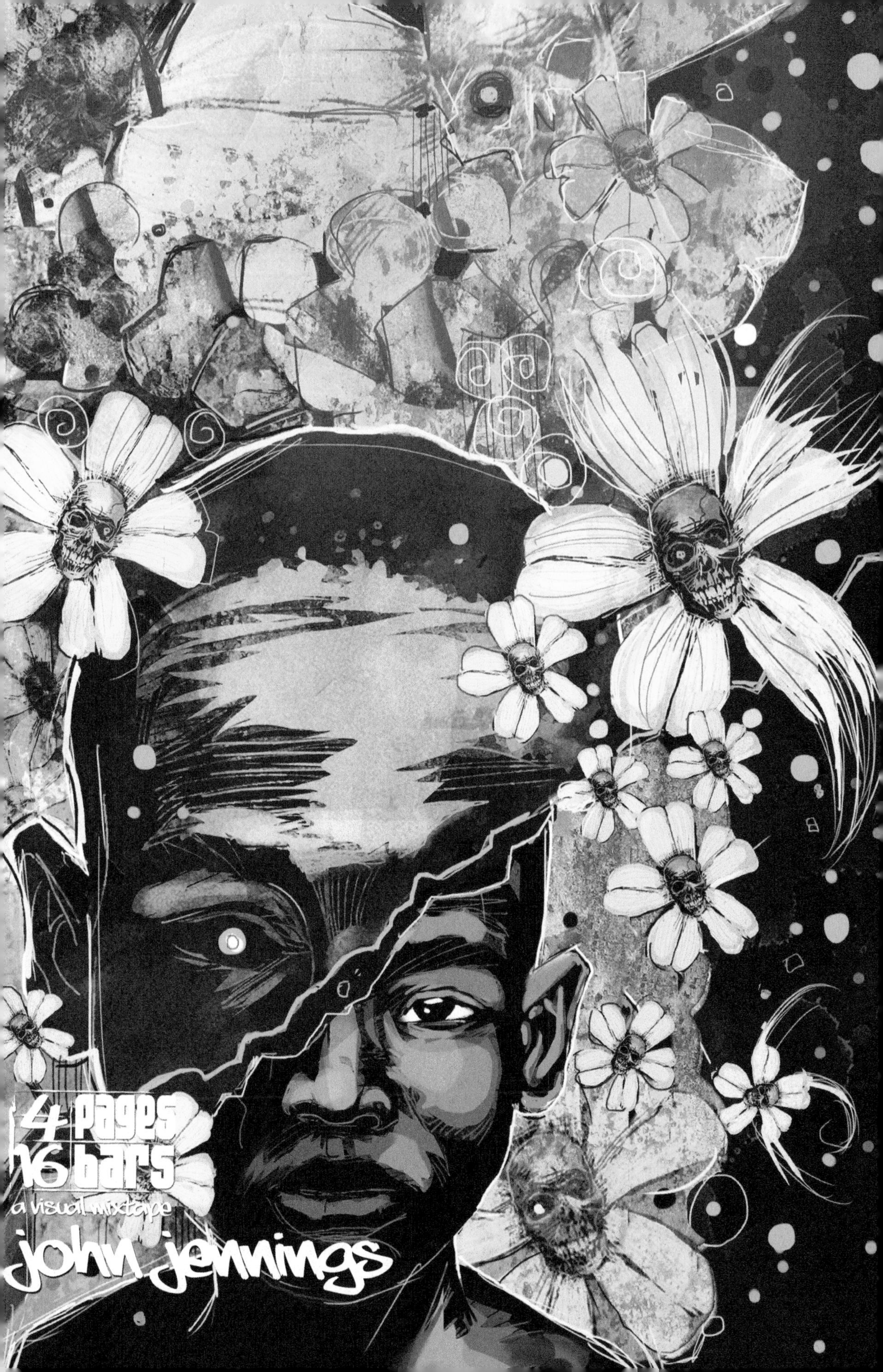

4 pages
16 bars
a visual mixtape
john jennings

John Jennings is an Associate Professor of Visual Studies at the **University of Buffalo SUNY**. His research and teaching focus on the analysis, explication, and disruption of African American stereotypes in popular visual media. He is an accomplished designer, curator, illustrator, and cartoonist.

Along with his long-time collaborator Damian Duffy, Jennings has co-authored and designed the books **Out of Sequence: Underrepresented Voices in American Comics, Black Comix: African American Independent Comics Art + Culture**, and the GLYPH Award winning graphic novel; **The Hole: Consumer Culture Vol. 1.**

His new projects include the supernatural crime story **Blue Hand Mojo: A Case of You** and the forthcoming graphic novel adaptation of Octavia Butler's classic dark fantasy novel **Kindred** (also with Duffy). He has also garnered acclaim for his artist collective **Black Kirby** along with his co-creator Stacey Robinson.

Currently, Jennings is working on among other things, **Kid Code: Channel Zero** with Stacey Robinson and Damian Duffy.

website: jjjennin70.tumblr.com

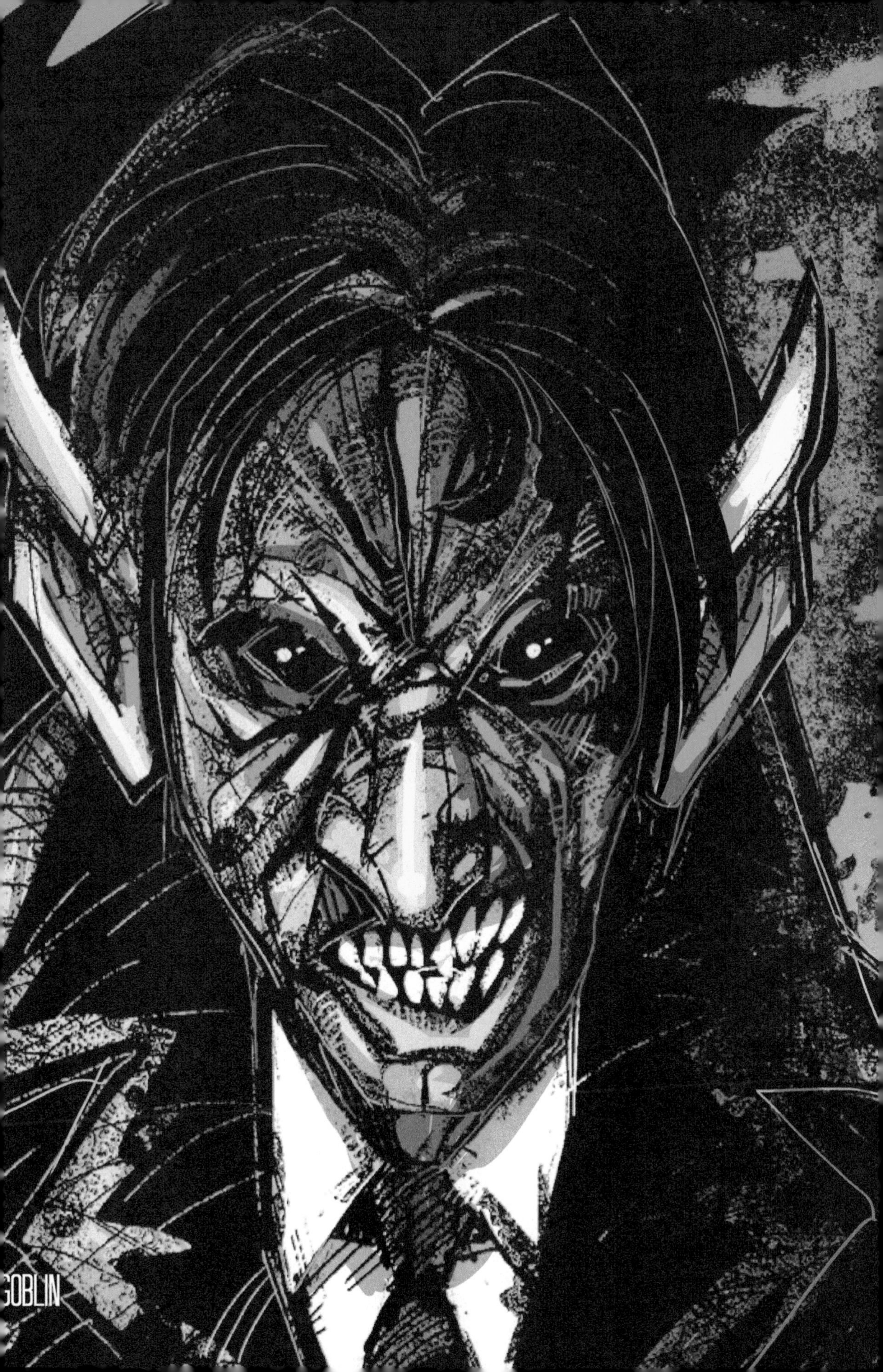
GOBLIN

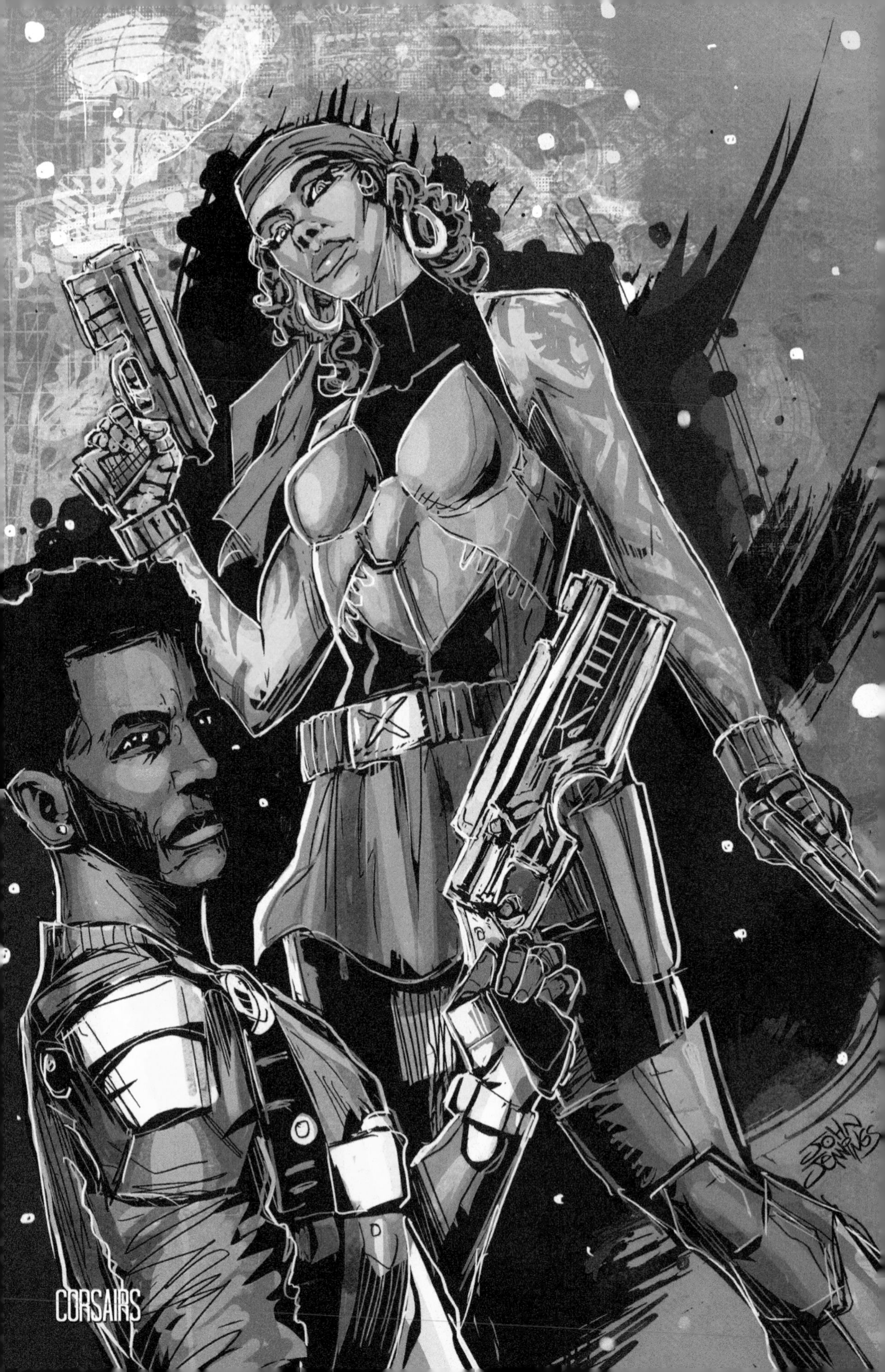
JOHN JENNINGS
CORSAIRS

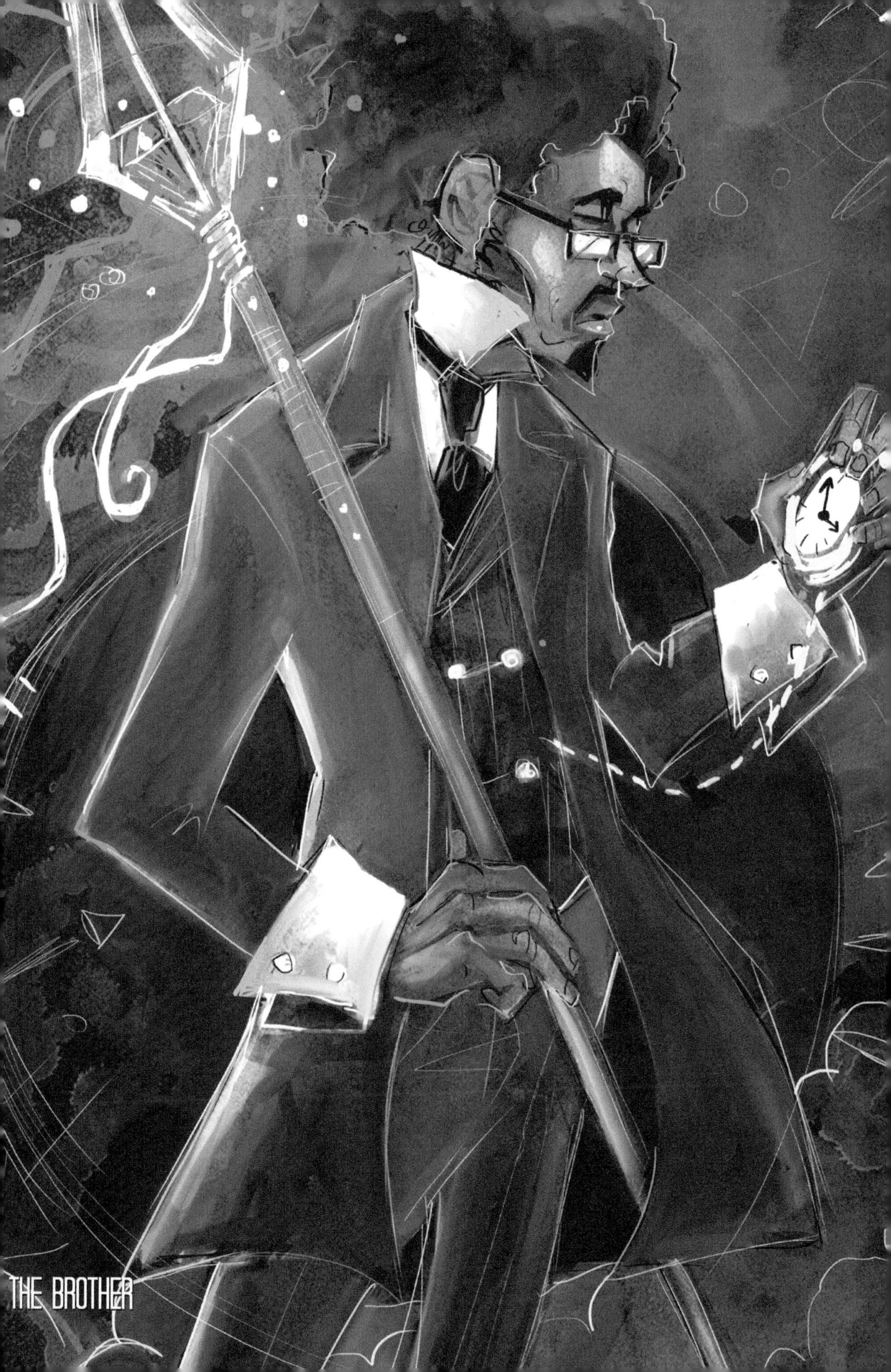
THE BROTHER

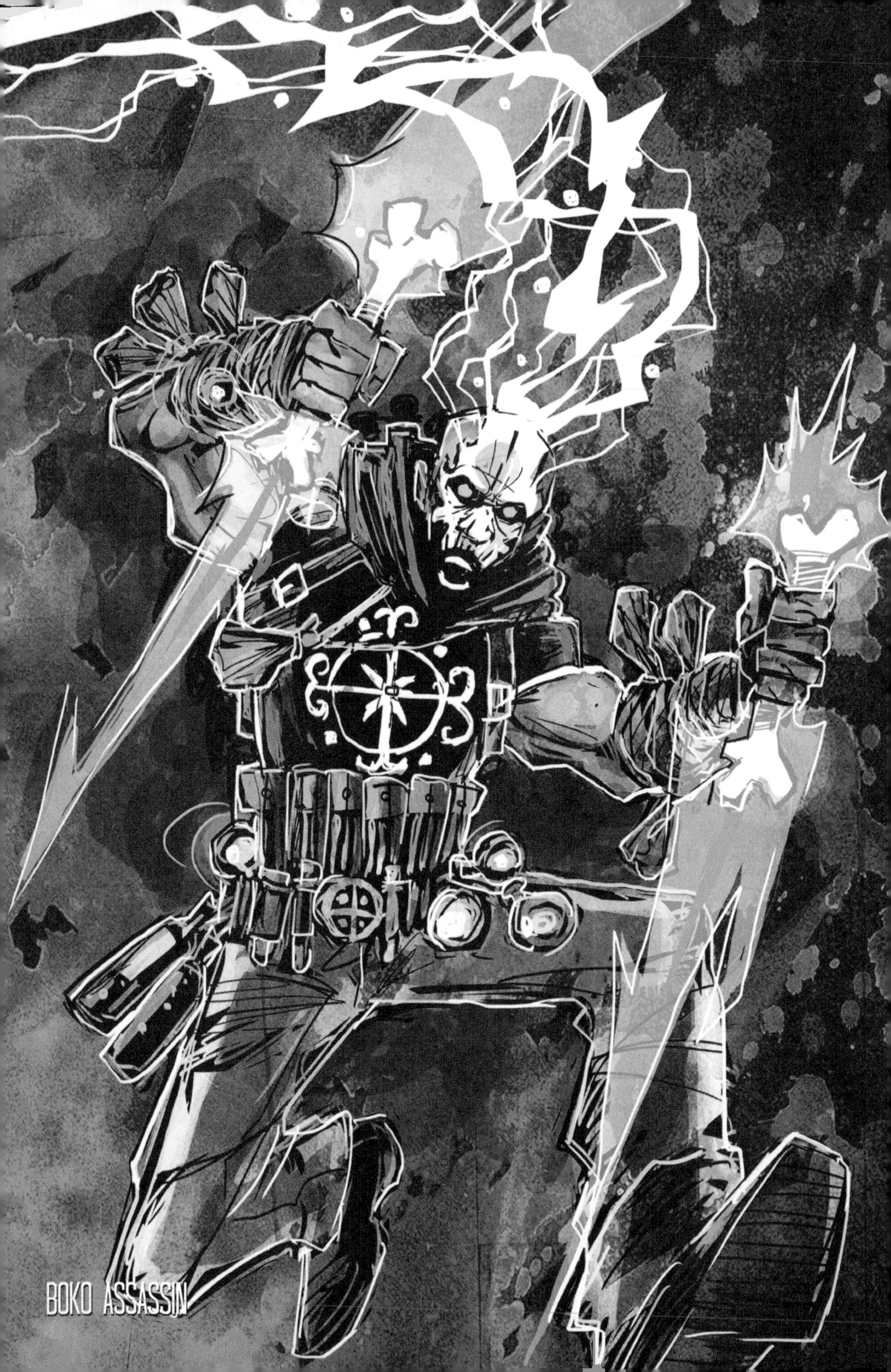
BOKO ASSASSIN

DOCTOR VOODOO

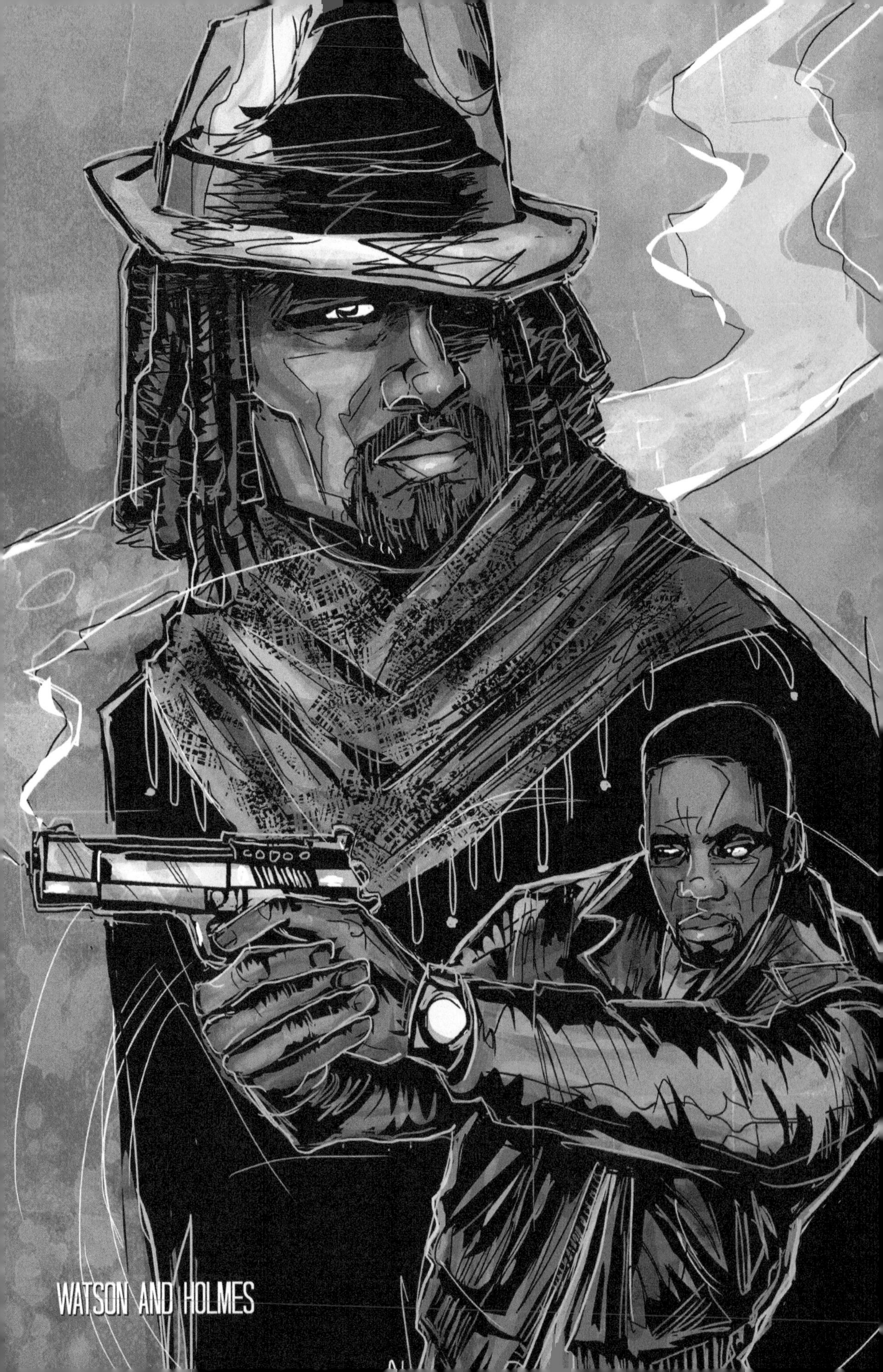
WATSON AND HOLMES

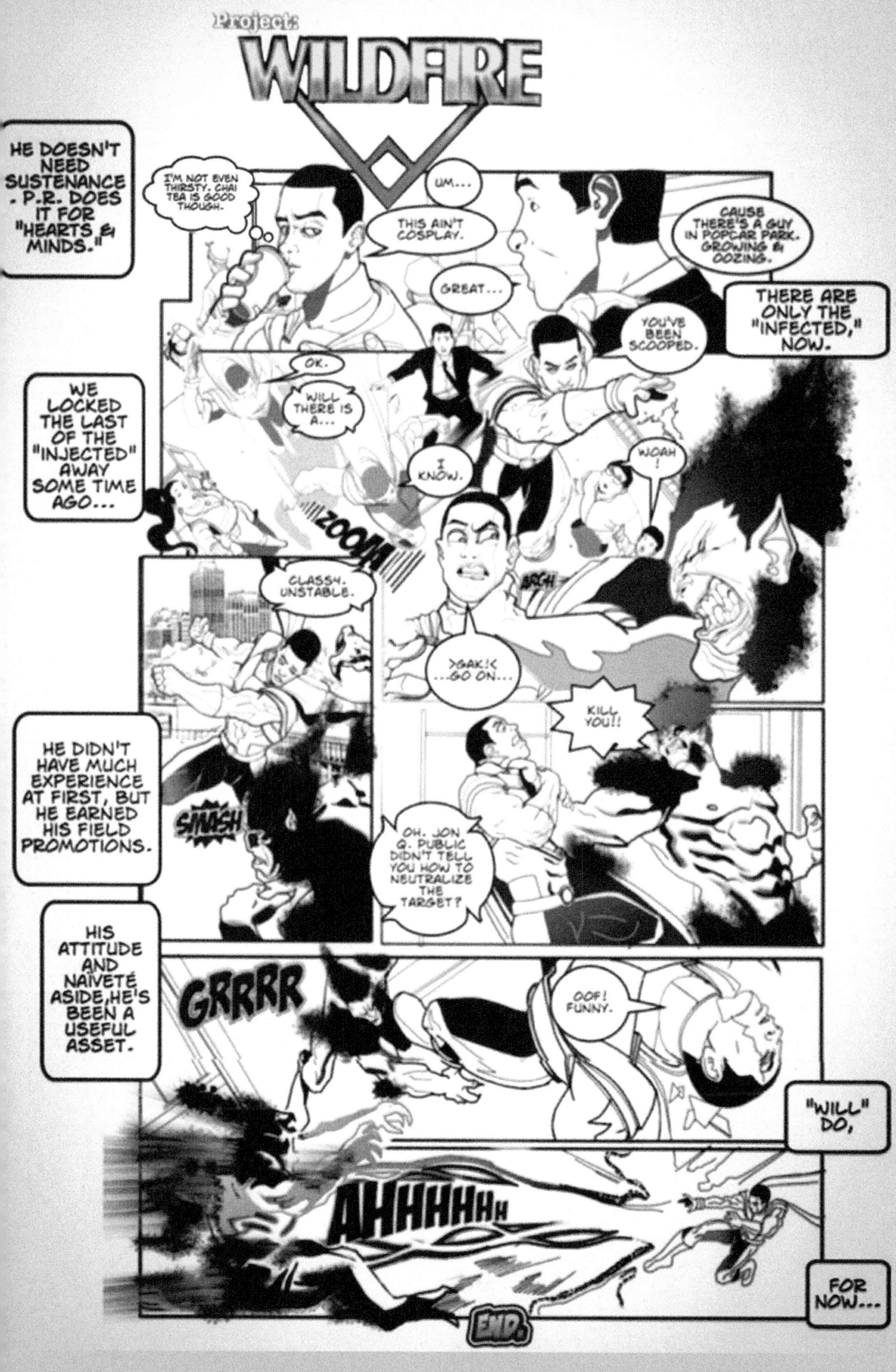
Project: WILDFIRE
HE DOESN'T NEED SUSTENANCE - P.R. DOES IT FOR "HEARTS & MINDS."
I'M NOT EVEN THIRSTY. CHAI TEA IS GOOD THOUGH.
UM...
THIS AIN'T COSPLAY.
CAUSE THERE'S A GUY IN POPCAR PARK. GROWING & OOZING.
GREAT...
THERE ARE ONLY THE "INFECTED," NOW.
YOU'VE BEEN SCOOPED.
WE LOCKED THE LAST OF THE "INJECTED" AWAY SOME TIME AGO...
OK.
WILL THERE IS A...
I KNOW.
WOAH !
ZOOM
CLASSY. UNSTABLE.
ARGH
>GAK!< ...GO ON...
KILL YOU!!
HE DIDN'T HAVE MUCH EXPERIENCE AT FIRST, BUT HE EARNED HIS FIELD PROMOTIONS.
SMASH
OH. JON Q. PUBLIC DIDN'T TELL YOU HOW TO NEUTRALIZE THE TARGET?
HIS ATTITUDE AND NAÏVETÉ ASIDE, HE'S BEEN A USEFUL ASSET.
GRRRR
OOF! FUNNY.
"WILL" DO,
AHHHHHH
FOR NOW...
END.

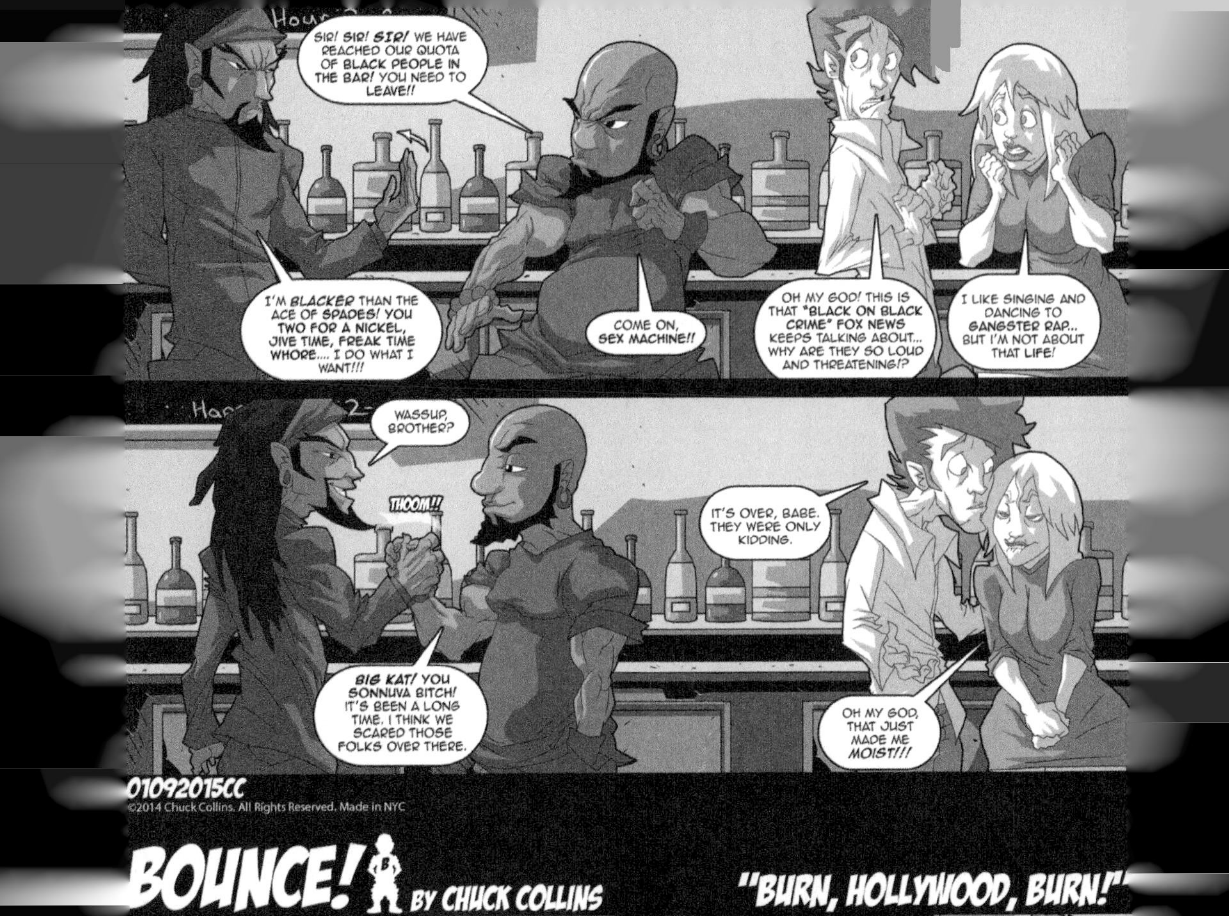
SIR! SIR! SIR! WE HAVE REACHED OUR QUOTA OF BLACK PEOPLE IN THE BAR! YOU NEED TO LEAVE!!
I'M BLACKER THAN THE ACE OF SPADES! YOU TWO FOR A NICKEL, JIVE TIME, FREAK TIME WHORE.... I DO WHAT I WANT!!!
COME ON, SEX MACHINE!!
OH MY GOD! THIS IS THAT "BLACK ON BLACK CRIME" FOX NEWS KEEPS TALKING ABOUT... WHY ARE THEY SO LOUD AND THREATENING!?
I LIKE SINGING AND DANCING TO GANGSTER RAP... BUT I'M NOT ABOUT THAT LIFE!
WASSUP, BROTHER?
THOOM!!
BIG KAT! YOU SONNUVA BITCH! IT'S BEEN A LONG TIME. I THINK WE SCARED THOSE FOLKS OVER THERE.
IT'S OVER, BABE. THEY WERE ONLY KIDDING.
OH MY GOD, THAT JUST MADE ME MOIST!!!

01092015CC

BOUNCE! BY CHUCK COLLINS

"BURN, HOLLYWOOD, BURN!"

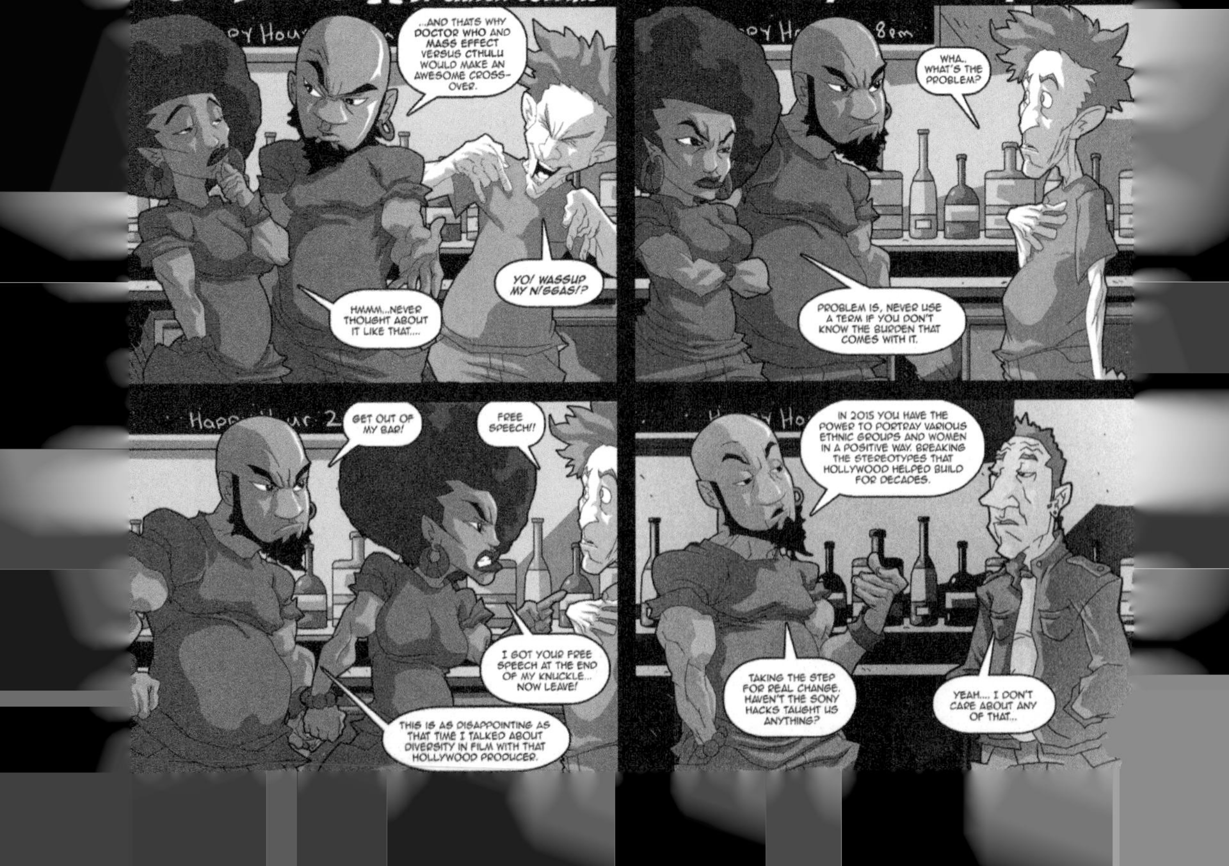
...AND THATS WHY DOCTOR WHO AND MASS EFFECT VERSUS CTHULU WOULD MAKE AN AWESOME CROSS-OVER.
HMMM...NEVER THOUGHT ABOUT IT LIKE THAT....
YO! WASSUP MY N!GGAS!?
WHA.. WHAT'S THE PROBLEM?
PROBLEM IS, NEVER USE A TERM IF YOU DON'T KNOW THE BURDEN THAT COMES WITH IT.
GET OUT OF MY BAR!
FREE SPEECH!!
I GOT YOUR FREE SPEECH AT THE END OF MY KNUCKLE... NOW LEAVE!
THIS IS AS DISAPPOINTING AS THAT TIME I TALKED ABOUT DIVERSITY IN FILM WITH THAT HOLLYWOOD PRODUCER.
IN 2015 YOU HAVE THE POWER TO PORTRAY VARIOUS ETHNIC GROUPS AND WOMEN IN A POSITIVE WAY. BREAKING THE STEREOTYPES THAT HOLLYWOOD HELPED BUILD FOR DECADES.
TAKING THE STEP FOR REAL CHANGE. HAVEN'T THE SONY HACKS TAUGHT US ANYTHING?
YEAH.... I DON'T CARE ABOUT ANY OF THAT...

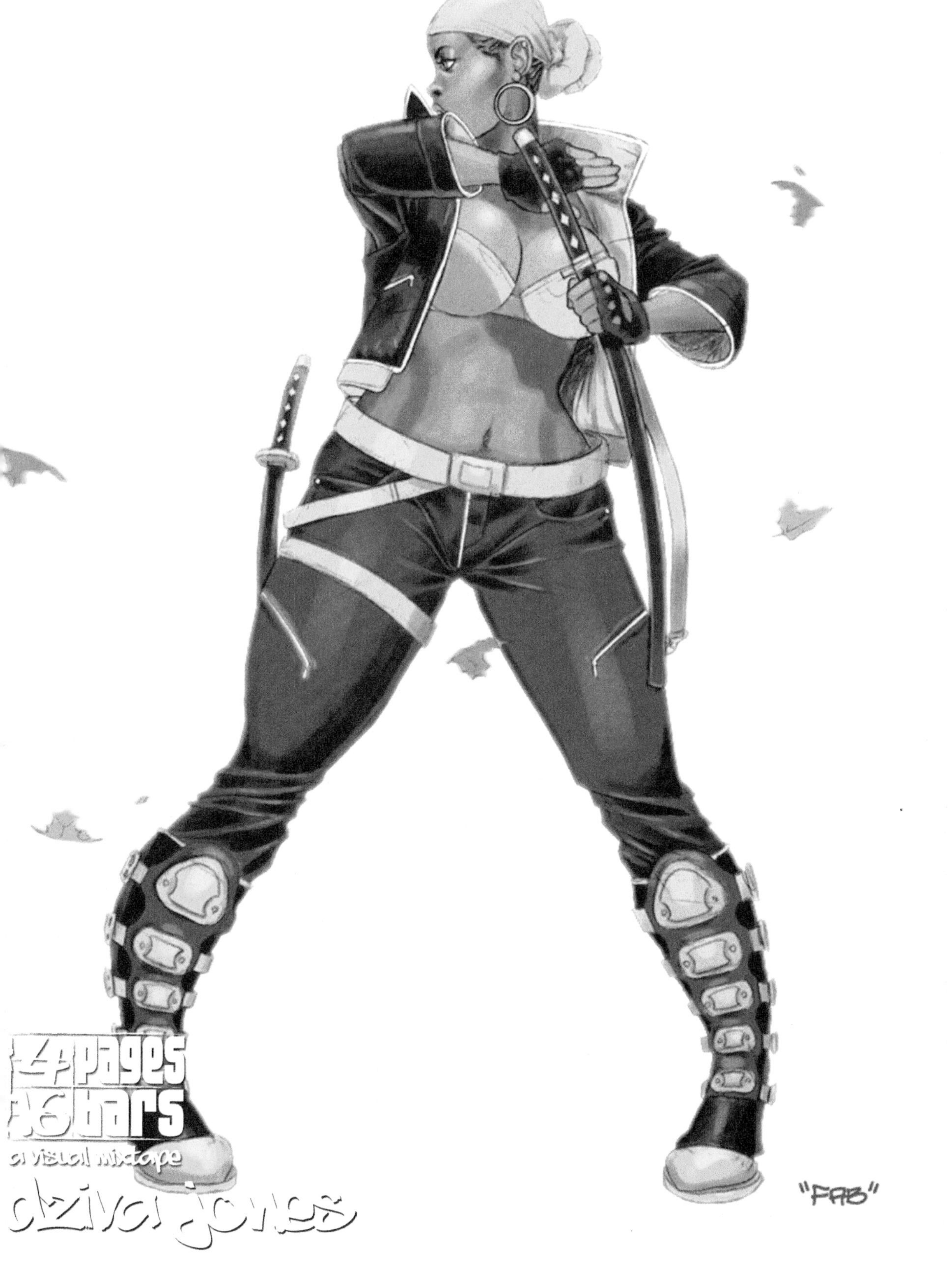
24 pages
16 bars
a visual mixtape
dziva jones
"FAB"

COVER ILLUSTRATION BY
CHARLIE "FAB" GOUBILE

INTERIOR ART BY
ASHLEY A. WOODS

Aminah Armour was born and raised in Chicago. Growing up in the '80s and '90s she was influence by cartoons like Thundercats, He-man and Jem as well as movies and television shows such as Wonder Woman and The Incredible Hulk.. It was only a matter of time before she would gravitate toward comics.

Influenced by writers such as Chris Claremont, Christopher Priest, and Fabian Nicieza, Aminah created **Dziva Jones**, the telepathic/telekenetic, fun, sexy and fierce bodyguard for hire.

website: dziva jones.wix.com/bodyguard

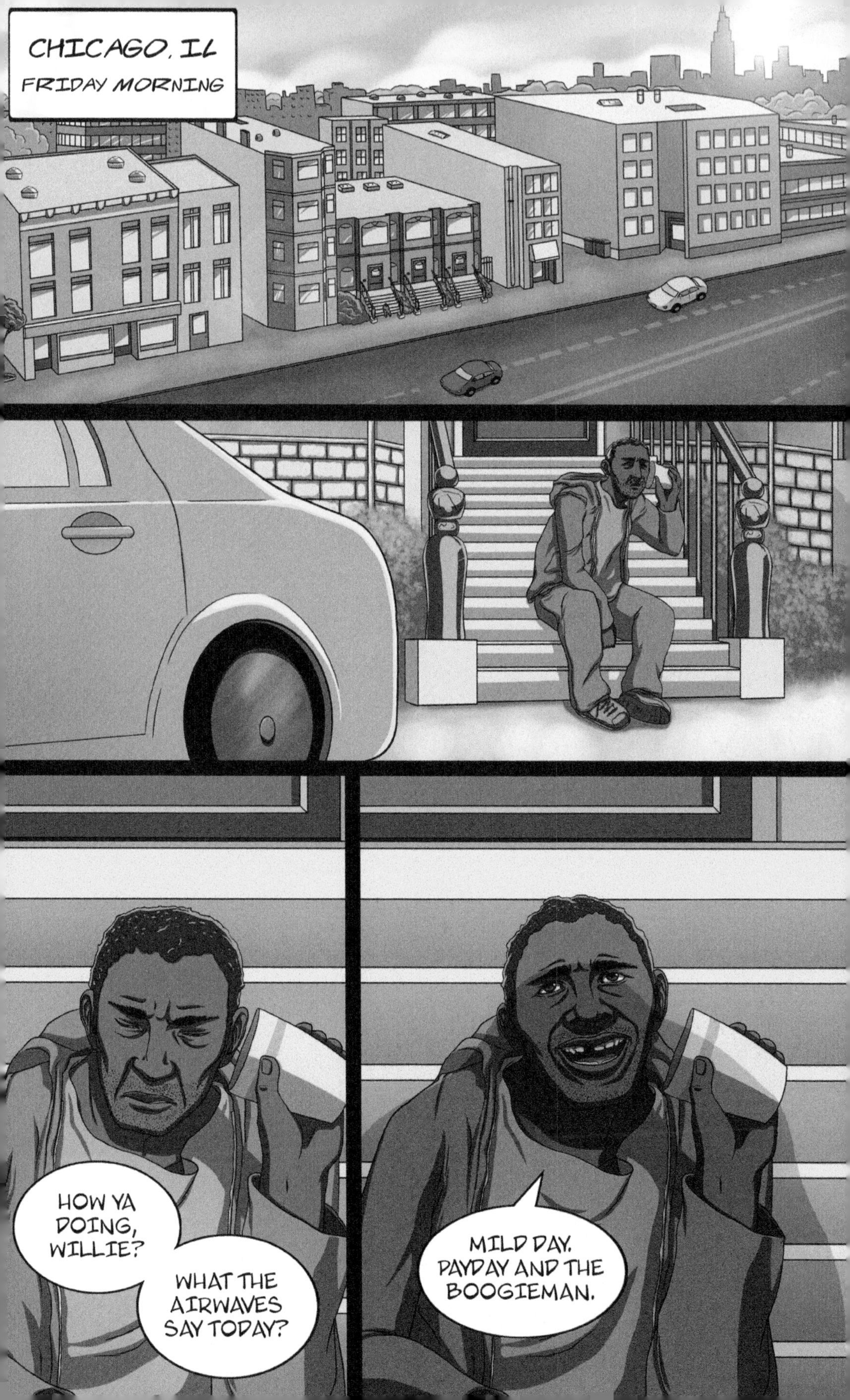
CHICAGO, IL
FRIDAY MORNING
HOW YA DOING, WILLIE?
WHAT THE AIRWAVES SAY TODAY?
MILD DAY. PAYDAY AND THE BOOGIEMAN.

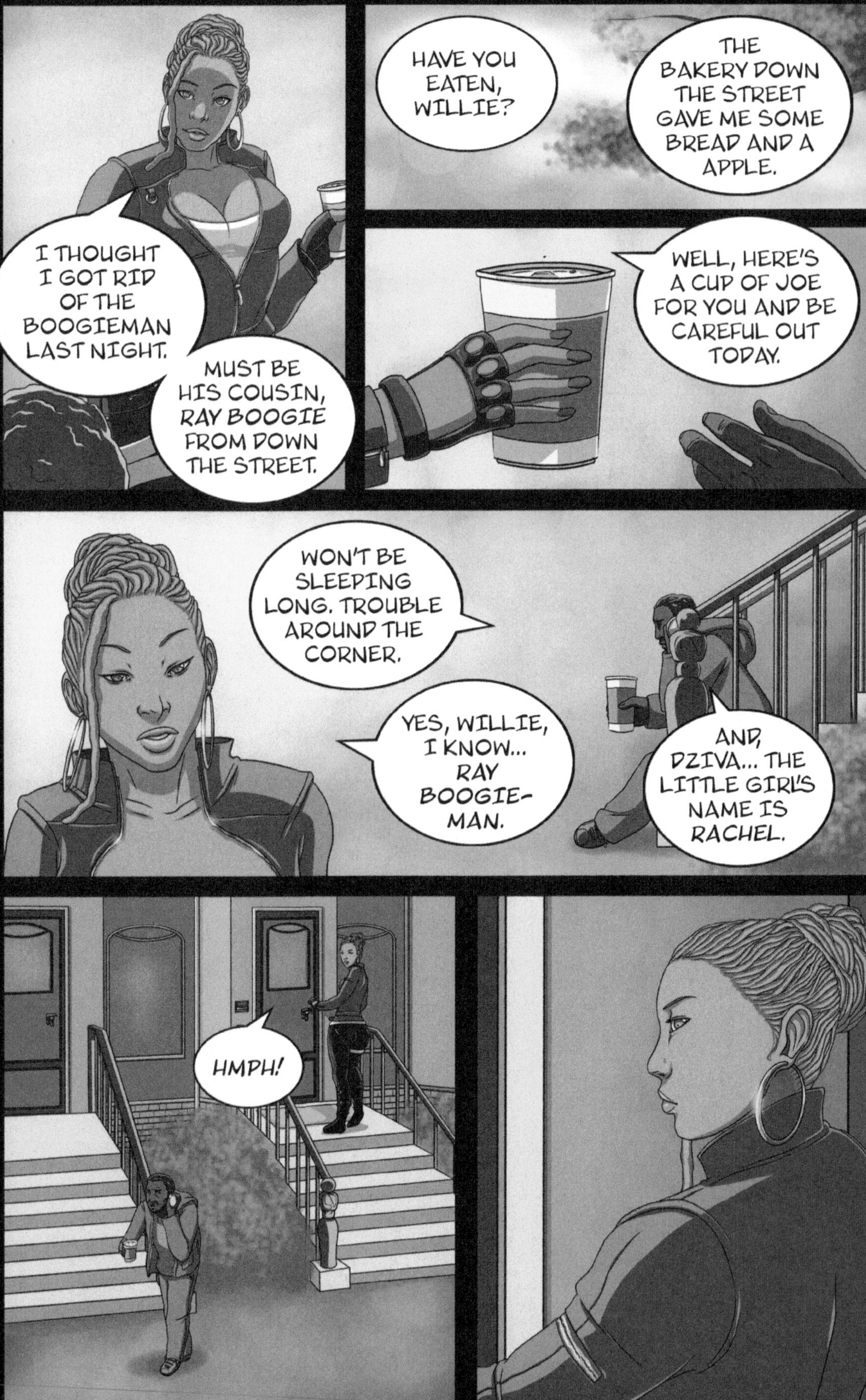
I THOUGHT I GOT RID OF THE BOOGIEMAN LAST NIGHT.
MUST BE HIS COUSIN, RAY BOOGIE FROM DOWN THE STREET.
HAVE YOU EATEN, WILLIE?
THE BAKERY DOWN THE STREET GAVE ME SOME BREAD AND A APPLE.
WELL, HERE'S A CUP OF JOE FOR YOU AND BE CAREFUL OUT TODAY.
WON'T BE SLEEPING LONG. TROUBLE AROUND THE CORNER.
YES, WILLIE, I KNOW... RAY BOOGIE-MAN.
AND, DZIVA... THE LITTLE GIRL'S NAME IS RACHEL.
HMPH!

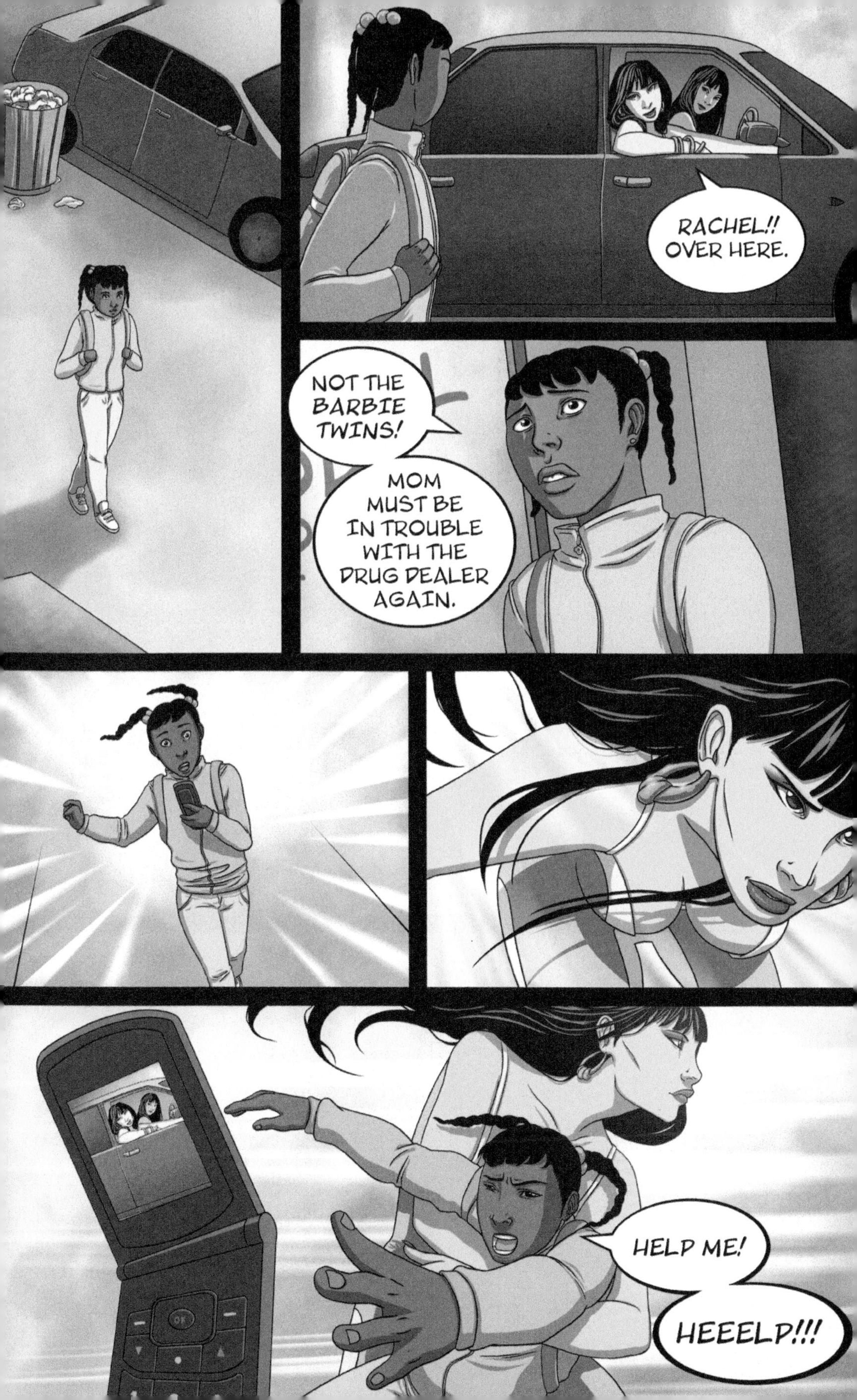
RACHEL!! OVER HERE.
NOT THE BARBIE TWINS!
MOM MUST BE IN TROUBLE WITH THE DRUG DEALER AGAIN.
HELP ME!
HEEELP!!!

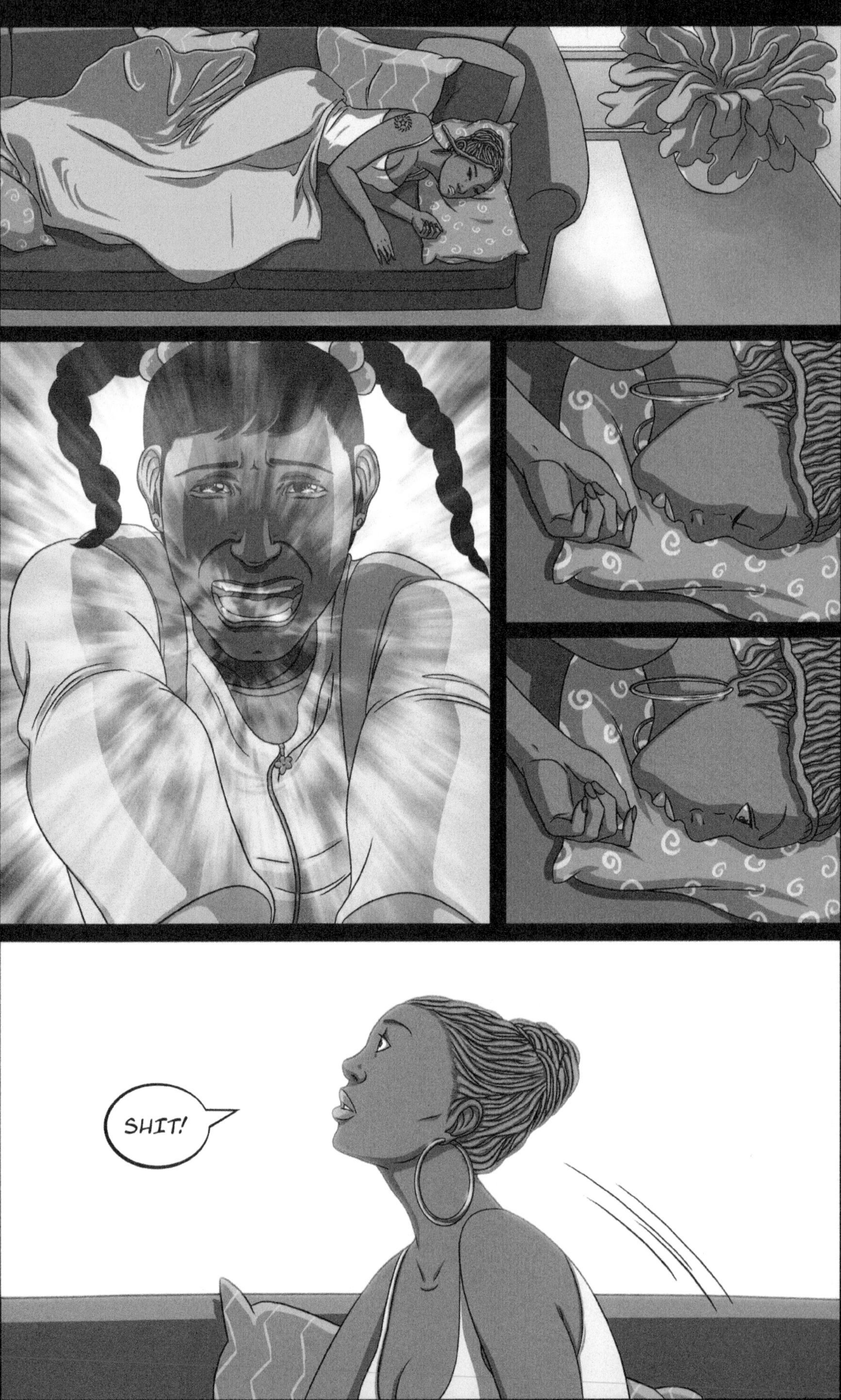
SHIT!

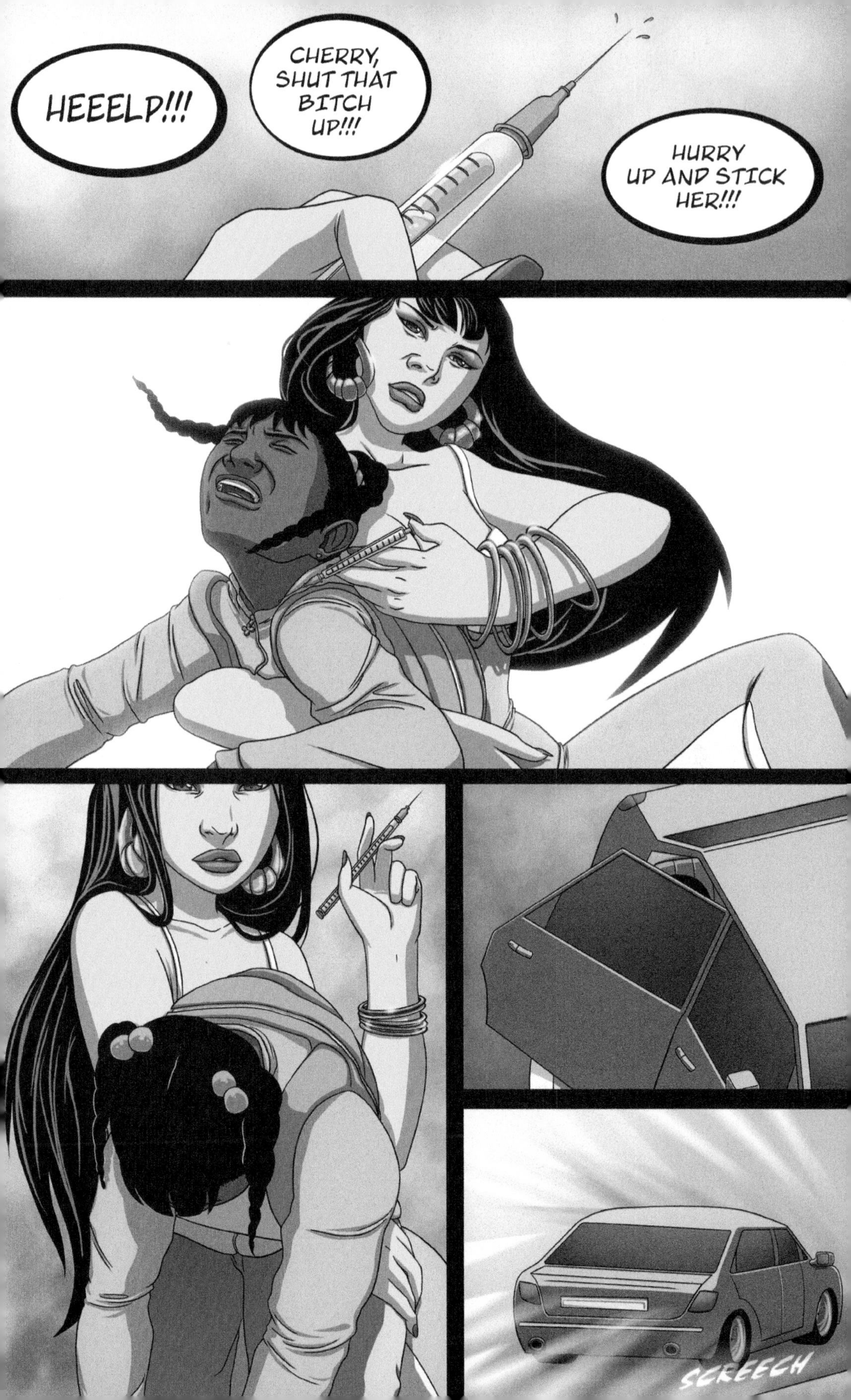
HEEELP!!!
CHERRY, SHUT THAT BITCH UP!!!
HURRY UP AND STICK HER!!!
SCREECH

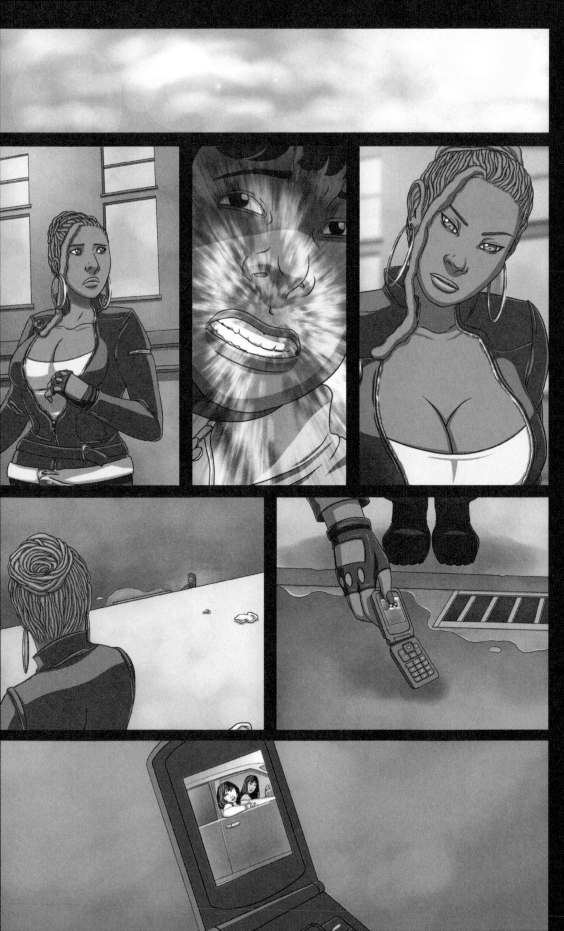

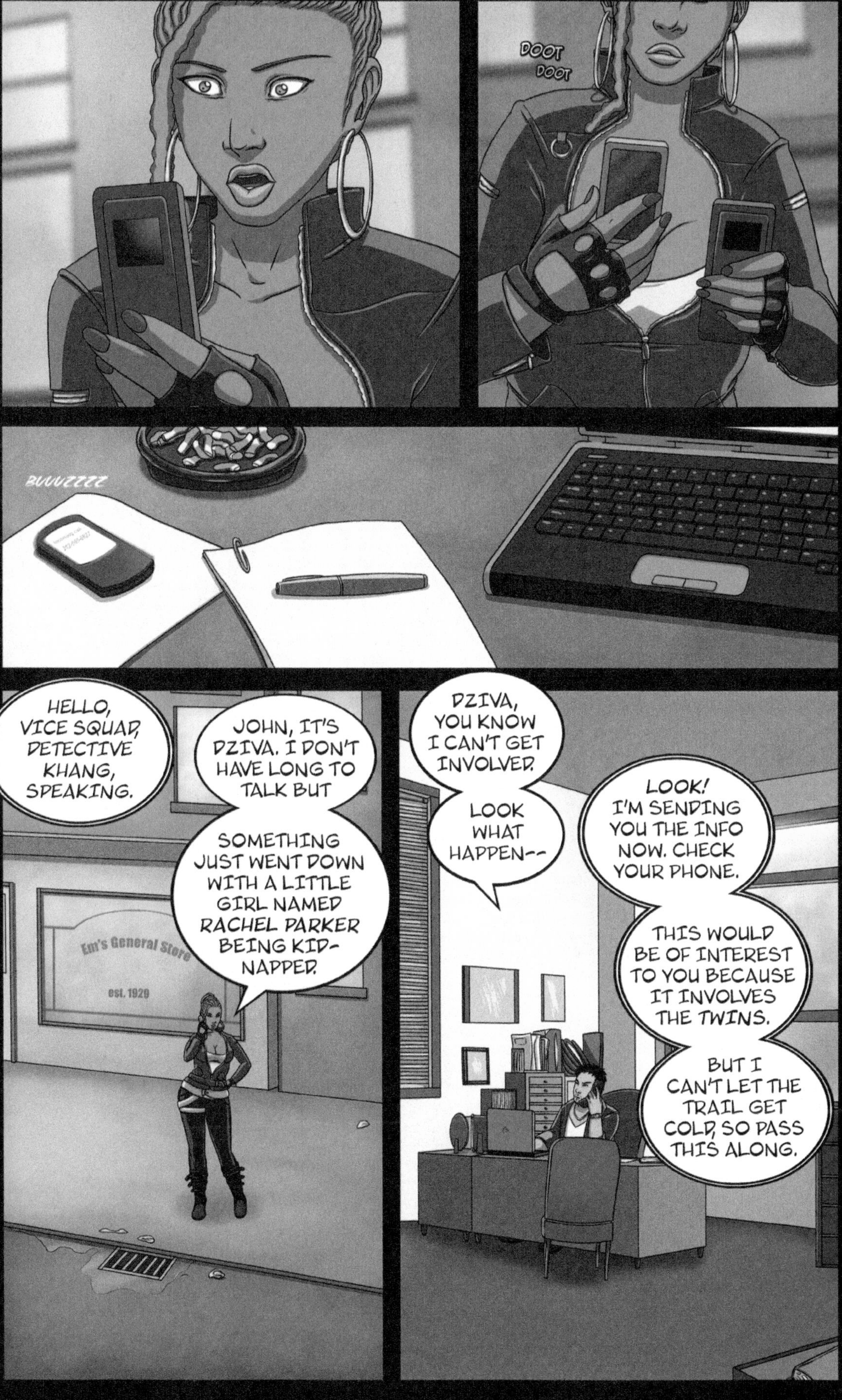
DOOT
DOOT
BUUUZZZZ
HELLO, VICE SQUAD, DETECTIVE KHANG, SPEAKING.
JOHN, IT'S DZIVA. I DON'T HAVE LONG TO TALK BUT
SOMETHING JUST WENT DOWN WITH A LITTLE GIRL NAMED RACHEL PARKER BEING KID-NAPPED.
Em's General Store
est. 1920
DZIVA, YOU KNOW I CAN'T GET INVOLVED.
LOOK WHAT HAPPEN--
LOOK! I'M SENDING YOU THE INFO NOW. CHECK YOUR PHONE.
THIS WOULD BE OF INTEREST TO YOU BECAUSE IT INVOLVES THE TWINS.
BUT I CAN'T LET THE TRAIL GET COLD, SO PASS THIS ALONG.

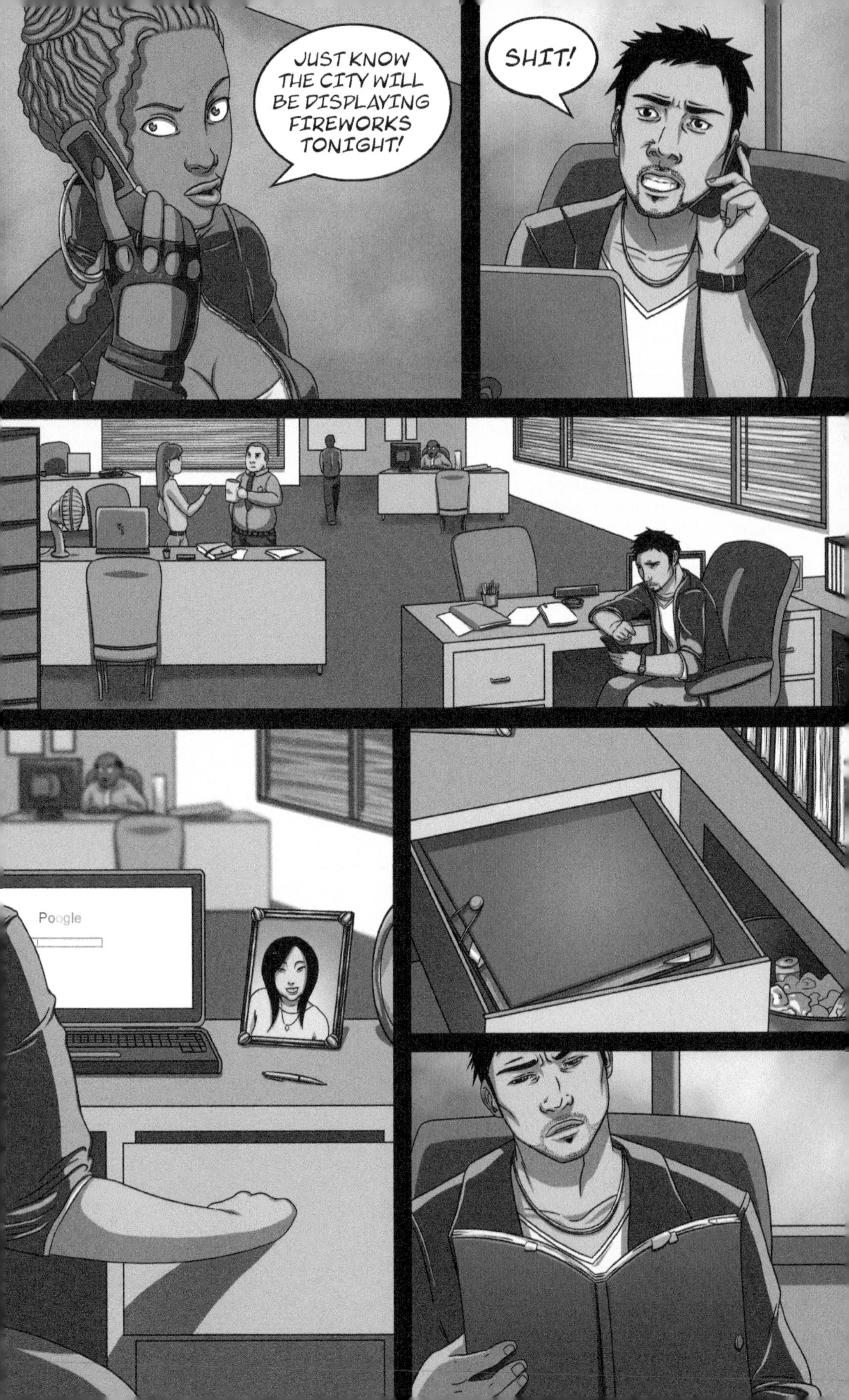
JUST KNOW THE CITY WILL BE DISPLAYING FIREWORKS TONIGHT!
SHIT!
Poogle

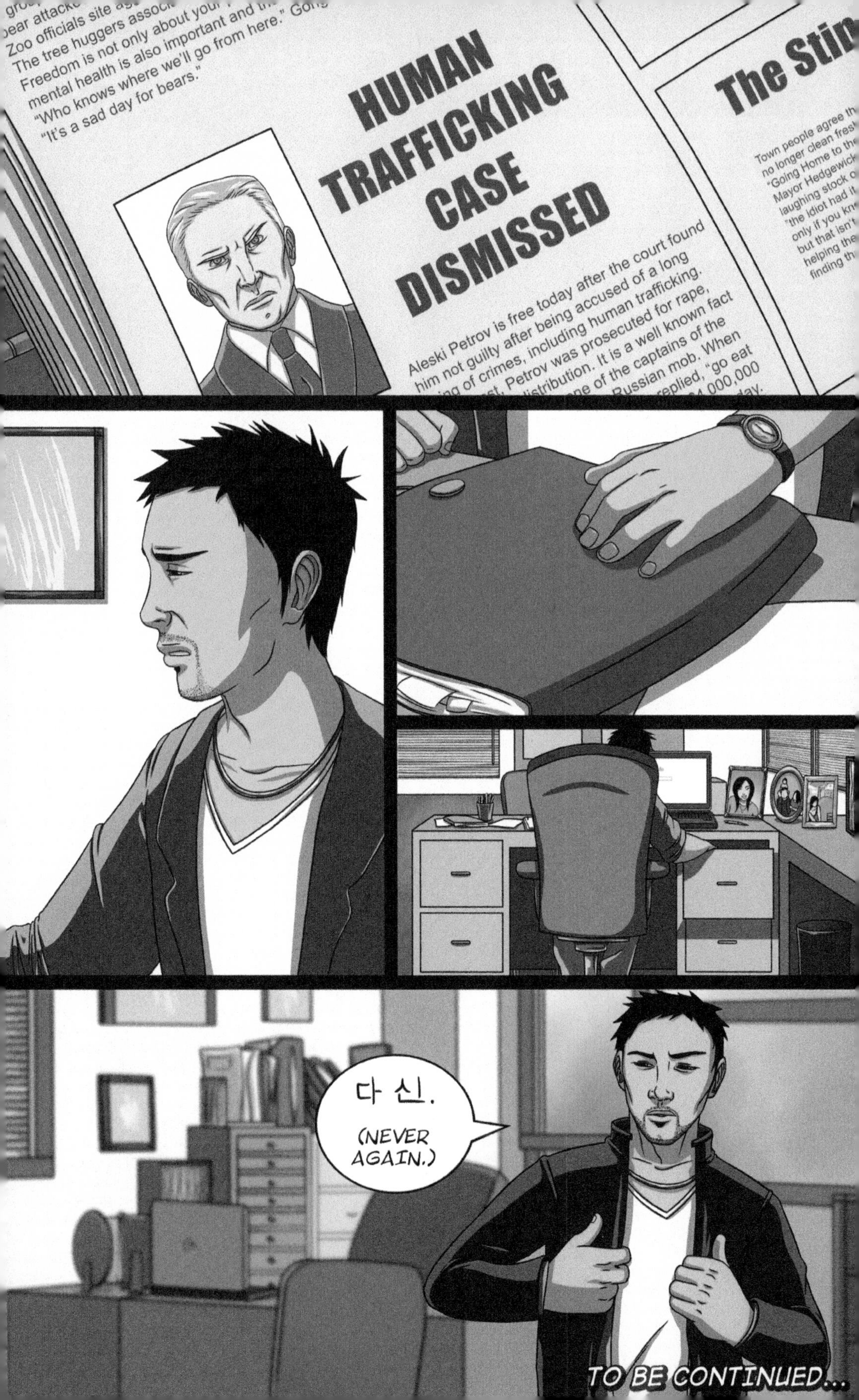

Freedom is not only about your
mental health is also important and
"Who knows where we'll go from here."
"It's a sad day for bears."
HUMAN TRAFFICKING CASE DISMISSED
Aleski Petrov is free today after the court found
him not guilty after being accused of a long
of crimes, including human trafficking.
Petrov was prosecuted for rape,
distribution. It is a well known fact
of the captains of the
Russian mob. When
replied, "go eat
The Sti
Town people agree th
no longer clean fres
"Going Home to the
Mayor Hedgewick
laughing stock o
"the idiot had it
only if you kn
but that isn't
helping the
finding th
다 신.
(NEVER AGAIN.)
TO BE CONTINUED...

THE SOUNDTRACK OF BLACK SCI-FI
MILE STONE
GHETTO OF THE MIND
ghetto
ghetto of the mind
pyrrhic
ghetto
LIBERATION SONG
GHETTO OF THE MIND
ghetto
FUNK SHUI
GHETTO OF THE MIND
ghetto
I battle the forces of mediocrity on a daily basis.
I walk the Eightfold Path of righteousness seeking the Universal Truth.
I stand on the rooftop with my barbaric yawp calling to the tribe.
I scream at the top of my lungs to the heavens letting them know that warriors have entered the celestial plane.
I change the world in my own way, with passion, with panache, and with style...
Episodes available now on Itunes

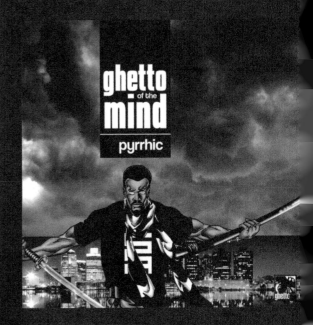

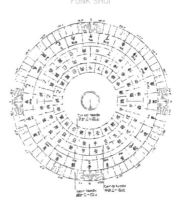

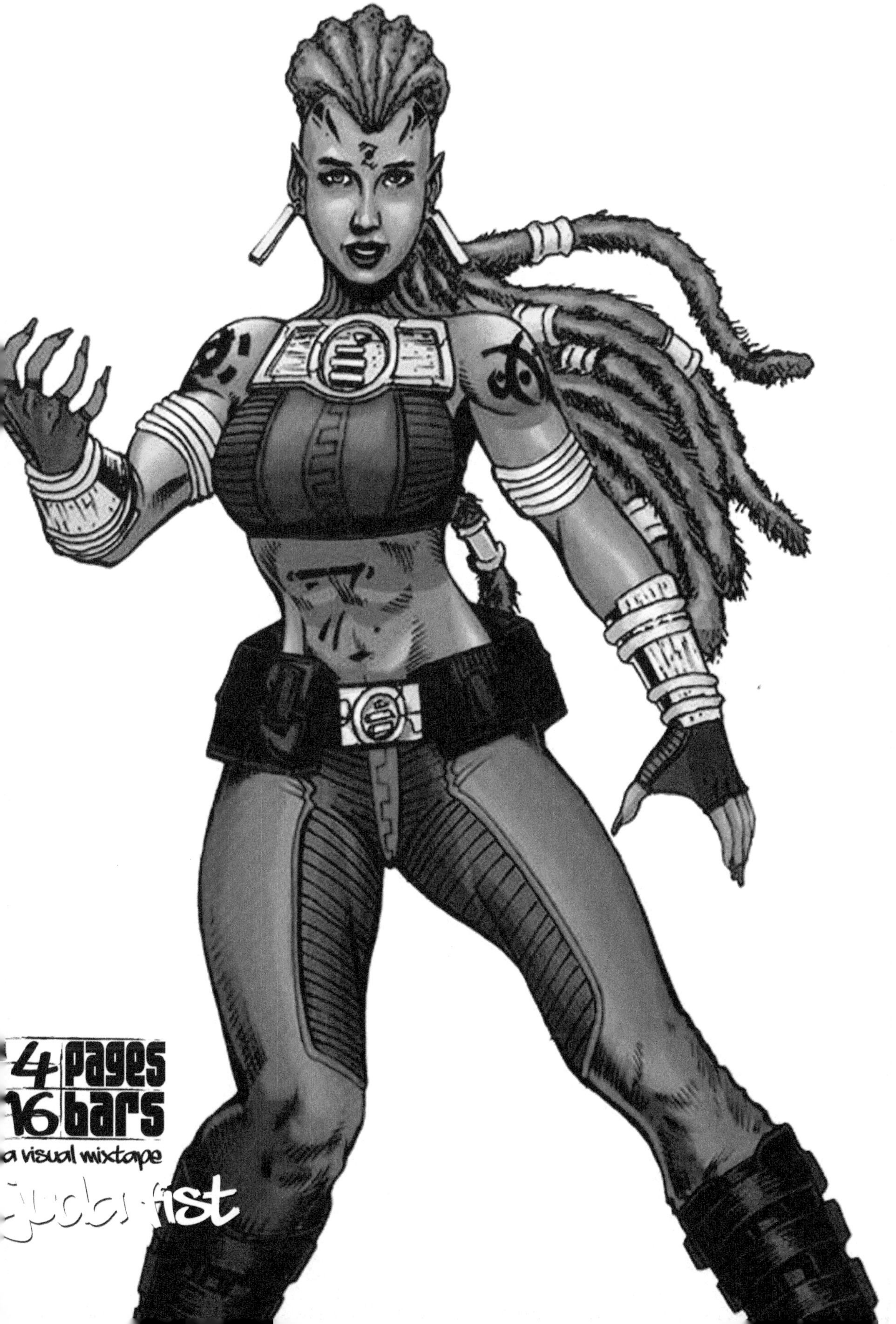
4 pages
16 bars
a visual mixtape

Mark C. Dudley is native of the Detroit Area. His love affair with artwork and comics started when he was a child, but his imagination found a new forum when he discovered the role-playing games of **Palladium Books**. Mark's first and all-time favorite *Palladium RPG: Heroes Unlimited™*. His next favorite: *Rifts®*.

His work appears under his own name as well as under **Drunken Style Studios** in many issues of The Rifter® as well as such notable RPG titles as *Heroes Unlimited™ RPG 2nd Edition, Armageddon Unlimited™, Rifts® Ultimate Edition, Rifts® New West™, Rifts® China Two, Rifts® MercTown™, Rifts® Merc Ops, Nightbane® Survival Guide, Heroes of the Megaverse®* and many others.

Mark Dudley's collaborations have gone beyond artwork on numerous Palladium projects, including concept and concept development, talent coordination, and work on one of Palladium's ill-fated MMORPG projects. Mark led a handpicked crew of artists and writers from Drunken Style Studios to develop a mature-themed Nightbane® animated TV series that Palladium hopes will someday find a home on a cable channel.

He is also the creator of the Afro futuristic *Juda Fist: 7 Deaths of the Yobi*. This dystopian, hip hop inspired tale is about Amaru Jones, a man turned into a bio organic weapon who awakes from a decades old sleep to rebuild his life. However, age old enemies await his resurrection and ready themselves to continue a battle in which the fate of our solar system hangs in the balance.

website: markcdudley.deviantart.com/?rwrd★35936

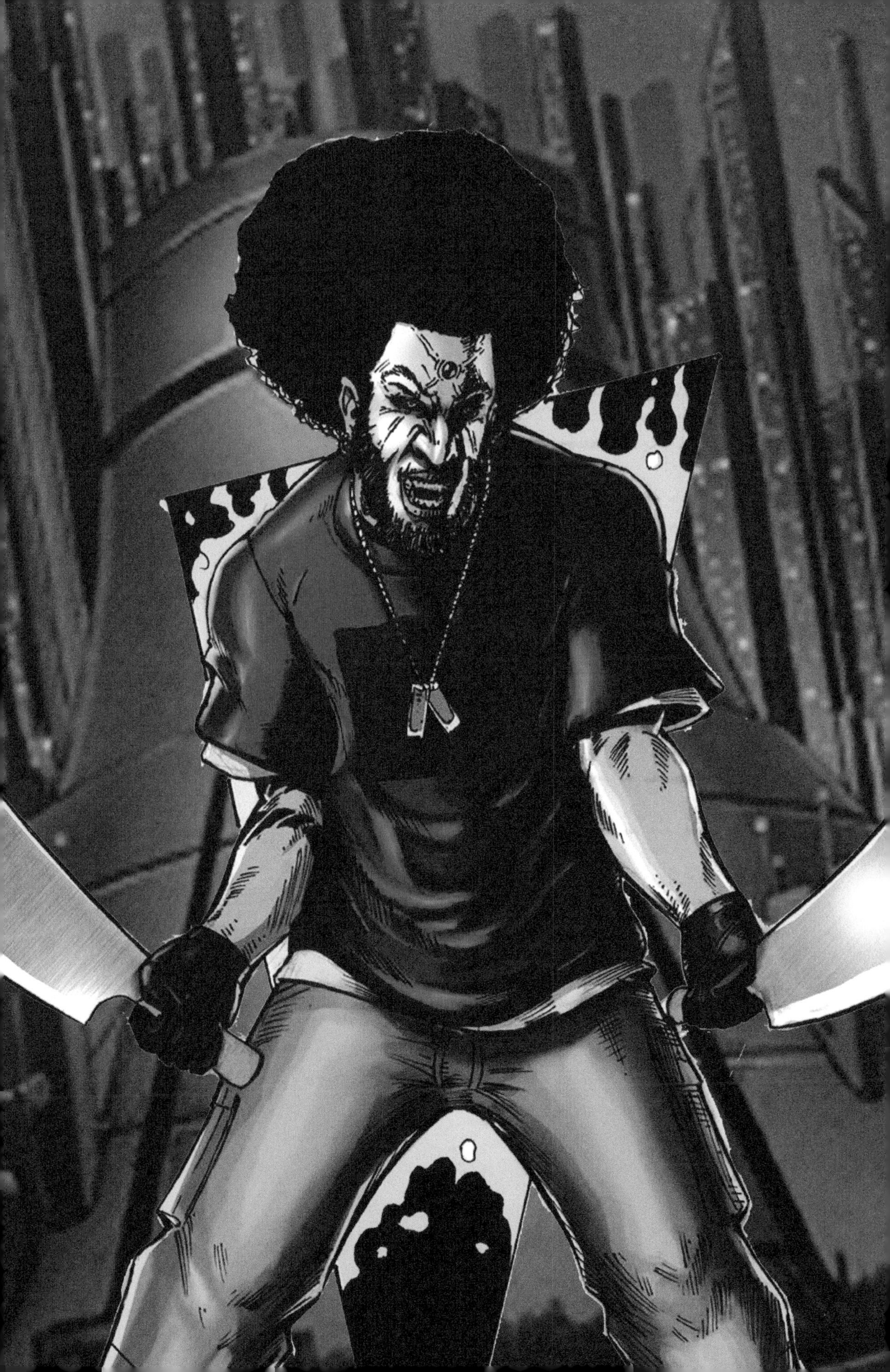

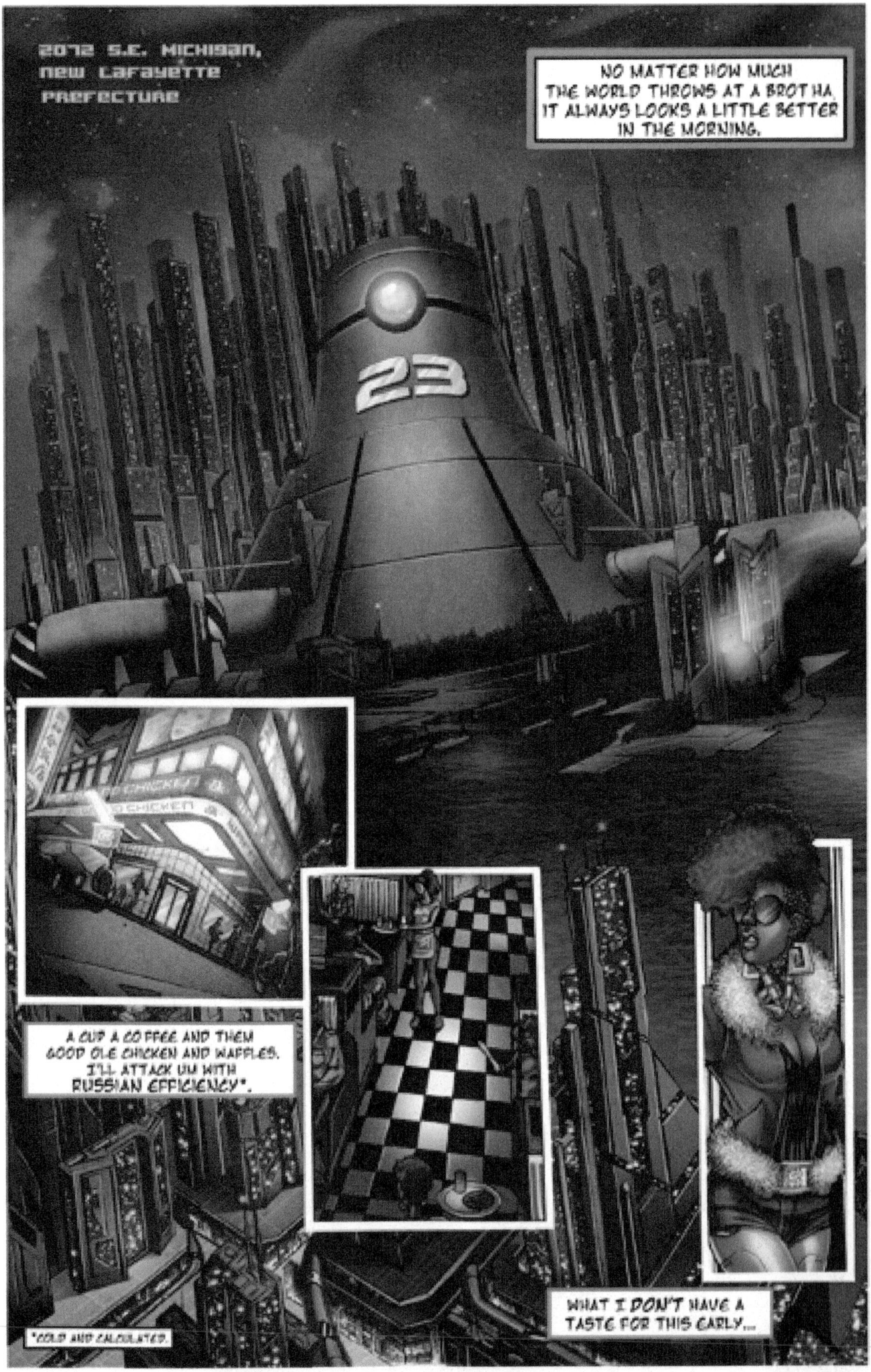
2072 S.E. MICHIGAN, NEW LAFAYETTE PREFECTURE
NO MATTER HOW MUCH THE WORLD THROWS AT A BROTHA IT ALWAYS LOOKS A LITTLE BETTER IN THE MORNING.
23
A CUP A COFFEE AND THEM GOOD OLE CHICKEN AND WAFFLES. I'LL ATTACK UM WITH RUSSIAN EFFICIENCY*.
WHAT I DON'T HAVE A TASTE FOR THIS EARLY...
*COLD AND CALCULATED.

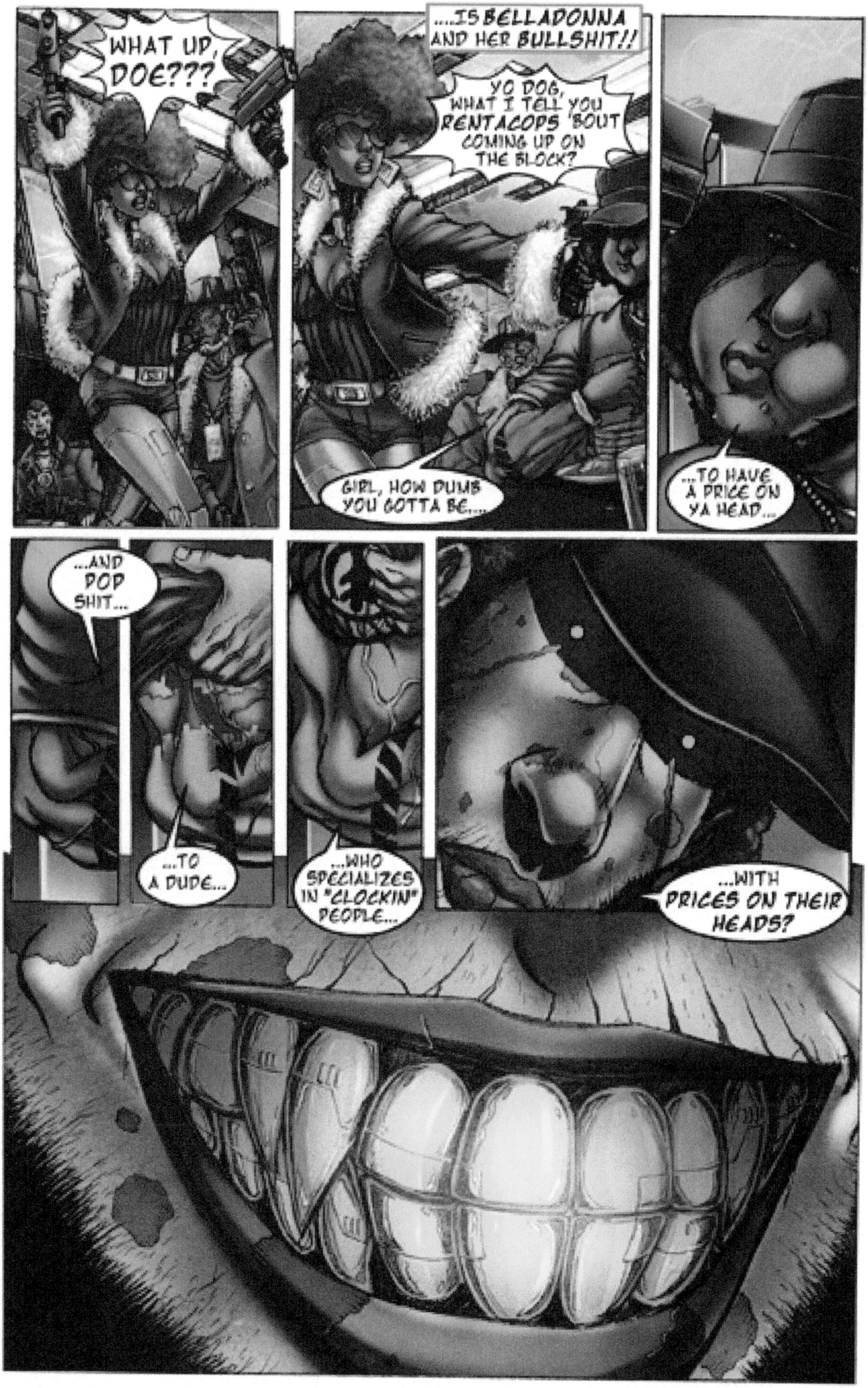
WHAT UP, DOE???
....IS BELLADONNA AND HER BULLSHIT!!
YO DOG, WHAT I TELL YOU RENTACOPS 'BOUT COMING UP ON THE BLOCK?
GIRL, HOW DUMB YOU GOTTA BE....
...TO HAVE A PRICE ON YA HEAD...
...AND POP SHIT...
...TO A DUDE...
...WHO SPECIALIZES IN "CLOCKIN" PEOPLE...
...WITH PRICES ON THEIR HEADS?

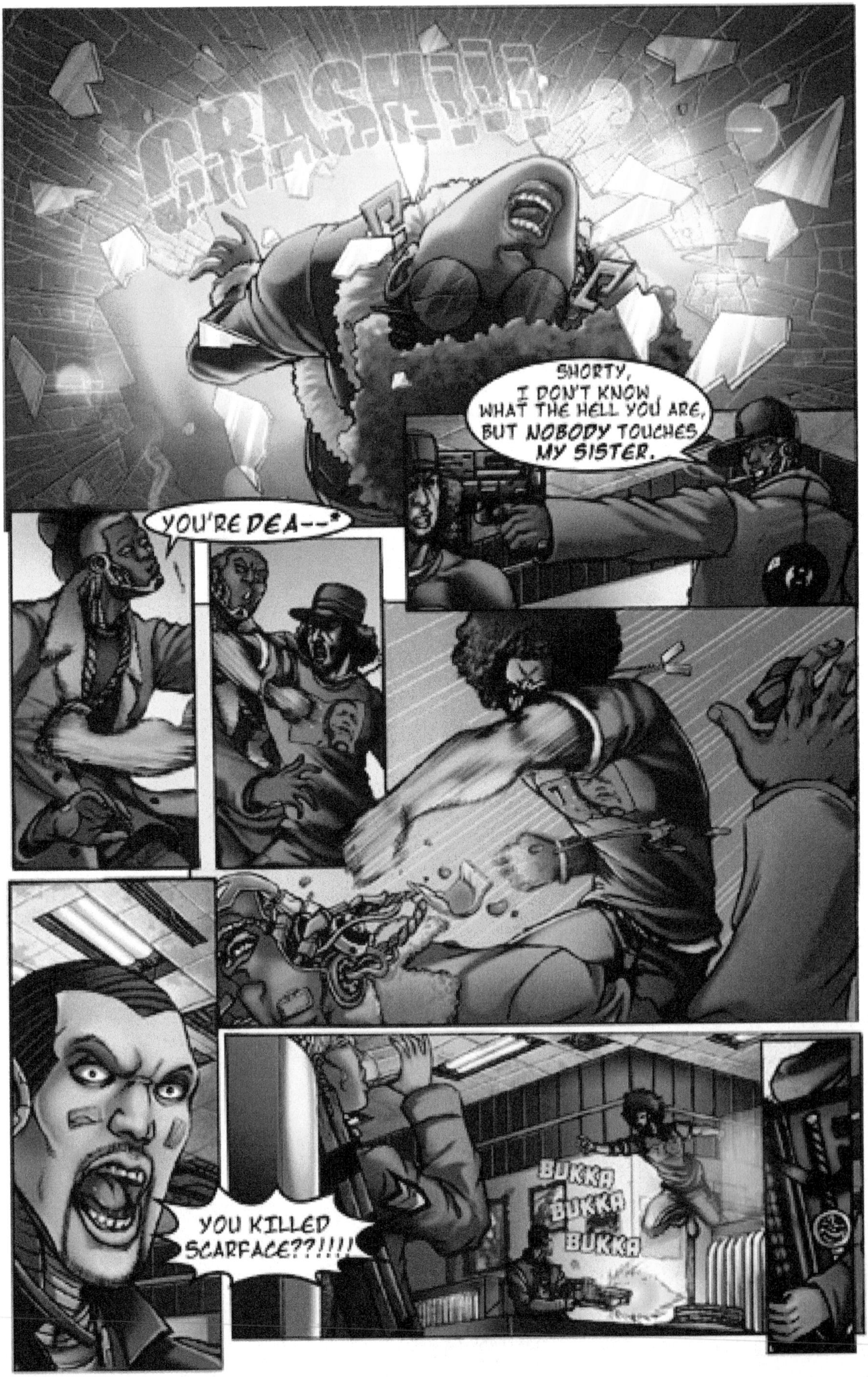
CRASH!!!
SHORTY, I DON'T KNOW WHAT THE HELL YOU ARE, BUT NOBODY TOUCHES MY SISTER.
YOU'RE DEA--*
YOU KILLED SCARFACE??!!!!
BUKKA
BUKKA
BUKKA

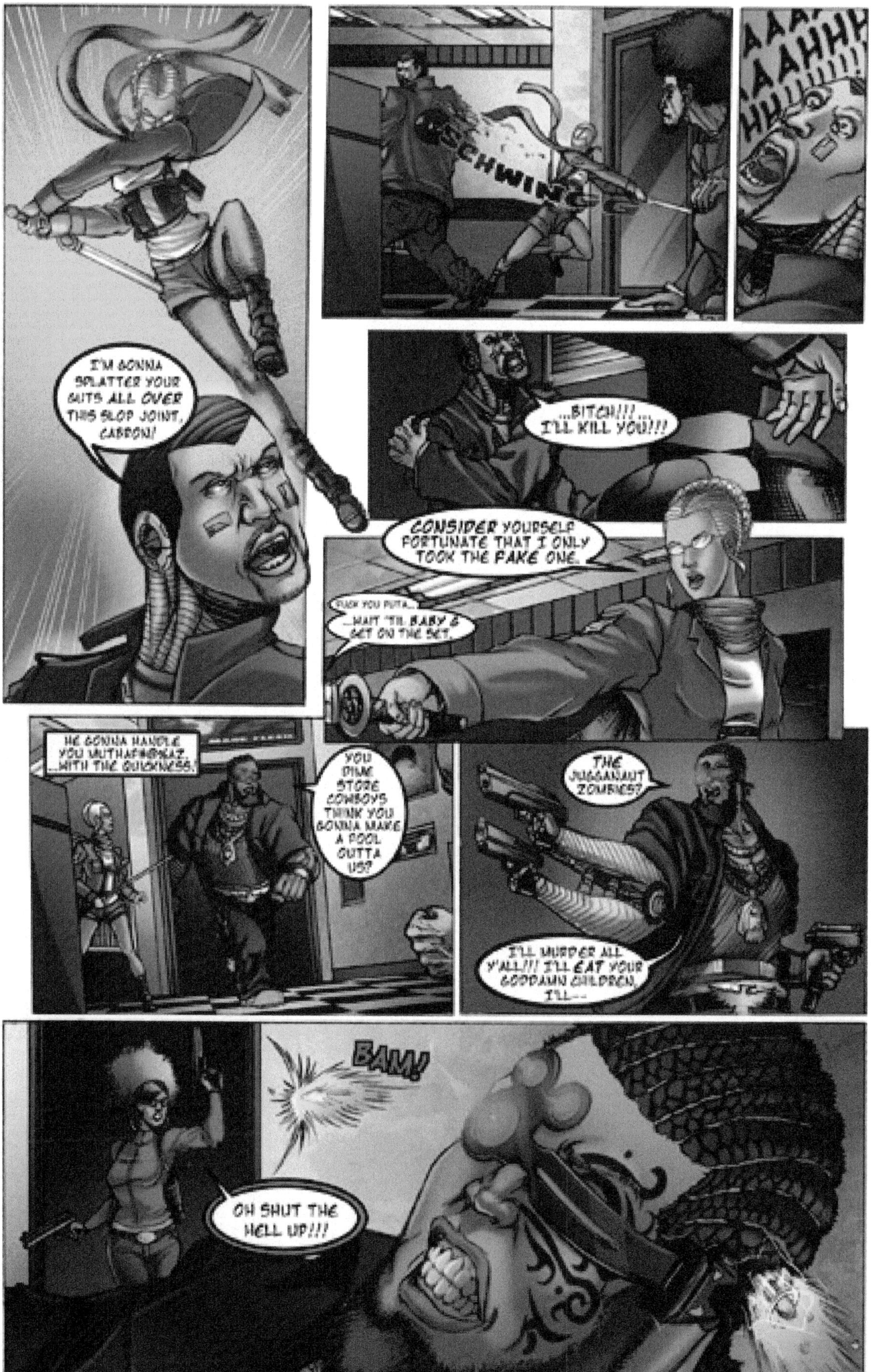

SCHWING
AAAAAHHH!!!!!
I'M GONNA SPLATTER YOUR GUTS ALL OVER THIS SLOP JOINT, CABRON!
...BITCH!!! ... I'LL KILL YOU!!!
CONSIDER YOURSELF FORTUNATE THAT I ONLY TOOK THE FAKE ONE.
FUCK YOU PUTA...
...WAIT 'TIL BABY G GET ON THE SET.
HE GONNA HANDLE YOU MUTHAF#@KAZ. ...WITH THE QUICKNESS.
YOU DIME STORE COWBOYS THINK YOU GONNA MAKE A FOOL OUTTA US?
THE JUGGANAUT ZOMBIES?
I'LL MURDER ALL Y'ALL!!! I'LL EAT YOUR GODDAMN CHILDREN. I'LL--
BAM!
OH SHUT THE HELL UP!!!

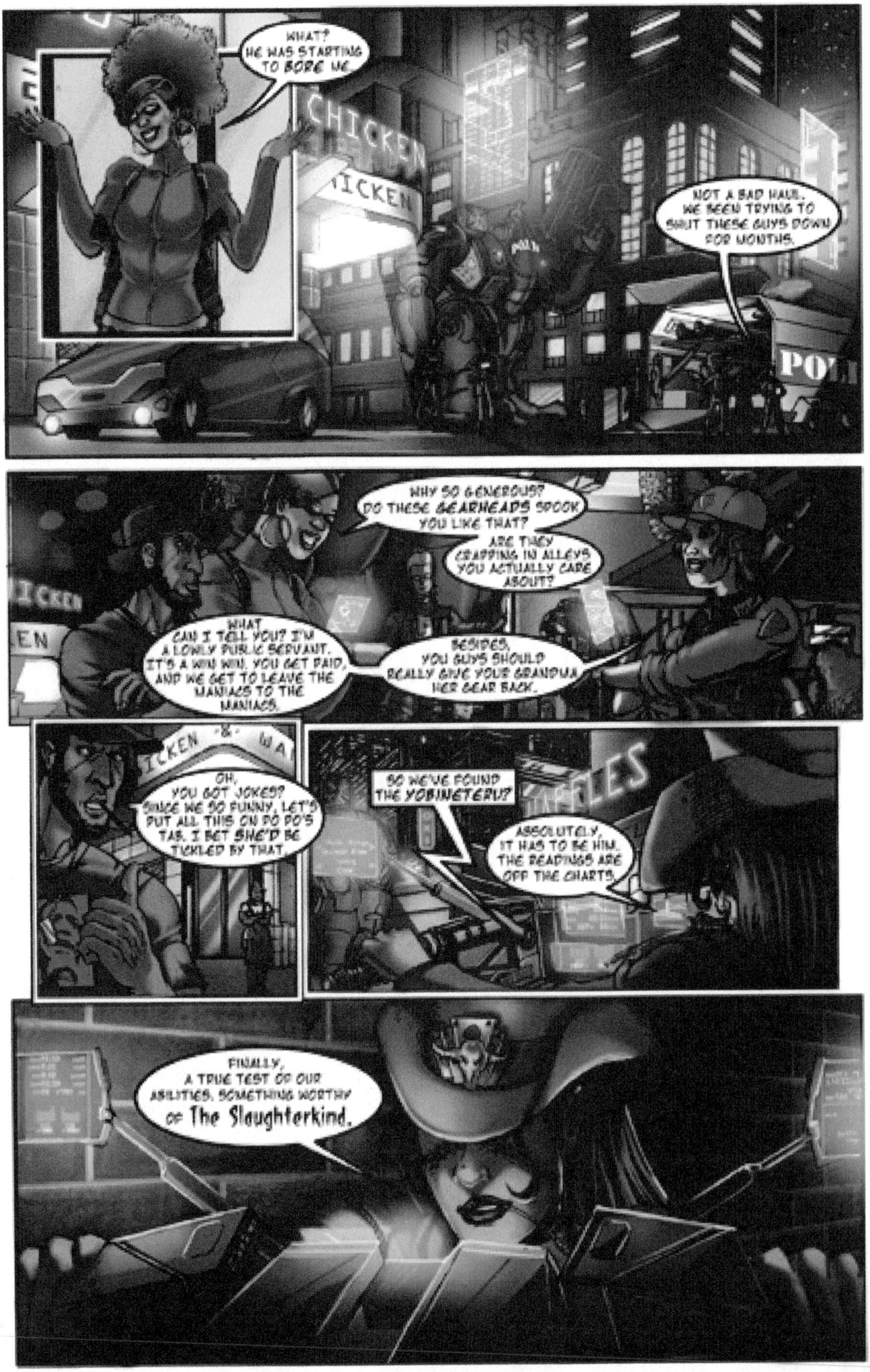
WHAT? HE WAS STARTING TO BORE ME.
NOT A BAD HAUL. WE BEEN TRYING TO SHUT THESE GUYS DOWN FOR MONTHS.
WHY SO GENEROUS? DO THESE GEARHEADS SPOOK YOU LIKE THAT?
ARE THEY CRAPPING IN ALLEYS YOU ACTUALLY CARE ABOUT?
WHAT CAN I TELL YOU? I'M A LOWLY PUBLIC SERVANT. IT'S A WIN WIN. YOU GET PAID, AND WE GET TO LEAVE THE MANIACS TO THE MANIACS.
BESIDES, YOU GUYS SHOULD REALLY GIVE YOUR GRANDMA HER GEAR BACK.
OH, YOU GOT JOKES? SINCE WE SO FUNNY, LET'S PUT ALL THIS ON DO DO'S TAB. I BET SHE'D BE TICKLED BY THAT.
SO WE'VE FOUND THE YOBINETERU?
ABSOLUTELY. IT HAS TO BE HIM. THE READINGS ARE OFF THE CHARTS.
FINALLY, A TRUE TEST OF OUR ABILITIES. SOMETHING WORTHY OF The Slaughterkind.

WILDFIRE CREATED BY
QUINN McGOWAN
www.quinnproart.com

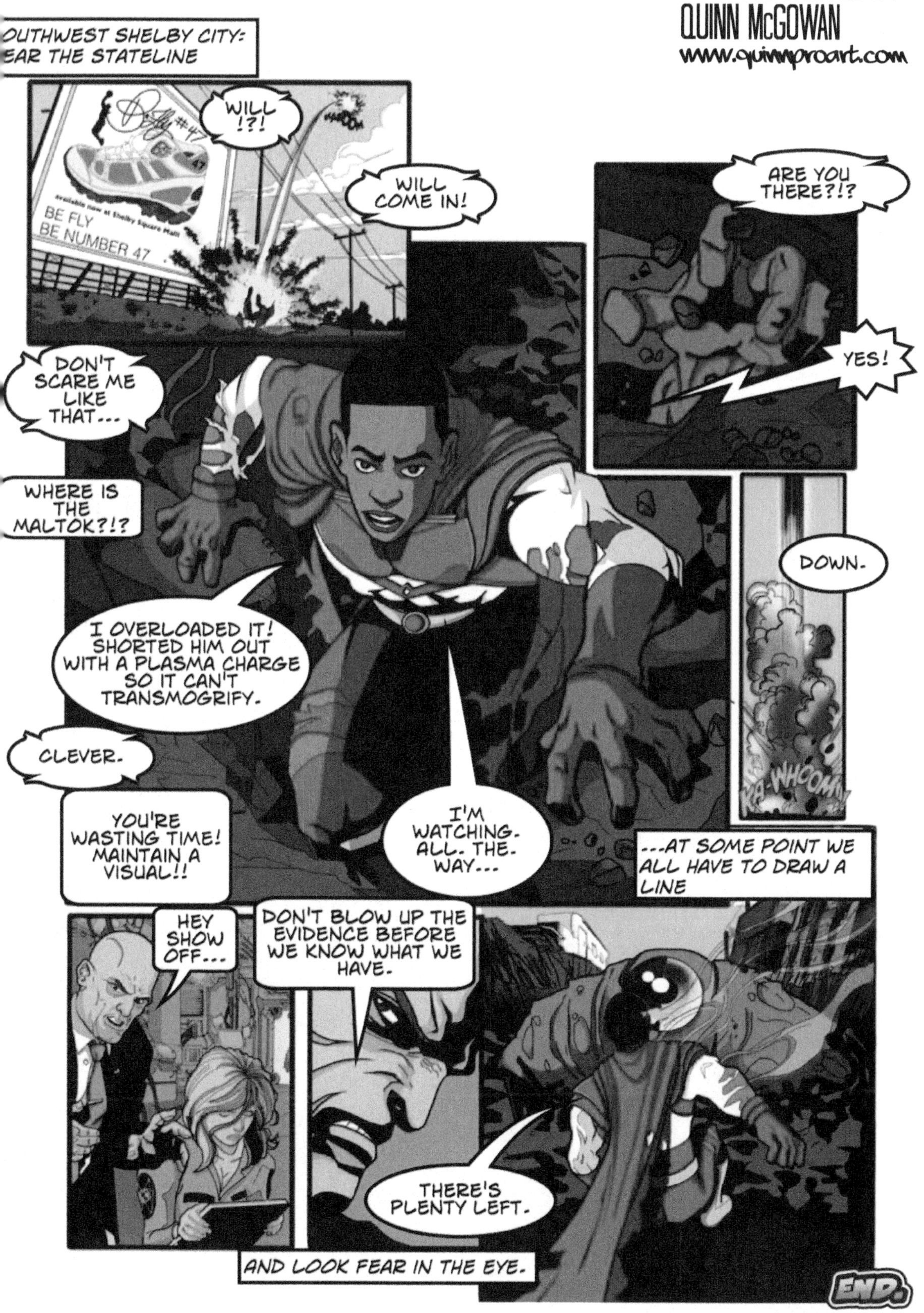
OUTHWEST SHELBY CITY:
EAR THE STATELINE
BE FLY
BE NUMBER 47
WILL !?!
WILL COME IN!
ARE YOU THERE?!?
YES!
DON'T SCARE ME LIKE THAT...
WHERE IS THE MALTOK?!?
DOWN.
I OVERLOADED IT! SHORTED HIM OUT WITH A PLASMA CHARGE SO IT CAN'T TRANSMOGRIFY.
CLEVER.
KA-WHOOM!
YOU'RE WASTING TIME! MAINTAIN A VISUAL!!
I'M WATCHING. ALL. THE. WAY...
...AT SOME POINT WE ALL HAVE TO DRAW A LINE
HEY SHOW OFF...
DON'T BLOW UP THE EVIDENCE BEFORE WE KNOW WHAT WE HAVE.
THERE'S PLENTY LEFT.
AND LOOK FEAR IN THE EYE.
END.

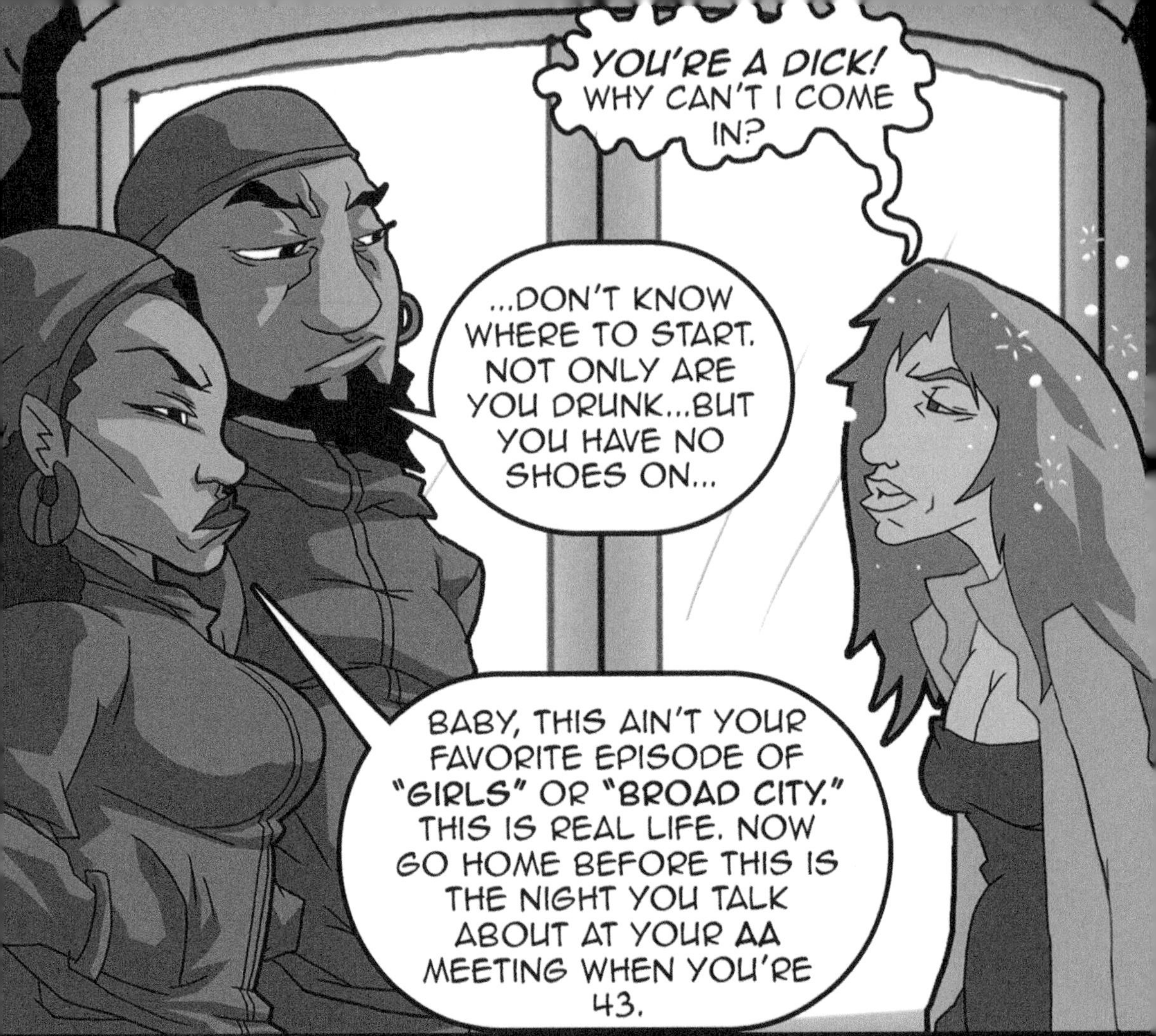
YOU'RE A DICK! WHY CAN'T I COME IN?
...DON'T KNOW WHERE TO START. NOT ONLY ARE YOU DRUNK...BUT YOU HAVE NO SHOES ON...
BABY, THIS AIN'T YOUR FAVORITE EPISODE OF "GIRLS" OR "BROAD CITY." THIS IS REAL LIFE. NOW GO HOME BEFORE THIS IS THE NIGHT YOU TALK ABOUT AT YOUR AA MEETING WHEN YOU'RE 43.

WHISKEYSHOT021814

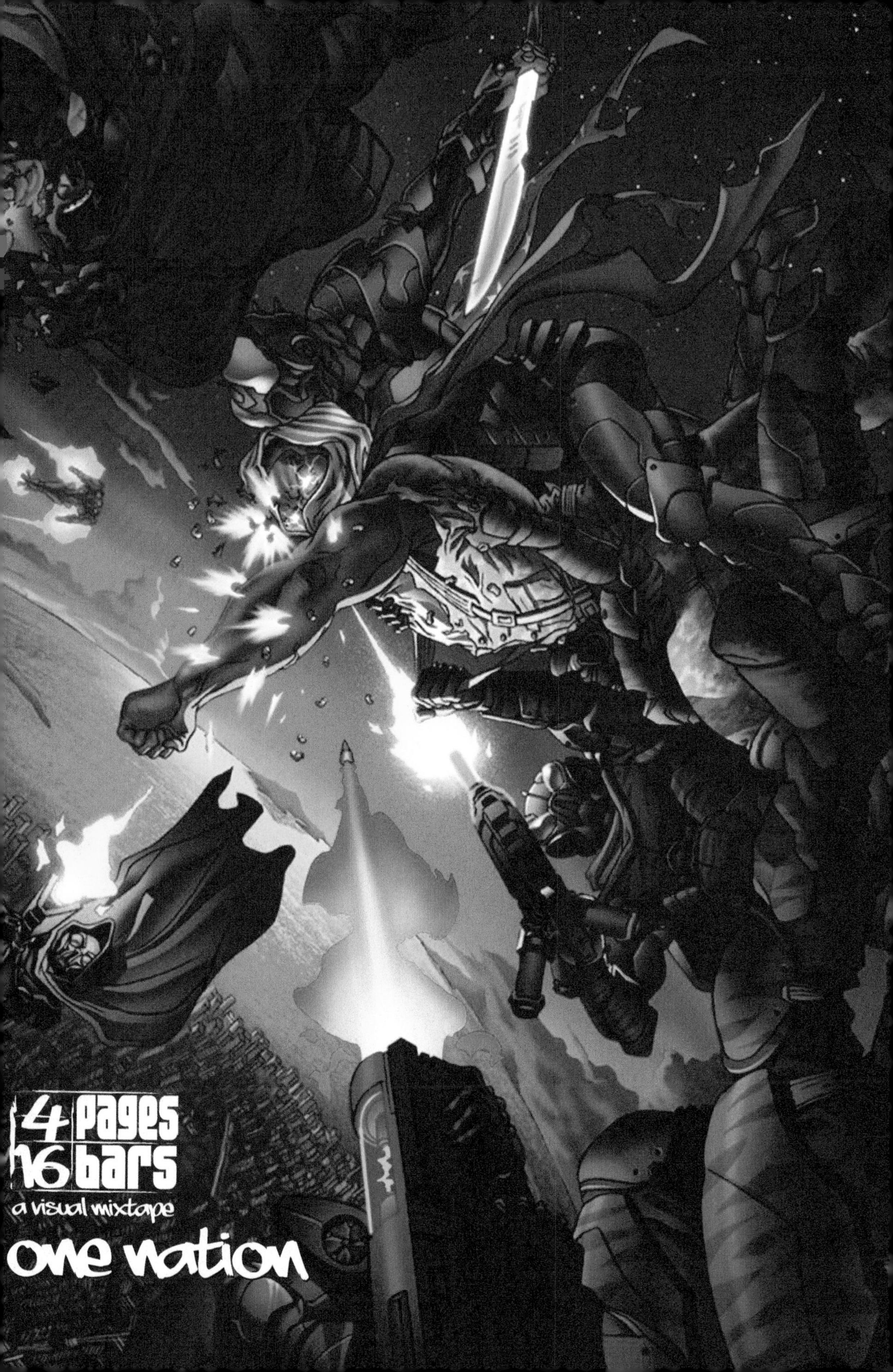
4 pages
16 bars
a visual mixtape
one nation

WRITTEN BY
ALVERNE BELL

INTERIOR ART BY
JASON REEVES & LUIS GUERRERO

Jason Reeves is a Los Angeles-based comics creator who has had his comics work published by **USA Today**, **Devil's Due Publishing** and **Arcana Studios**. In addition to comics, he has done illustration for Esquire Magazine, USAToday. com's 'F-00 Fighters' series and HASBRO's G.I. Joe and Transformers toylines. He is currently working on the award-winning *OneNation* comic series with Alverne Ball and is co-owner of the design studio **133Art**.

website: 133art.com

Now, I dialed 911 a long time ago--

MUSIC'S KINDA LOUD CAN YOU TURN IT DOWN?

...UH-HUH.

--Don't care...

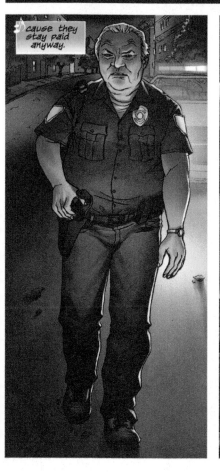

cause they stay paid anyway.

DO YOU KNOW HOW FAST--?

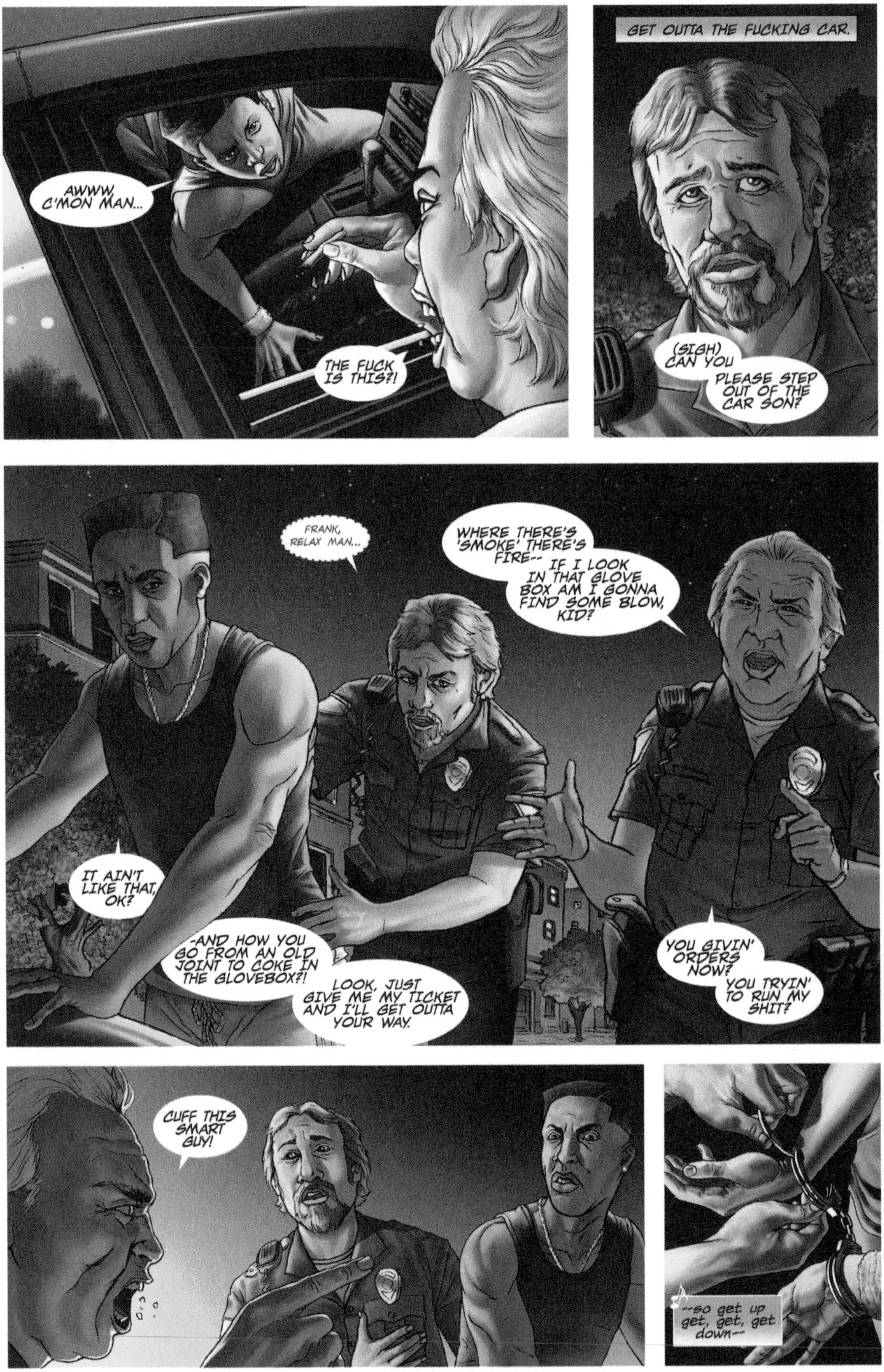
AWWW, C'MON MAN...
THE FUCK IS THIS?!
GET OUTTA THE FUCKING CAR.
(SIGH) CAN YOU
PLEASE STEP OUT OF THE CAR SON?
FRANK, RELAX MAN...
WHERE THERE'S 'SMOKE' THERE'S FIRE--
IF I LOOK IN THAT GLOVE BOX AM I GONNA FIND SOME BLOW, KID?
IT AIN'T LIKE THAT, OK?
-AND HOW YOU GO FROM AN OLD JOINT TO COKE IN THE GLOVEBOX?!
LOOK, JUST GIVE ME MY TICKET AND I'LL GET OUTTA YOUR WAY.
YOU GIVIN' ORDERS NOW?
YOU TRYIN' TO RUN MY SHIT?
CUFF THIS SMART GUY!
--so get up get, get, get down--

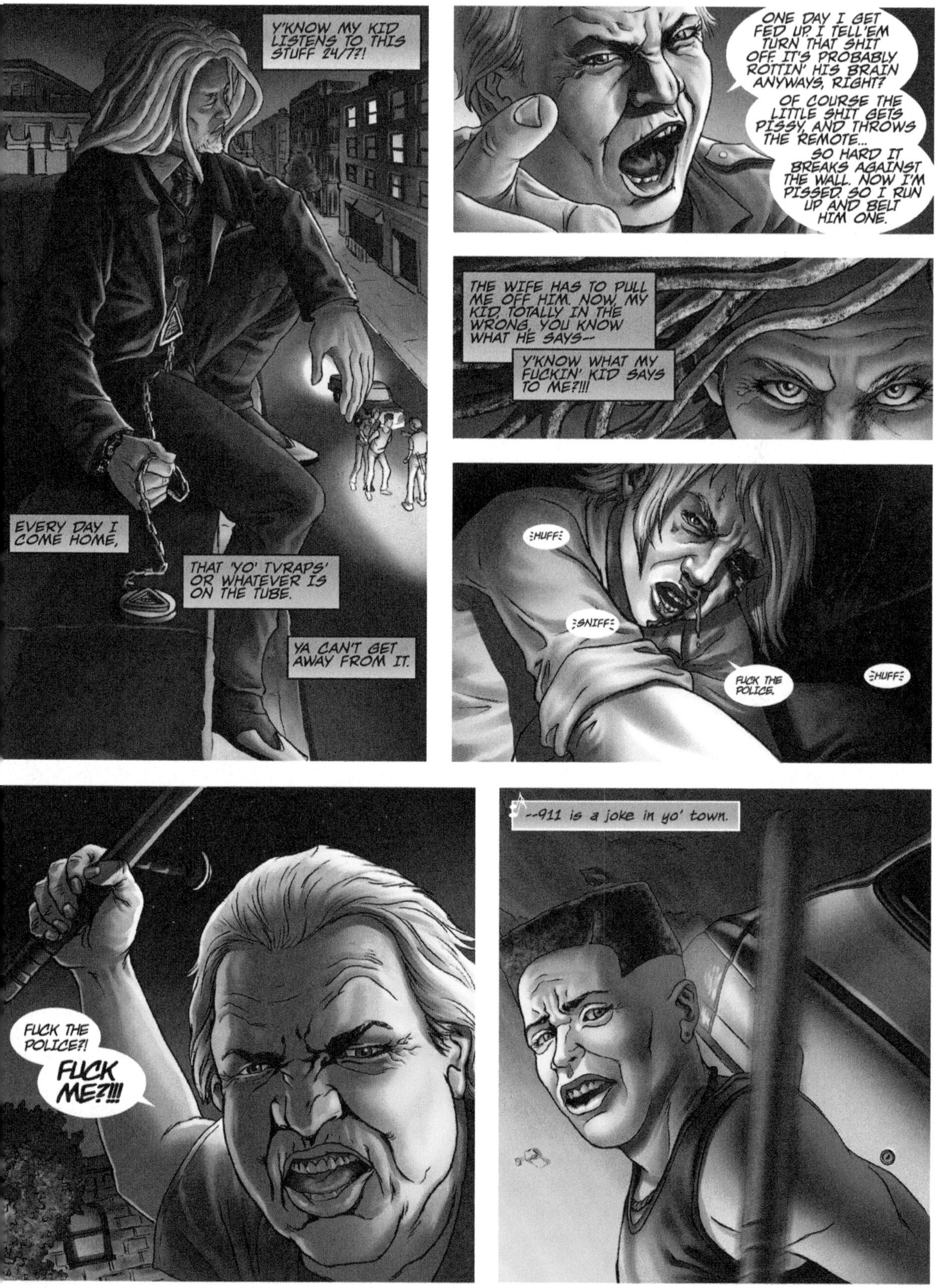
Y'KNOW MY KID LISTENS TO THIS STUFF 24/7?!
EVERY DAY I COME HOME,
THAT 'YO' TVRAPS' OR WHATEVER IS ON THE TUBE.
YA CAN'T GET AWAY FROM IT.
ONE DAY I GET FED UP. I TELL'EM TURN THAT SHIT OFF. IT'S PROBABLY ROTTIN' HIS BRAIN ANYWAYS, RIGHT?
OF COURSE THE LITTLE SHIT GETS PISSY, AND THROWS THE REMOTE...
SO HARD IT BREAKS AGAINST THE WALL. NOW I'M PISSED. SO I RUN UP AND BELT HIM ONE.
THE WIFE HAS TO PULL ME OFF HIM. NOW, MY KID, TOTALLY IN THE WRONG, YOU KNOW WHAT HE SAYS--
Y'KNOW WHAT MY FUCKIN' KID SAYS TO ME?!!!
HUFF
SNIFF
FUCK THE POLICE.
HUFF
FUCK THE POLICE?!
FUCK ME?!!!
--911 is a joke in yo' town.

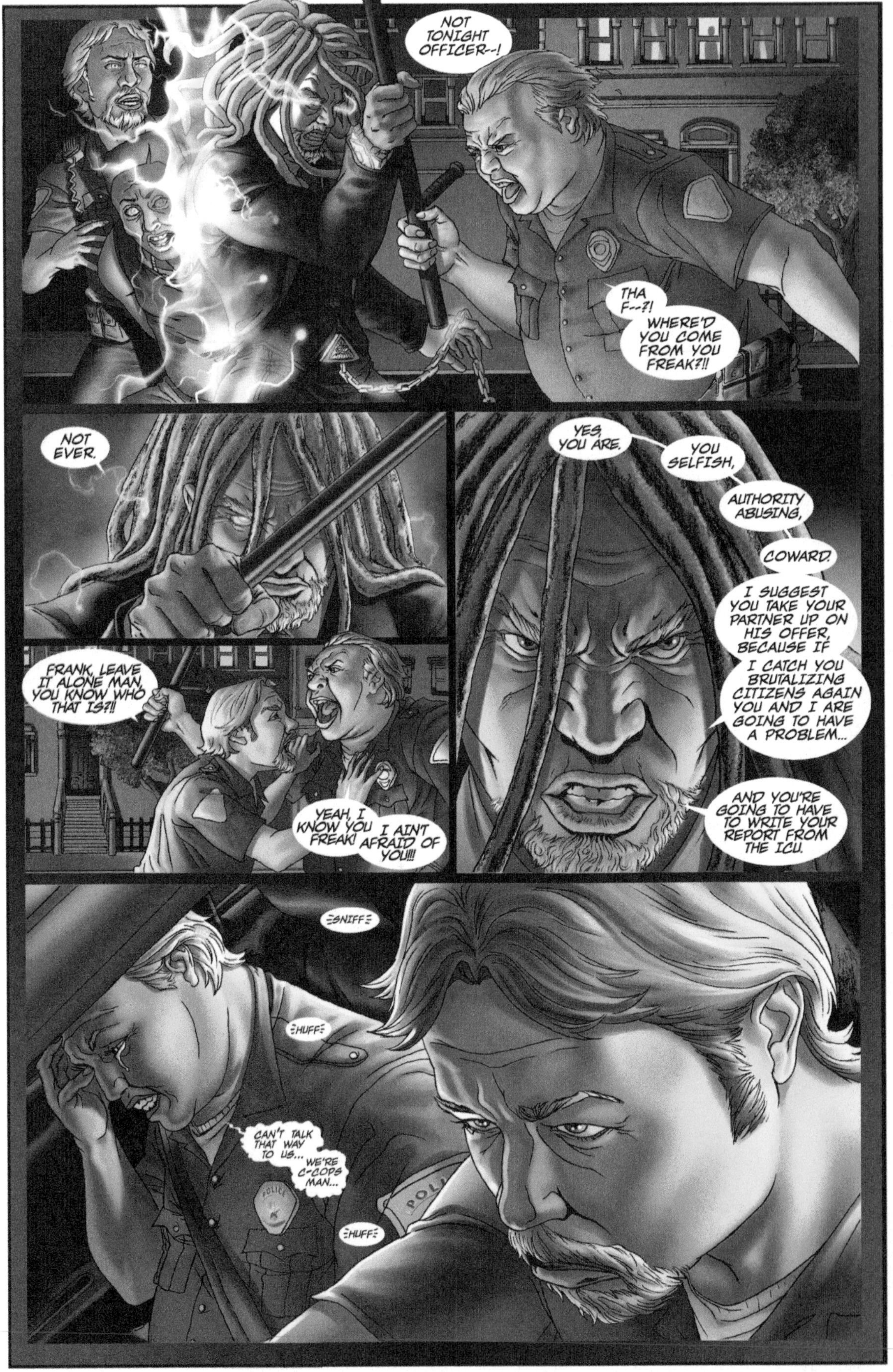
NOT TONIGHT OFFICER--!
THA F--?! WHERE'D YOU COME FROM YOU FREAK?!!
NOT EVER.
FRANK, LEAVE IT ALONE MAN, YOU KNOW WHO THAT IS?!!
YEAH, I KNOW YOU FREAK!
I AIN'T AFRAID OF YOU!!!
YES, YOU ARE.
YOU SELFISH,
AUTHORITY ABUSING,
COWARD.
I SUGGEST YOU TAKE YOUR PARTNER UP ON HIS OFFER, BECAUSE IF
I CATCH YOU BRUTALIZING CITIZENS AGAIN YOU AND I ARE GOING TO HAVE A PROBLEM...
AND YOU'RE GOING TO HAVE TO WRITE YOUR REPORT FROM THE ICU.
SNIFF
HUFF
CAN'T TALK THAT WAY TO US... WE'RE C-COPS MAN...
HUFF

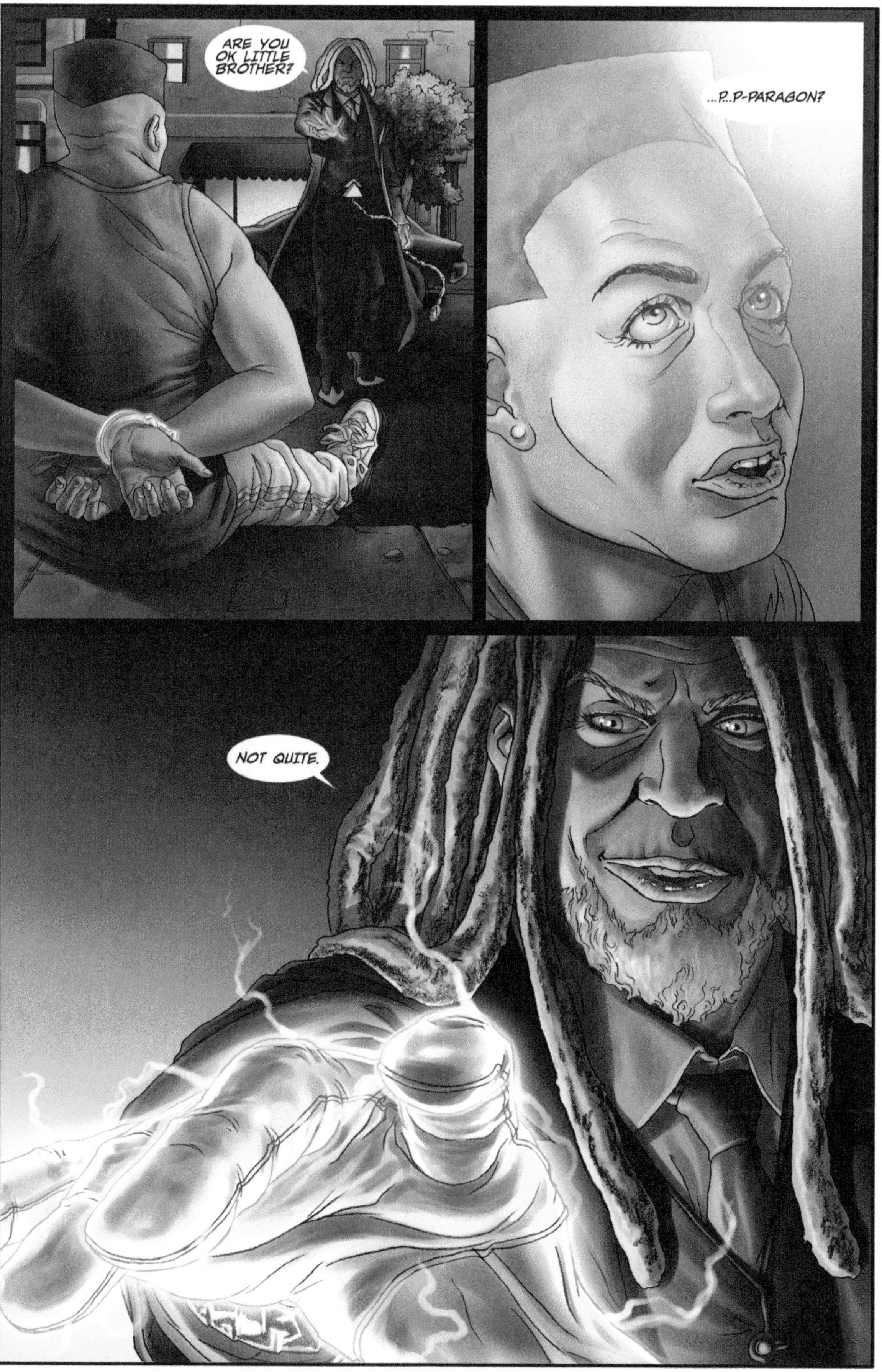
ARE YOU OK LITTLE BROTHER?
...P...P-PARAGON?
NOT QUITE.

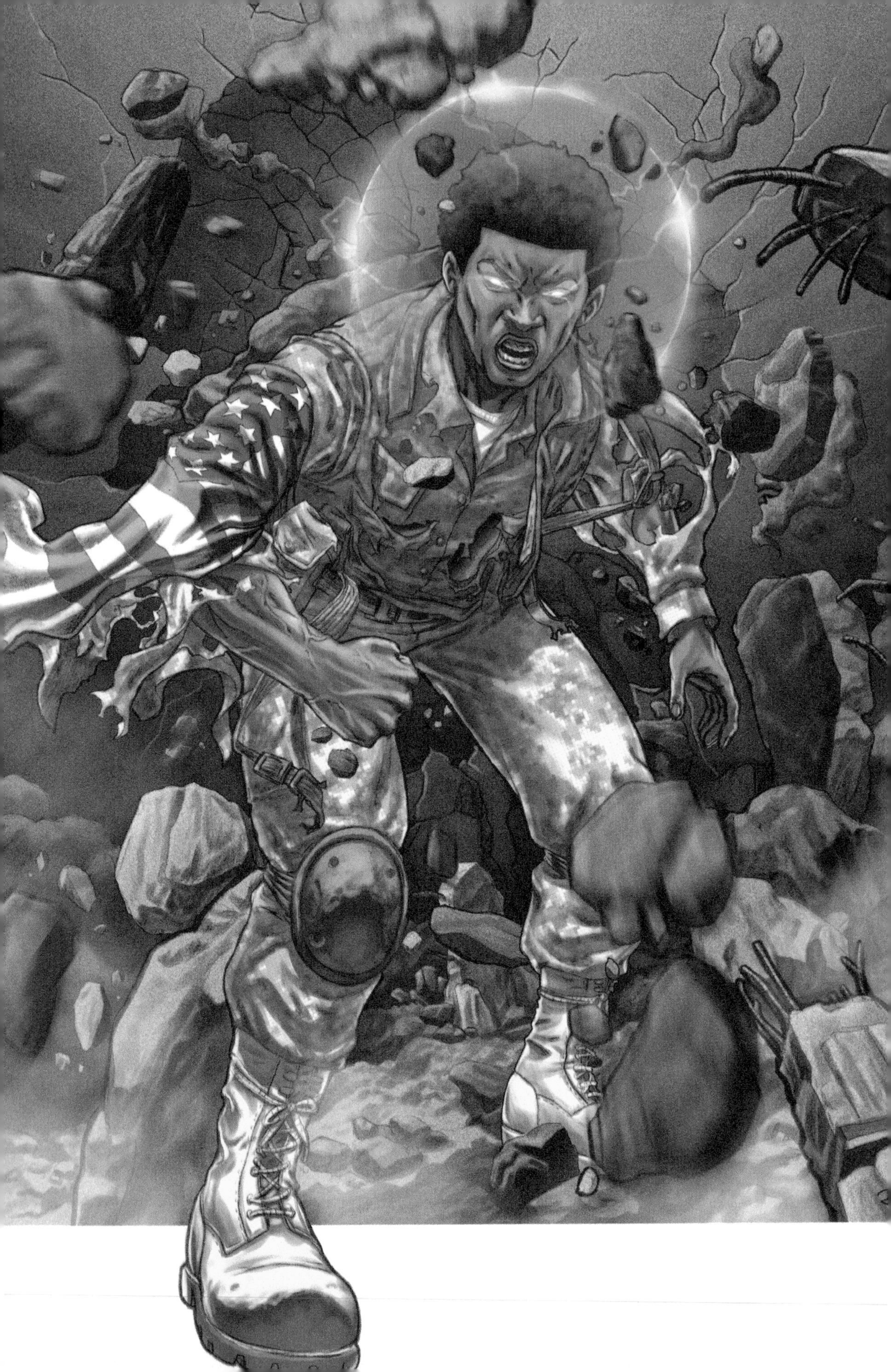

getchu some!

BY DAMON ALUMS

"What hath God wrought?"

Holy Bible, Book of Numbers, Chapter 22, verse 23

Also, the first message transmitted on the
Baltimore-Washington telegraph line, May 24, 1844.

Being a Blerd (Black nerd) is a lonely road. We follow
our interests those topics that resonate to us, despite
the surprise and consternation of those that would
pigeonhole or choose what we enjoy for us. I literally
thought I was the only one. I mean, I had heads in my
circle who liked a **Star Trek** episode or two and came
up watching **Sasquatch and Wildboy** like I did, but
Brothers and Sisters with the same mental warehouses
of Star Wars miscellany, garages full of longboxes, and
secret desires to costume up and take on the persona
of favorite characters? Yeah, I was sure I was the only
Brother breathing entertaining the option.

August 2012, I was getting acquainted with the basics
of social media on this widget called **Facebook**, with
a mind to get out of the game. I mean, it was A'IGHT,
but I'd connected with the folks from high school I'd a
mind connect with, done the creeper thing with past
loves, and had felt that's all there was to it. Checking
in on a high school homeboy, I take note of a thread
that is blowing up. The topic: **The Perfect Fan-Cast
For The Black Panther Movie**. Over that night, and a
portion of the next day, opinions were shared, gallows
humor about a movie we thought would never see the
light of day was expressed (Marvel hadn't dropped
the bombshell that the movie was in the works at
the time), and we traded friendly barbs and as many
laughs as imdb citations and OHOTMU references.

The conversation died down, as with all things, but I
wasn't done. Hanging out with this group of friends
I'd stumbled across by happenstance, I found that not
only was I not alone, there were Brothers and Sisters
out there with knowledge I didn't have, some actually
participating in the industry I love, and said I'd get
around to getting into. I had more I wanted to share,
more questions to ask, and more good times to enjoy.
Counter to my jaded adult exterior, I asked if there
was a club, page, group, or gathering place where
we could continue the good times. Rather than take
the digital shrug of ambivalence to heart, I discovered
Facebook's capacity for creating groups, and a few
keystrokes later, **Comic Nerds of Color** was born.

In the time since its inception, **CNOC** has become
much more than a standard Blerd group. Having
encountered the many sections of the Blerdosphere
on Facebook's groups since, Comic Nerds of
Color's collective focus on civil discourse, adherence
to mission, focus on the joys of being a Black Nerd
and dedicated focus on elevating the game, both as
fans and content creators, make it the first and best

place for Nerds to come, learn, share, laugh, critique,
and enjoy sequential art and its children in the way
only Nerds can.

This is the message on the "front door", the mission
statement of Comic Nerds of Color. Since **Day One**
we have chopped it up like play cousins, shared what
we love in the comics and pop culture world, both
mainstream and independent, come up with house
rules that make everything operate more smoothly,
gone to war with one another, and gone to war **for**
one another, and during this roller coaster ride,
become an online extended family, one nation
under a (Blerd) groove.

Since founding the group, I have discovered the
wonderful spectrum of groups dedicated specifically
to African American Fans of sci-fi-, pop culture, and
comic books. Some examples are to be aspired to,
some not. The takeaways I have had, and the
influence they have had on the Comic Nerds of Color
forum shape up like this:

Support and be supported: The Big Two have the
lion's share of the industry, but there is still room for
independent creators to make a living if they receive
proper support and exposure. However, comic book
that go beyond the offerings of the largest companies
groups turn into rioting bazaars of creators, employing
louder and louder tactics to get closer to the margin
that will get them over. Because the beginning of
the CNOC started in a chill dialogue among friends
and friendly people, that good vibe conversational
tone continued to those who are in the industry: a
sale is more likely from a friend than a cold call, so the
emphasis is on making introductions and getting ac-
climated, and *then* introducing the "next big thing"is
the CNOC tradition. The group is a dynamic force
of exposure and support, and it's fair that those who
receive that support invest in the group by dialogue,
posting relevant topics, and the like. If not, the result
is a whole lot of shouting, accomplishing nothing.

BAN HAMMER

OMIC N RDS OF COLOR
U DiG iT?
CA OU DiG iT?
CA YOU DiG iT?

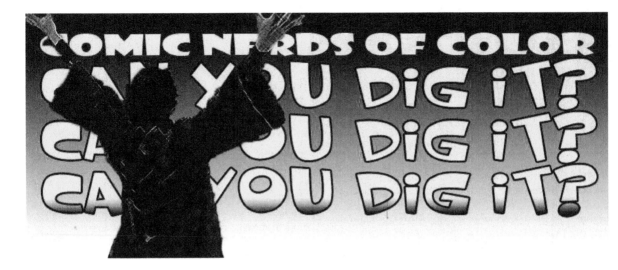

As we have grown, there has been a more formal addition to the support provided in the CNOC. Every month, time is taken out to lend some shine to an independent creator of Color making top notch product with the CNOC Creator's spotlight, helping to increase positive exposure and connect hungry creators with hungry consumers, so that way everyone gets fed.

Let the toys of youth be: Now this may seem strange, being that it concerns a group whose focus is all about comics, videogames and pop culture, but it stems from the biggest crisis from the beginning of the CNOC. Ever since we were kids, comic nerds of all kinds engaged in the classic *Who'd Win* debate. Prep time, no prep time, real world locations or thunderdome scenario, mind control or friendly sparring, on and on, ad infinitum. The number of these posts in our opening days had become so pervasive that information about the new hotness got lost amid all the fingers-in-the-ears screaming disguised as debate.

So as a topic for discussion in the forum, it was removed. It seems drastic, but it has caused a mushrooming of quality news and content to take its place. Nowadays, the only way a vs./Who'd Win post is allowed is if a fan steps up their game and creates a complete work of fine art, sequential art, or prose telling the story of who would win, and how. When presented with the challenge of becoming more than simply a keyboard jockey, many have quailed, and the strife has been replaced by an effort to see and be seen. There are many who are surprised at this policy, feel it's intrusive, and log protests, but with so many other things to discuss, an overwhelming majority join in the fun we have here, and the good times continue.

Not "Everyone Earns a Ribbon": A sentiment gaining traction in this day and age, as the consequences of "Everyone Gets a Ribbon" self-entitlement become evident. This applies to accountability for words posted, as well as creative works displayed. If it's posted, it becomes fair game. Outlandish statements will be expected to be verified, and art posted will be eligible for fair critique, rather than a simple, traditional, reflexive "That's tight". More often than not, folks that aren't feeling it will say so, and leave it at that. If someone is into the work and has an idea on how it can be improved, that will justifiably be offered as well. With as many folks in the group able to find work in comics and other nerd-friendly industries, an overwhelming amount of it will be very apt.

That's how we do. This online family has been going strong for three years now, with no sign of stopping. We have rallied to help members get through hard times, come together to mourn the passing of members gone too soon, and even have life partners who choose to spend the rest of their lives bickering with each other who met while chopping it up and bickering in the forum. We have members from all walks of life, all over the world, and in every shade of the human rainbow, coming together, sifting through the chaff to find the best wheat that nerddom has to offer. We're human. There are times the flame wars pop up, and times when the higher angels of folks' natures aren't even in sight, much less within reach. There are days where basic nerdboy complaining holds sway, and the humor gets so blue that somebody has to pull the emergency brake, and we have to take a group reset. We're not a bunch of proper-acting robots. We folks.

And me? I have the distinctive honor of saying I was the one that flipped the switch and got all this started. I look at the forum bubbling away, and ponder the interactions of folks who never would have met had I not clicked that button, creators who would never had made that sale, and fans who never would have found a current favorite if I hadn't taken a step outside myself, and said, "Go ahead. What's the worst that could happen?"

In thinking of the results, what can I think of riding this wave, of guiding this ship on the information superhighway but, "What hath god wrought?"

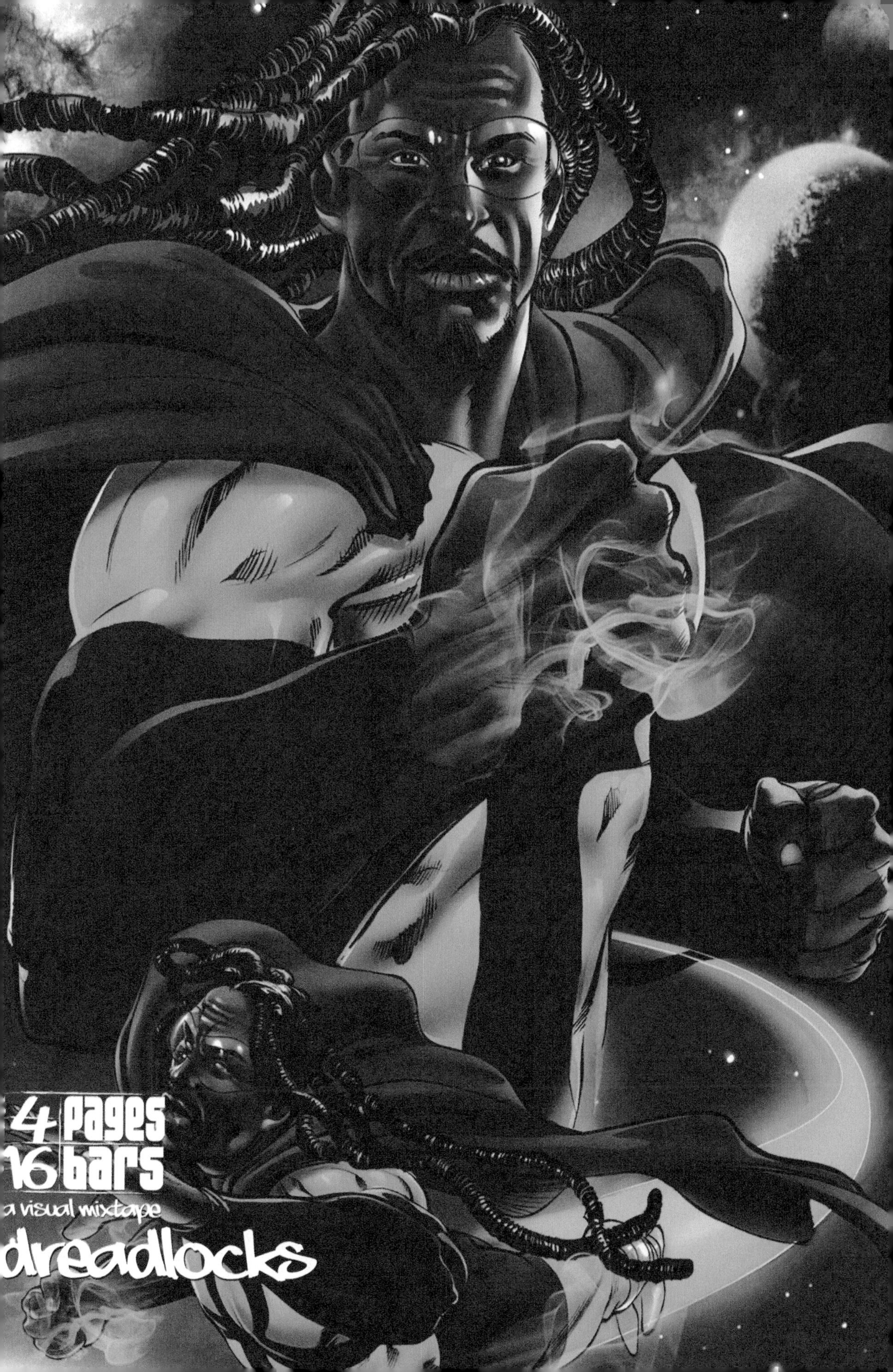
4 pages
16 bars
a visual mixtape
dreadlocks

COVER ILLUSTRATION BY
ALBERTO FOCHE

PIN-UP ART BY
ABDUL RASHID & JOHN JENNINGS

Andre L.Batts is the creator and founder of **Urban Style Comics**. Although his characters have strong Afro-centric themes that are similar to the current Afro-futurism movement popular in a lot of "underground" comic book creators he feels that anyone who enjoys the genre will enjoy his work.

Urban Style's flagship character, ***Dreadlocks***, is guided by the Gods of Alkebulan (Africa) and born as a sacrificial lamb to the Gods of ancient Alkebulan. Dreadlocks has no physical sight for the Gods are his guiding light from within his third eye (spirit/conscious). He is a revolutionary hero based in the urban world. His primary task is bringing Ma'at (universal order, justice and righteousness) to the lost tribes of Alkebulan. Dreadlocks is a hero for the people. He serves only the Gods/ancestors that walked before him.

website: urbanstylecomics.com

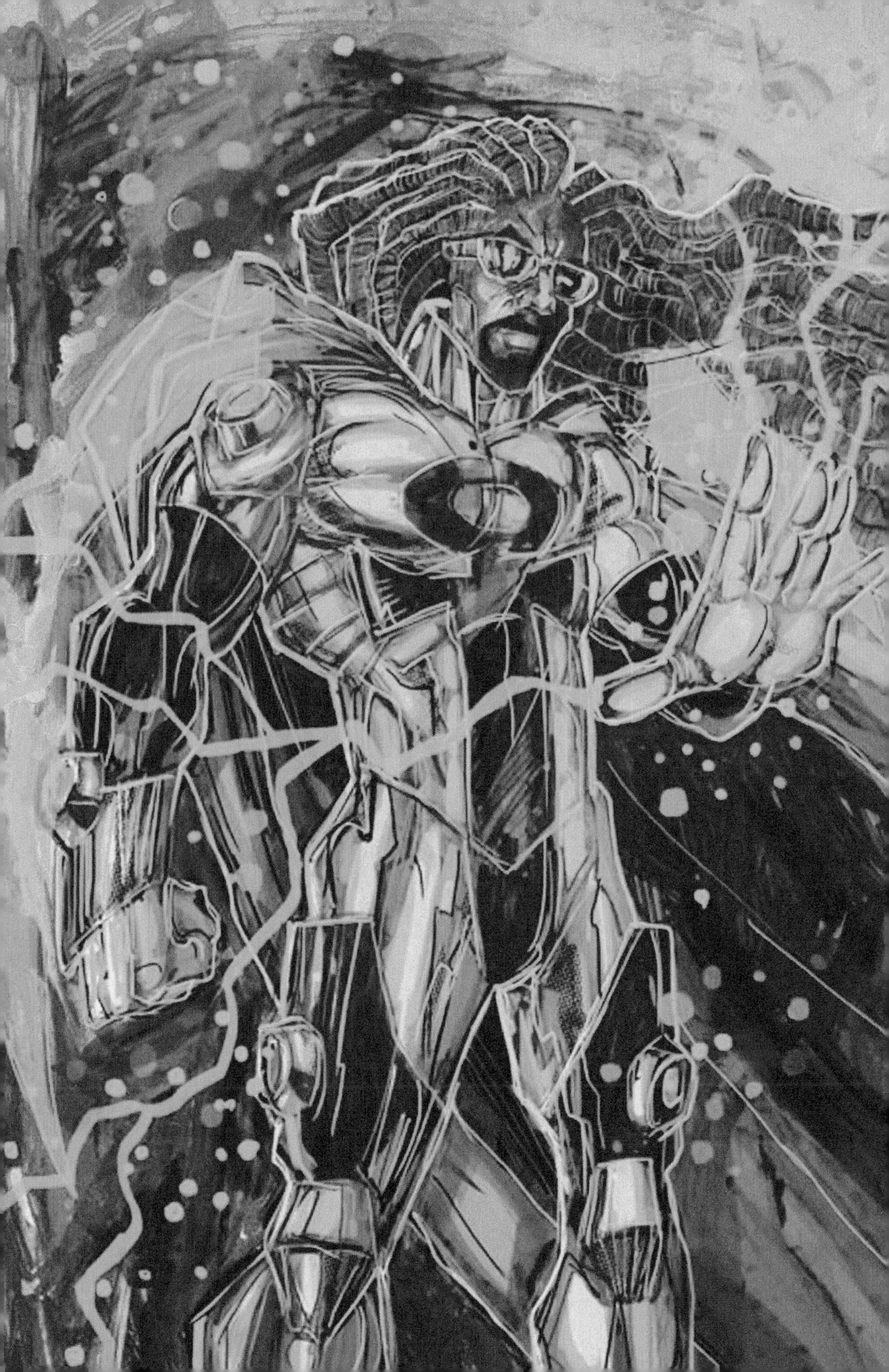

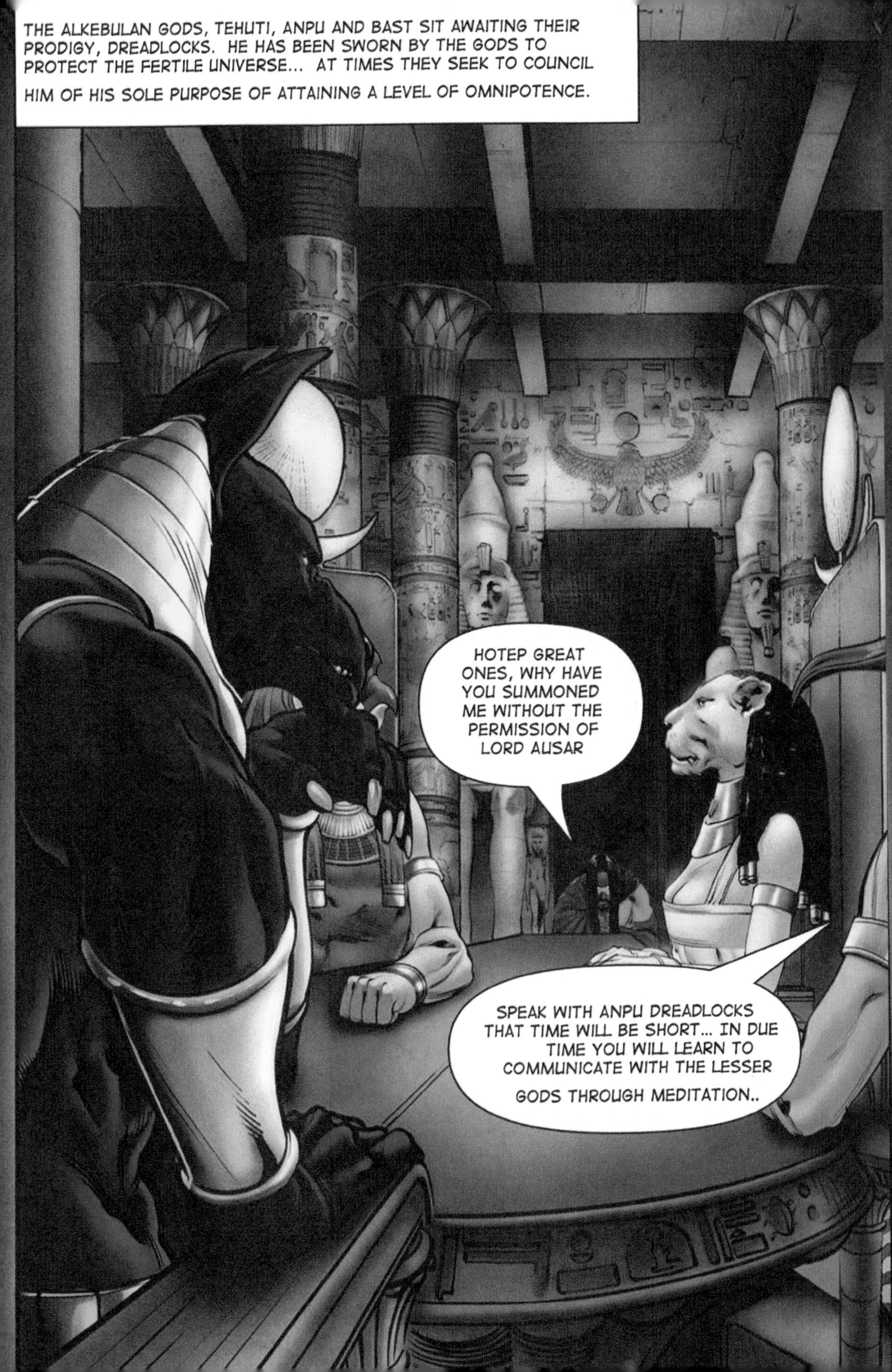
THE ALKEBULAN GODS, TEHUTI, ANPU AND BAST SIT AWAITING THEIR PRODIGY, DREADLOCKS. HE HAS BEEN SWORN BY THE GODS TO PROTECT THE FERTILE UNIVERSE... AT TIMES THEY SEEK TO COUNCIL HIM OF HIS SOLE PURPOSE OF ATTAINING A LEVEL OF OMNIPOTENCE.
HOTEP GREAT ONES, WHY HAVE YOU SUMMONED ME WITHOUT THE PERMISSION OF LORD AUSAR
SPEAK WITH ANPU DREADLOCKS THAT TIME WILL BE SHORT... IN DUE TIME YOU WILL LEARN TO COMMUNICATE WITH THE LESSER GODS THROUGH MEDITATION..

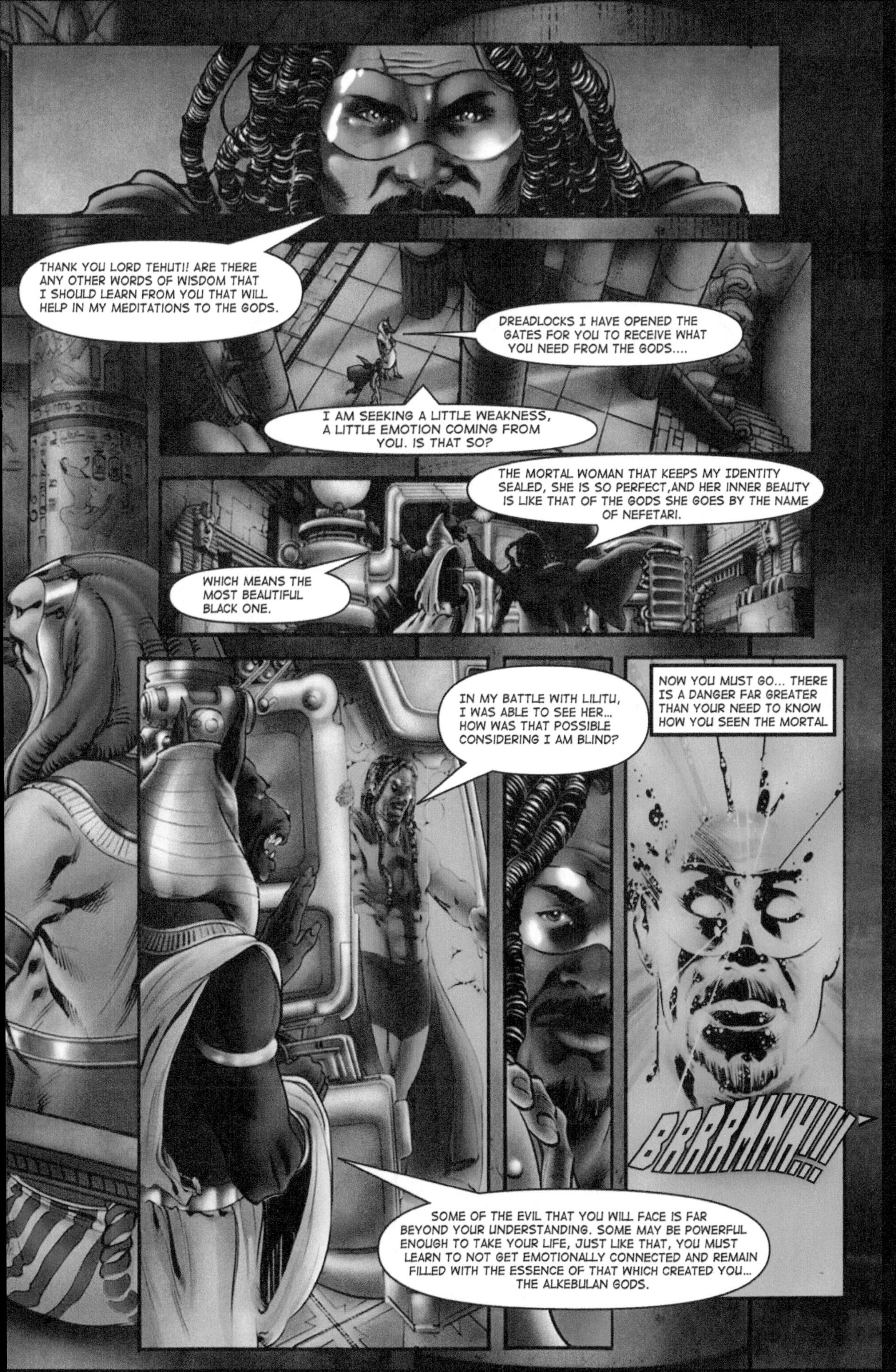
THANK YOU LORD TEHUTI! ARE THERE ANY OTHER WORDS OF WISDOM THAT I SHOULD LEARN FROM YOU THAT WILL HELP IN MY MEDITATIONS TO THE GODS.
DREADLOCKS I HAVE OPENED THE GATES FOR YOU TO RECEIVE WHAT YOU NEED FROM THE GODS....
I AM SEEKING A LITTLE WEAKNESS, A LITTLE EMOTION COMING FROM YOU. IS THAT SO?
THE MORTAL WOMAN THAT KEEPS MY IDENTITY SEALED, SHE IS SO PERFECT,AND HER INNER BEAUTY IS LIKE THAT OF THE GODS SHE GOES BY THE NAME OF NEFETARI.
WHICH MEANS THE MOST BEAUTIFUL BLACK ONE.
IN MY BATTLE WITH LILITU, I WAS ABLE TO SEE HER... HOW WAS THAT POSSIBLE CONSIDERING I AM BLIND?
NOW YOU MUST GO... THERE IS A DANGER FAR GREATER THAN YOUR NEED TO KNOW HOW YOU SEEN THE MORTAL
BRRRMMH!!!...
SOME OF THE EVIL THAT YOU WILL FACE IS FAR BEYOND YOUR UNDERSTANDING. SOME MAY BE POWERFUL ENOUGH TO TAKE YOUR LIFE, JUST LIKE THAT, YOU MUST LEARN TO NOT GET EMOTIONALLY CONNECTED AND REMAIN FILLED WITH THE ESSENCE OF THAT WHICH CREATED YOU... THE ALKEBULAN GODS.

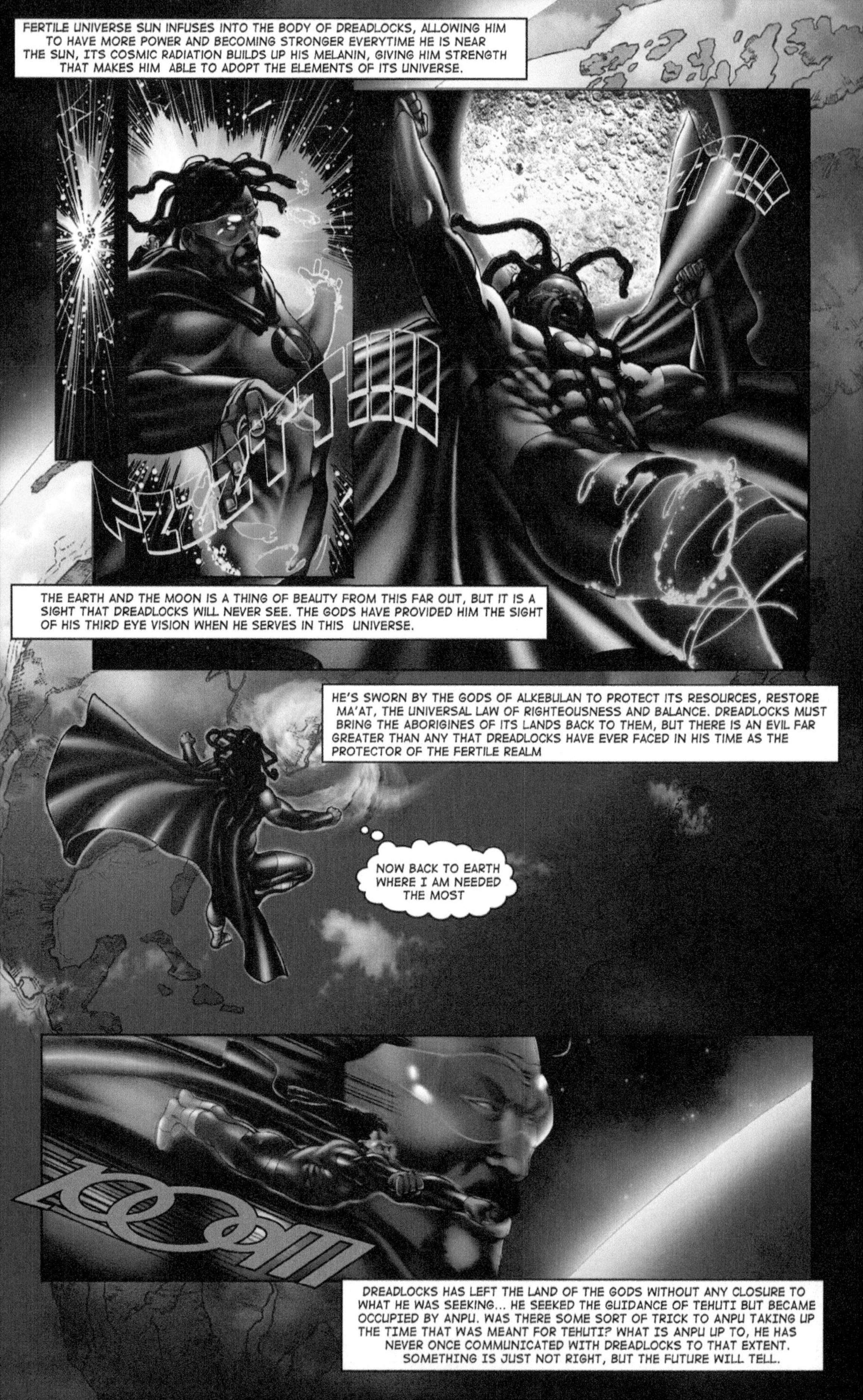
FERTILE UNIVERSE SUN INFUSES INTO THE BODY OF DREADLOCKS, ALLOWING HIM TO HAVE MORE POWER AND BECOMING STRONGER EVERYTIME HE IS NEAR THE SUN, ITS COSMIC RADIATION BUILDS UP HIS MELANIN, GIVING HIM STRENGTH THAT MAKES HIM ABLE TO ADOPT THE ELEMENTS OF ITS UNIVERSE.
THE EARTH AND THE MOON IS A THING OF BEAUTY FROM THIS FAR OUT, BUT IT IS A SIGHT THAT DREADLOCKS WILL NEVER SEE. THE GODS HAVE PROVIDED HIM THE SIGHT OF HIS THIRD EYE VISION WHEN HE SERVES IN THIS UNIVERSE.
HE'S SWORN BY THE GODS OF ALKEBULAN TO PROTECT ITS RESOURCES, RESTORE MA'AT, THE UNIVERSAL LAW OF RIGHTEOUSNESS AND BALANCE. DREADLOCKS MUST BRING THE ABORIGINES OF ITS LANDS BACK TO THEM, BUT THERE IS AN EVIL FAR GREATER THAN ANY THAT DREADLOCKS HAVE EVER FACED IN HIS TIME AS THE PROTECTOR OF THE FERTILE REALM
NOW BACK TO EARTH WHERE I AM NEEDED THE MOST
DREADLOCKS HAS LEFT THE LAND OF THE GODS WITHOUT ANY CLOSURE TO WHAT HE WAS SEEKING... HE SEEKED THE GUIDANCE OF TEHUTI BUT BECAME OCCUPIED BY ANPU. WAS THERE SOME SORT OF TRICK TO ANPU TAKING UP THE TIME THAT WAS MEANT FOR TEHUTI? WHAT IS ANPU UP TO, HE HAS NEVER ONCE COMMUNICATED WITH DREADLOCKS TO THAT EXTENT. SOMETHING IS JUST NOT RIGHT, BUT THE FUTURE WILL TELL.

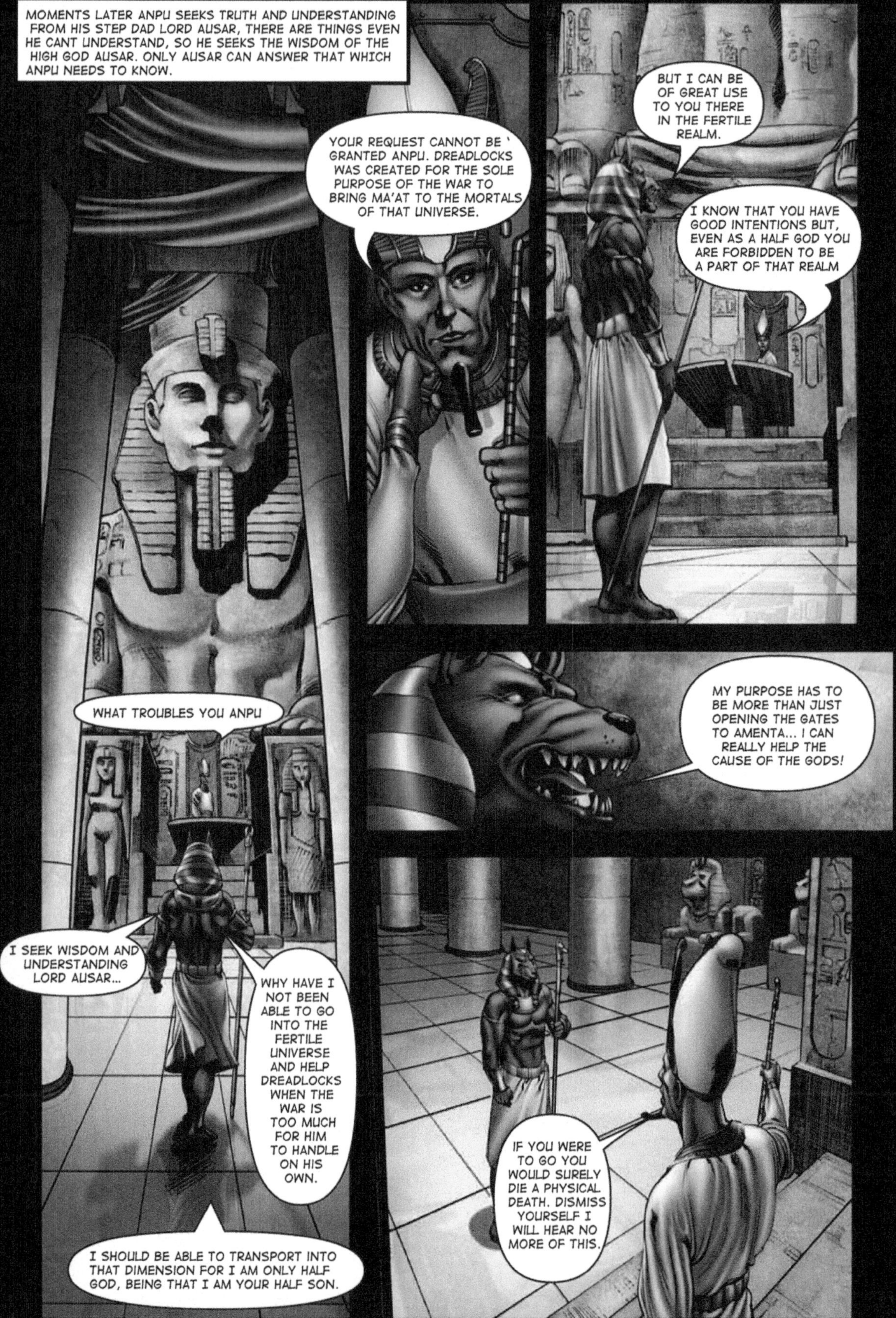

MOMENTS LATER ANPU SEEKS TRUTH AND UNDERSTANDING FROM HIS STEP DAD LORD AUSAR, THERE ARE THINGS EVEN HE CANT UNDERSTAND, SO HE SEEKS THE WISDOM OF THE HIGH GOD AUSAR. ONLY AUSAR CAN ANSWER THAT WHICH ANPU NEEDS TO KNOW.
WHAT TROUBLES YOU ANPU
I SEEK WISDOM AND UNDERSTANDING LORD AUSAR...
WHY HAVE I NOT BEEN ABLE TO GO INTO THE FERTILE UNIVERSE AND HELP DREADLOCKS WHEN THE WAR IS TOO MUCH FOR HIM TO HANDLE ON HIS OWN.
I SHOULD BE ABLE TO TRANSPORT INTO THAT DIMENSION FOR I AM ONLY HALF GOD, BEING THAT I AM YOUR HALF SON.
YOUR REQUEST CANNOT BE ` GRANTED ANPU. DREADLOCKS WAS CREATED FOR THE SOLE PURPOSE OF THE WAR TO BRING MA'AT TO THE MORTALS OF THAT UNIVERSE.
BUT I CAN BE OF GREAT USE TO YOU THERE IN THE FERTILE REALM.
I KNOW THAT YOU HAVE GOOD INTENTIONS BUT, EVEN AS A HALF GOD YOU ARE FORBIDDEN TO BE A PART OF THAT REALM
MY PURPOSE HAS TO BE MORE THAN JUST OPENING THE GATES TO AMENTA... I CAN REALLY HELP THE CAUSE OF THE GODS!
IF YOU WERE TO GO YOU WOULD SURELY DIE A PHYSICAL DEATH. DISMISS YOURSELF I WILL HEAR NO MORE OF THIS.

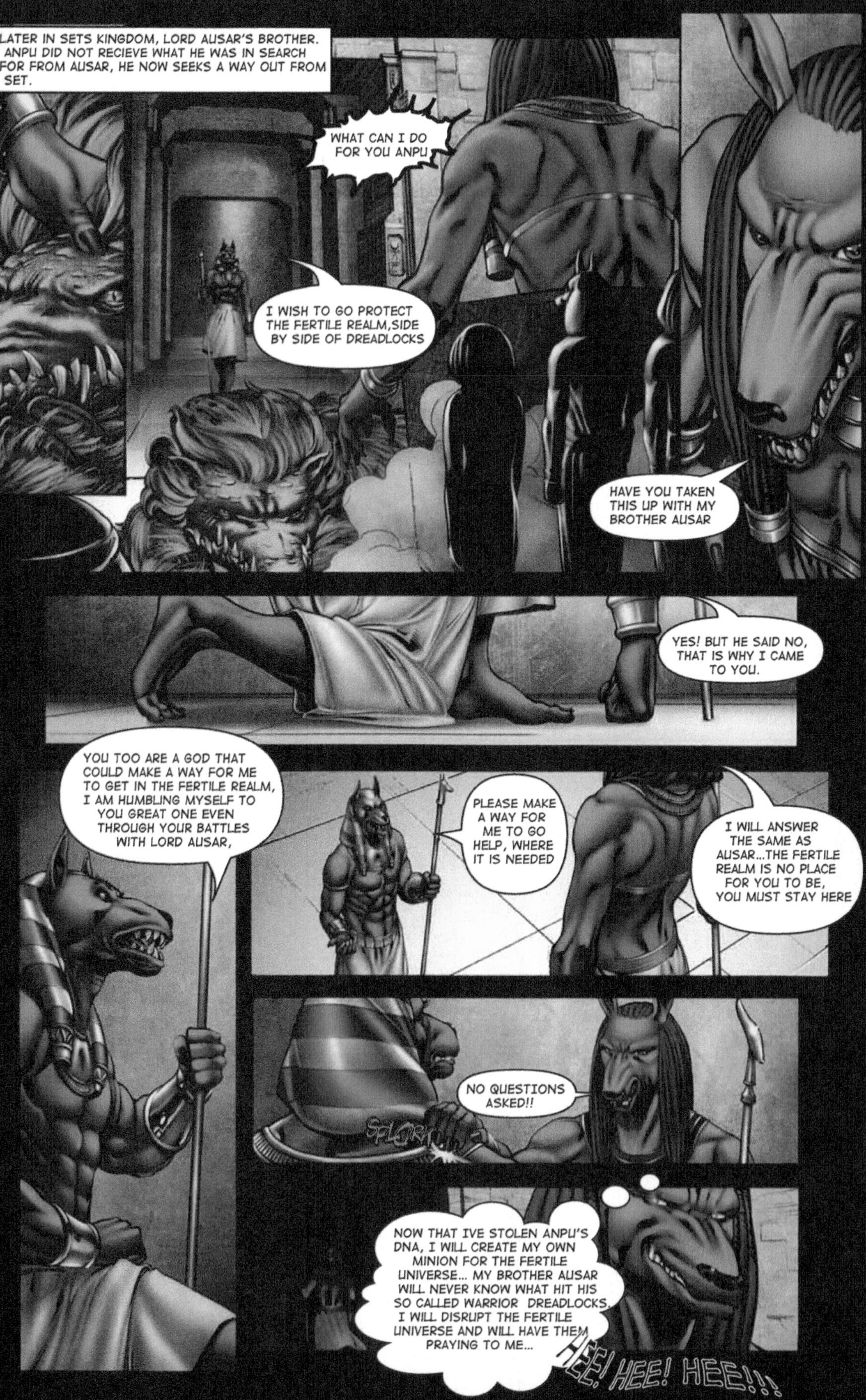
LATER IN SETS KINGDOM, LORD AUSAR'S BROTHER. ANPU DID NOT RECIEVE WHAT HE WAS IN SEARCH FOR FROM AUSAR, HE NOW SEEKS A WAY OUT FROM SET.
WHAT CAN I DO FOR YOU ANPU
I WISH TO GO PROTECT THE FERTILE REALM,SIDE BY SIDE OF DREADLOCKS
HAVE YOU TAKEN THIS UP WITH MY BROTHER AUSAR
YES! BUT HE SAID NO, THAT IS WHY I CAME TO YOU.
YOU TOO ARE A GOD THAT COULD MAKE A WAY FOR ME TO GET IN THE FERTILE REALM, I AM HUMBLING MYSELF TO YOU GREAT ONE EVEN THROUGH YOUR BATTLES WITH LORD AUSAR,
PLEASE MAKE A WAY FOR ME TO GO HELP, WHERE IT IS NEEDED
I WILL ANSWER THE SAME AS AUSAR...THE FERTILE REALM IS NO PLACE FOR YOU TO BE, YOU MUST STAY HERE
NO QUESTIONS ASKED!!
SPLORK
NOW THAT IVE STOLEN ANPU'S DNA, I WILL CREATE MY OWN MINION FOR THE FERTILE UNIVERSE... MY BROTHER AUSAR WILL NEVER KNOW WHAT HIT HIS SO CALLED WARRIOR DREADLOCKS. I WILL DISRUPT THE FERTILE UNIVERSE AND WILL HAVE THEM PRAYING TO ME...
HEE! HEE! HEE!!!

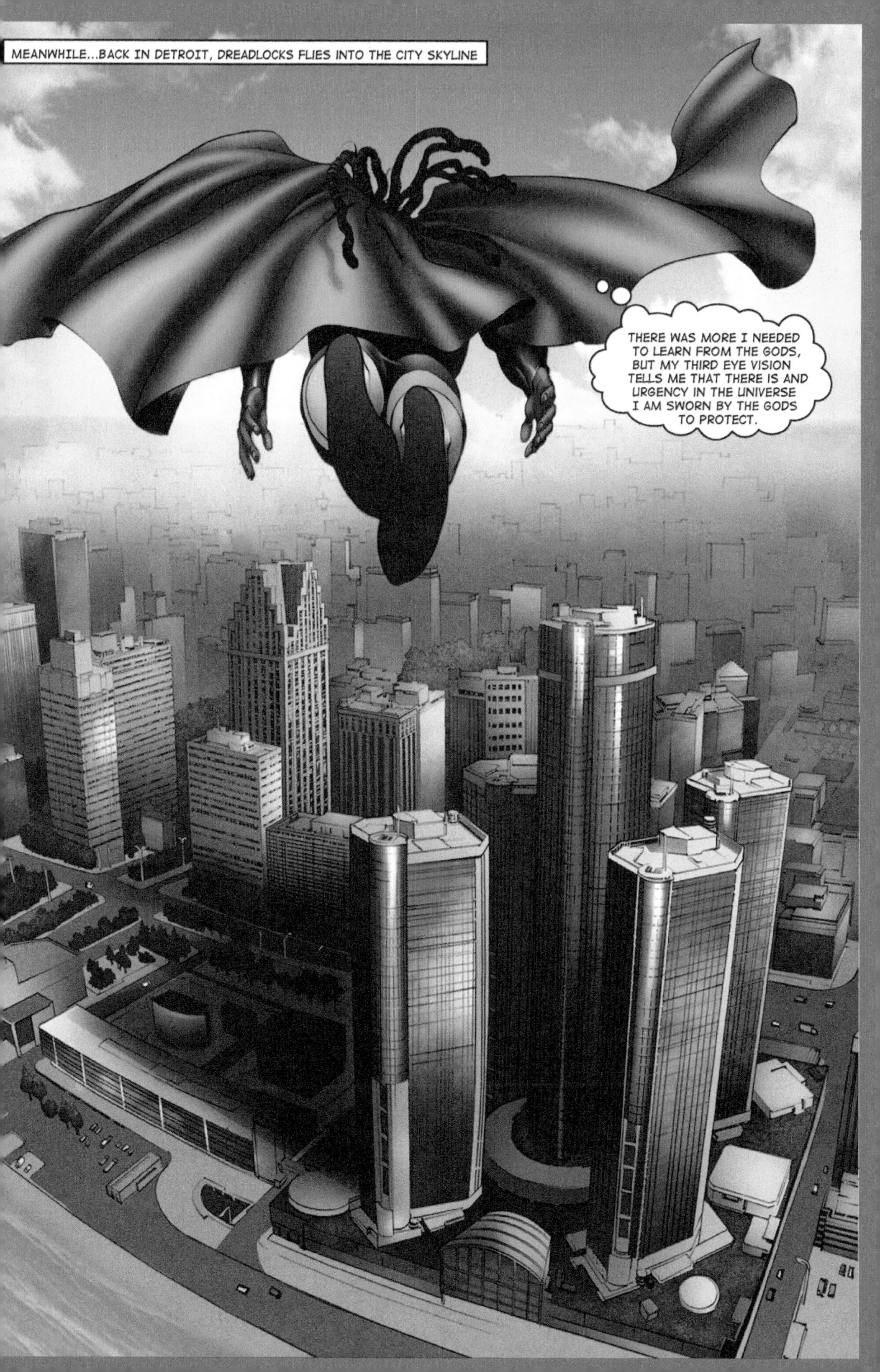
MEANWHILE...BACK IN DETROIT, DREADLOCKS FLIES INTO THE CITY SKYLINE
THERE WAS MORE I NEEDED TO LEARN FROM THE GODS, BUT MY THIRD EYE VISION TELLS ME THAT THERE IS AND URGENCY IN THE UNIVERSE I AM SWORN BY THE GODS TO PROTECT.

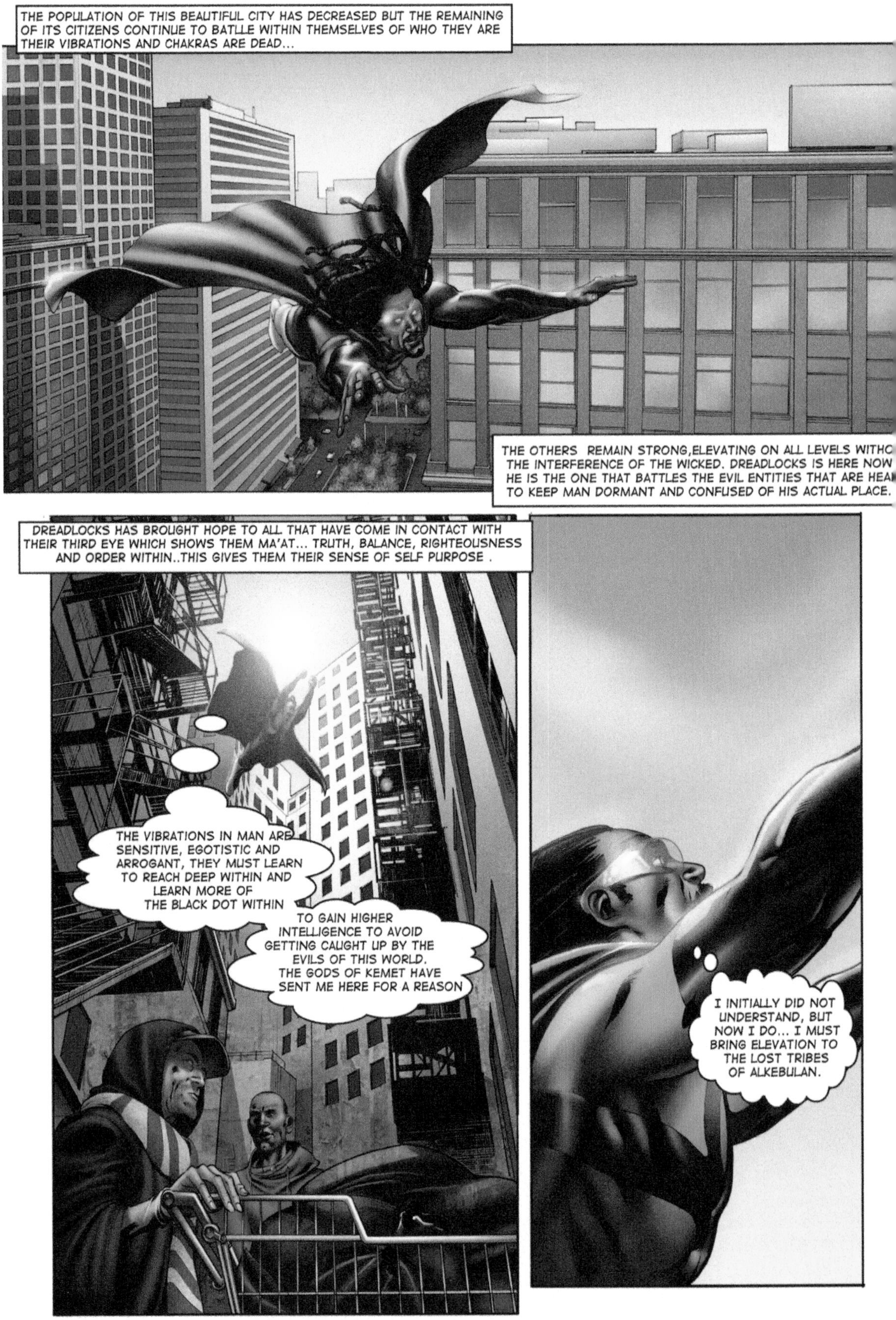
THE POPULATION OF THIS BEAUTIFUL CITY HAS DECREASED BUT THE REMAINING OF ITS CITIZENS CONTINUE TO BATLLE WITHIN THEMSELVES OF WHO THEY ARE THEIR VIBRATIONS AND CHAKRAS ARE DEAD...
THE OTHERS REMAIN STRONG,ELEVATING ON ALL LEVELS WITHO THE INTERFERENCE OF THE WICKED. DREADLOCKS IS HERE NOW HE IS THE ONE THAT BATTLES THE EVIL ENTITIES THAT ARE HEA TO KEEP MAN DORMANT AND CONFUSED OF HIS ACTUAL PLACE.
DREADLOCKS HAS BROUGHT HOPE TO ALL THAT HAVE COME IN CONTACT WITH THEIR THIRD EYE WHICH SHOWS THEM MA'AT... TRUTH, BALANCE, RIGHTEOUSNESS AND ORDER WITHIN..THIS GIVES THEM THEIR SENSE OF SELF PURPOSE .
THE VIBRATIONS IN MAN ARE SENSITIVE, EGOTISTIC AND ARROGANT, THEY MUST LEARN TO REACH DEEP WITHIN AND LEARN MORE OF THE BLACK DOT WITHIN
TO GAIN HIGHER INTELLIGENCE TO AVOID GETTING CAUGHT UP BY THE EVILS OF THIS WORLD. THE GODS OF KEMET HAVE SENT ME HERE FOR A REASON
I INITIALLY DID NOT UNDERSTAND, BUT NOW I DO... I MUST BRING ELEVATION TO THE LOST TRIBES OF ALKEBULAN.

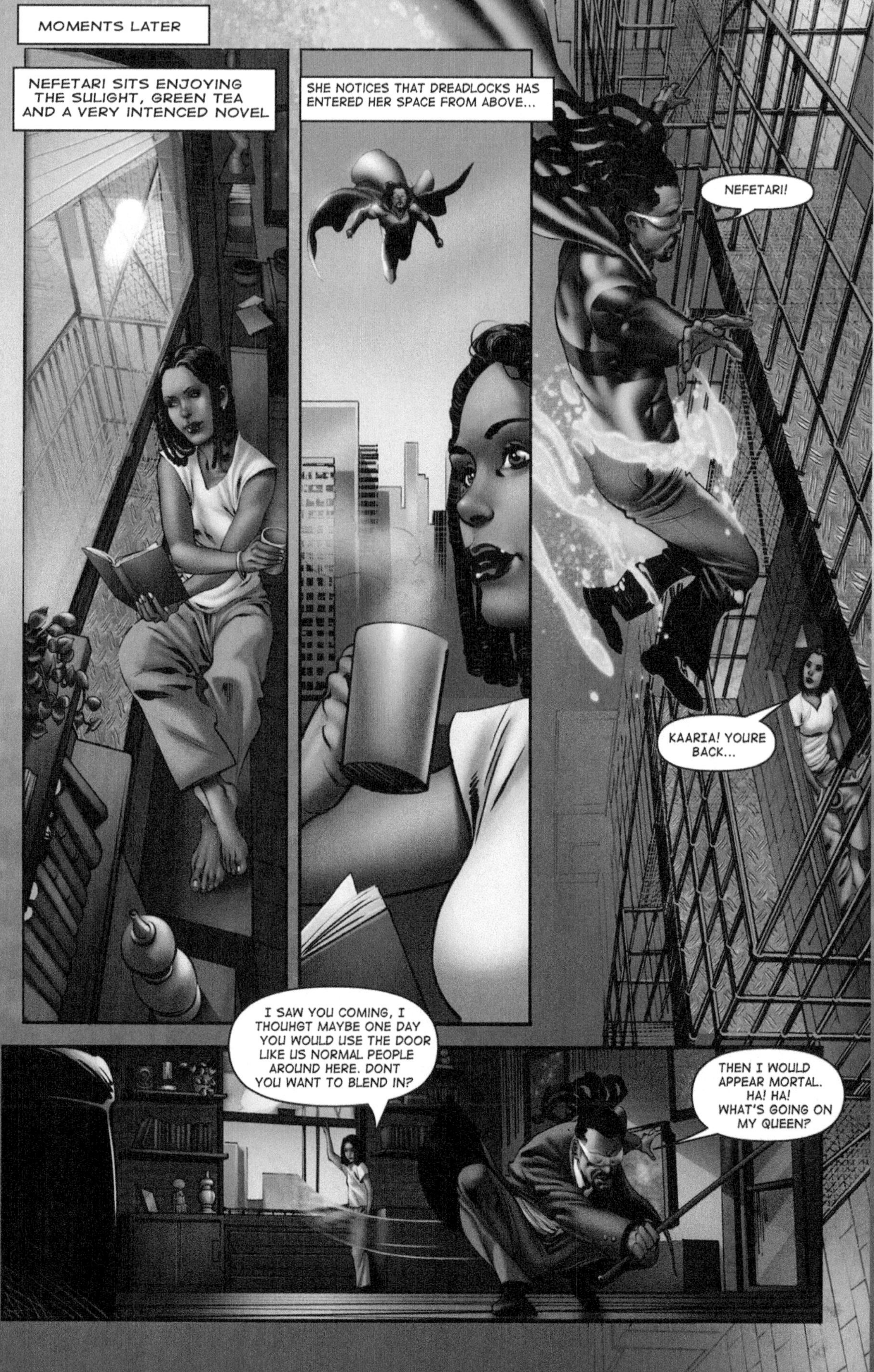
MOMENTS LATER
NEFETARI SITS ENJOYING THE SULIGHT, GREEN TEA AND A VERY INTENCED NOVEL
SHE NOTICES THAT DREADLOCKS HAS ENTERED HER SPACE FROM ABOVE...
NEFETARI!
KAARIA! YOURE BACK...
I SAW YOU COMING, I THOUHGT MAYBE ONE DAY YOU WOULD USE THE DOOR LIKE US NORMAL PEOPLE AROUND HERE. DONT YOU WANT TO BLEND IN?
THEN I WOULD APPEAR MORTAL. HA! HA! WHAT'S GOING ON MY QUEEN?

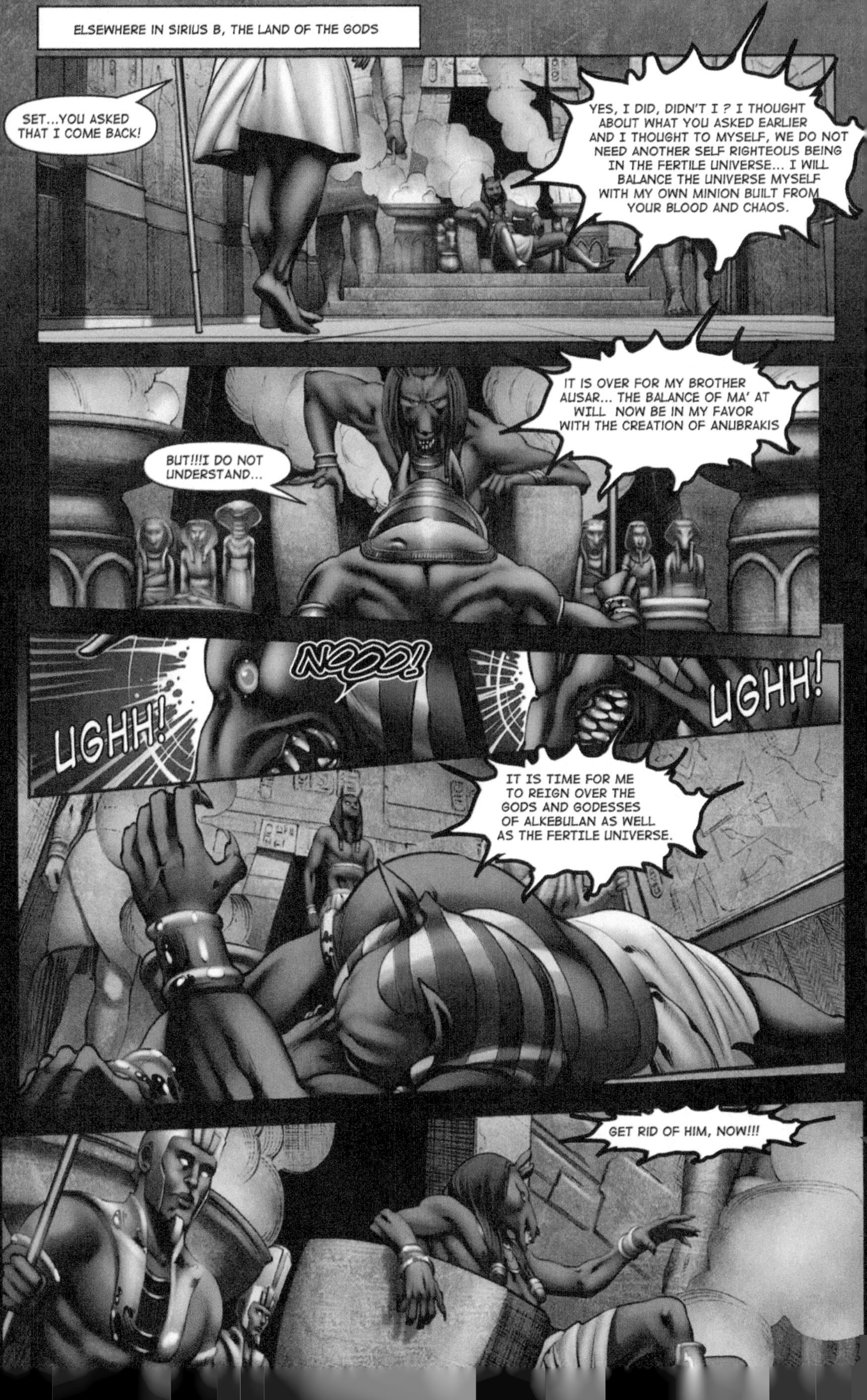

ELSEWHERE IN SIRIUS B, THE LAND OF THE GODS
SET...YOU ASKED THAT I COME BACK!
YES, I DID, DIDN'T I ? I THOUGHT ABOUT WHAT YOU ASKED EARLIER AND I THOUGHT TO MYSELF, WE DO NOT NEED ANOTHER SELF RIGHTEOUS BEING IN THE FERTILE UNIVERSE... I WILL BALANCE THE UNIVERSE MYSELF WITH MY OWN MINION BUILT FROM YOUR BLOOD AND CHAOS.
IT IS OVER FOR MY BROTHER AUSAR... THE BALANCE OF MA' AT WILL NOW BE IN MY FAVOR WITH THE CREATION OF ANUBRAKIS
BUT!!!I DO NOT UNDERSTAND...
UGHH!
NOOO!
UGHH!
IT IS TIME FOR ME TO REIGN OVER THE GODS AND GODESSES OF ALKEBULAN AS WELL AS THE FERTILE UNIVERSE.
GET RID OF HIM, NOW!!!

MOMENTS LATER NORTERN ETHIOPIA

THERE ARE MEN THAT SEARCH THE THE STEP PYRAMIDS IN SEARCH OF THE STORY OF ANUBIS ALSO KNOWN AS ANPU. WESTERN MAN HAS NO UNDERSTANDING OF ANPU AND HIS PURPOSE IN THE EGYPTIAN PANTHEON OF GODS.

THE STEP PYRAMID THAT HAS BEEN DISCOVERED ARE SOME OF THE OLDEST OF PYRAMIDS EXISTING OVER 10,000 YEARS AGO ARE AT THE BORDER OF ETHIOPIA AND EGYPT WITH EACH COUNTRY CLAIMING IT AS PART OF THEIR MODERN COUNTRY, NOT REALIZING THAT ALL OF THIS WAS PART OF ONE LAND KNOWN IN ANCIENT TIMES AS KEMET.

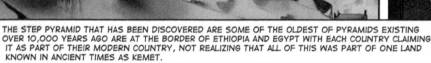

THE HIEROGLYPHICS (SACRED LANGUAGE OF THE GODS) ON THE WALLS OF THIS PYRAMID REVEALS THAT IT WAS SACRED GROUND WHERE THE ANCIENTS WORSHIPED AND CARRIED OUT THEIR RITUALS TO THE GODS OF THE SIRIUS STAR SYSTEM KNOWN AS THE LAND OF THE BLACK GODS.

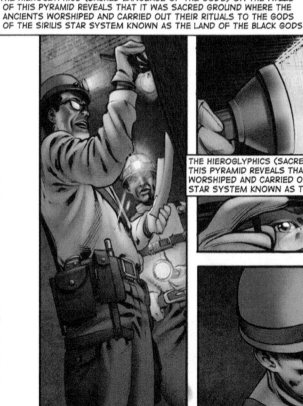

THE HIEROGLYPHICS (SACRED LANGUAGE OF THE GODS) ON THE WALLS OF THIS PYRAMID REVEALS THAT IT WAS SACRED GROUND WHERE THE ANCIENTS WORSHIPED AND CARRIED OUT THEIR RITUALS TO THE GODS OF THE SIRIUS STAR SYSTEM KNOWN AS THE LAND OF THE BLACK GODS.

WHAT ARE WE GOING TO DO SIR? WE CANT SHARE WHAT WE HAVE FOUND!

MODERN DAY ARCHAEOLOGIST AND ANTHROPOLOGIST CANNOT BELIEVE THAT THE BLACK GODS EVER EXISTED SO THEY SET OUT TO COVER UP THE TRUTH AND DISPEL THE TRUTHS AS FABLES AND MYTHS SO TO DISCREDIT THE ORIGINAL PEOPLE OF THE LAND OF AFRICA.

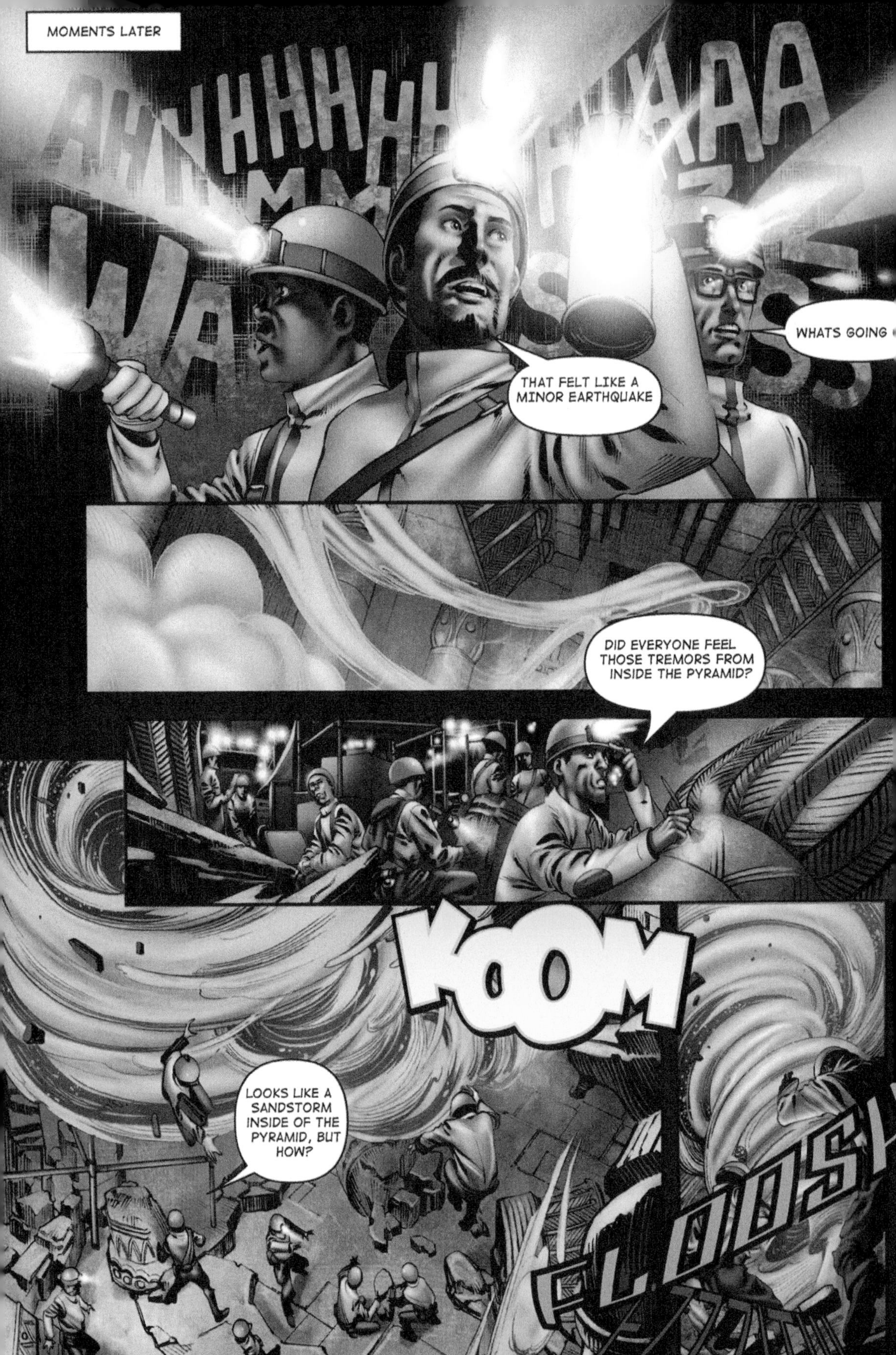
MOMENTS LATER
THAT FELT LIKE A MINOR EARTHQUAKE
WHATS GOING
DID EVERYONE FEEL THOSE TREMORS FROM INSIDE THE PYRAMID?
KOOM
LOOKS LIKE A SANDSTORM INSIDE OF THE PYRAMID, BUT HOW?

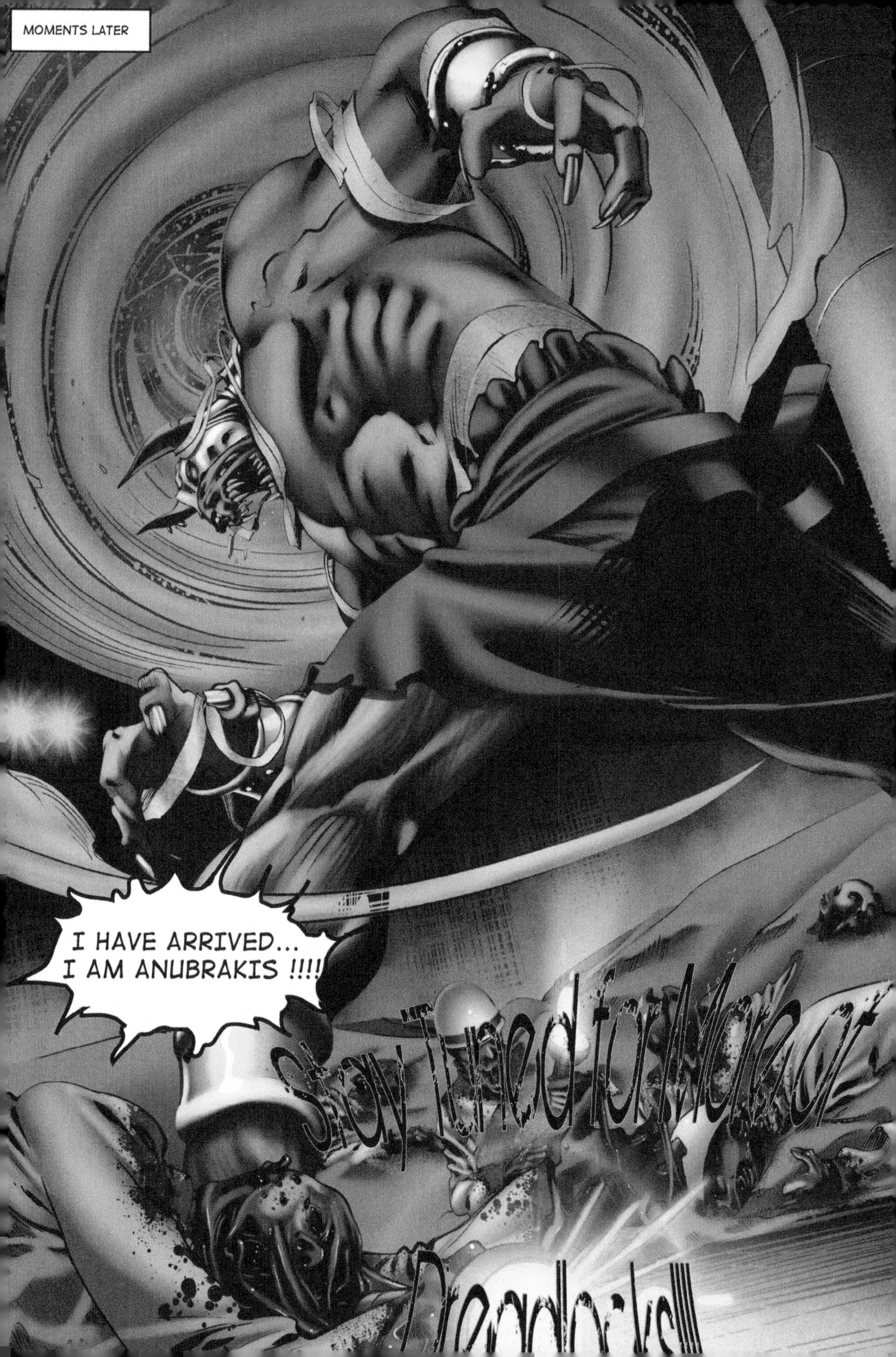
MOMENTS LATER
I HAVE ARRIVED... I AM ANUBRAKIS !!!!
Stay Tuned for More of

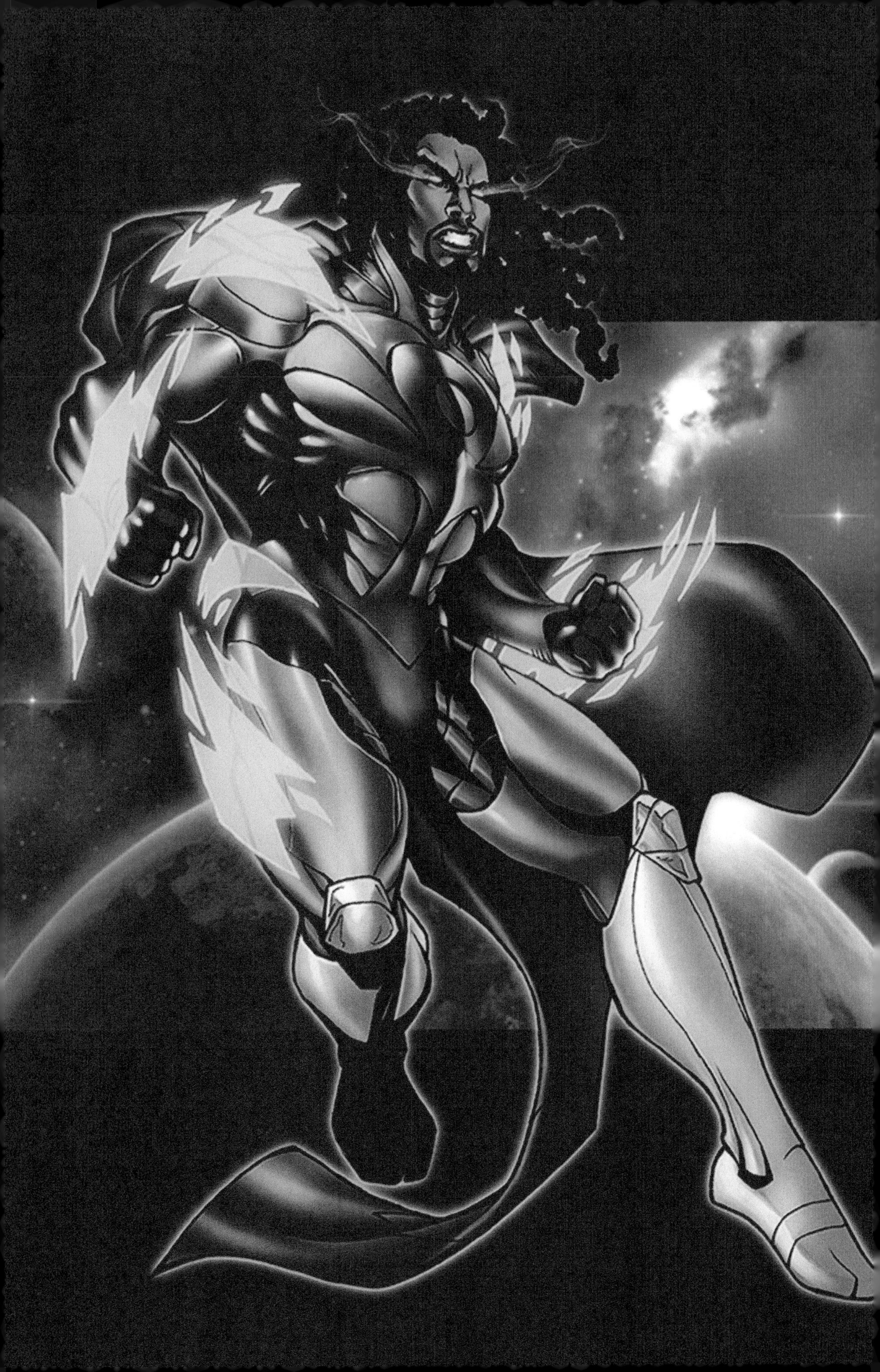

NEXT ON DECK:

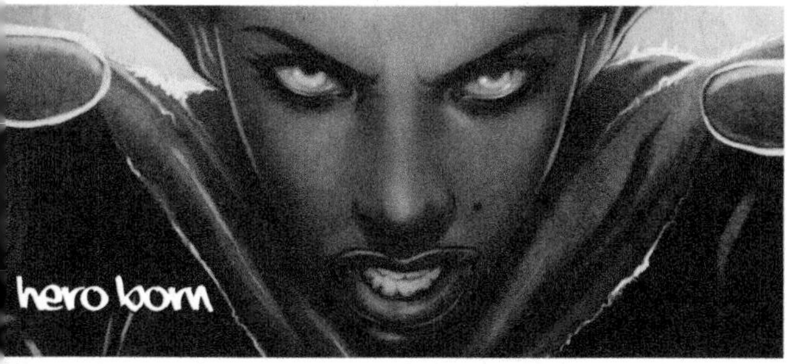
hero born

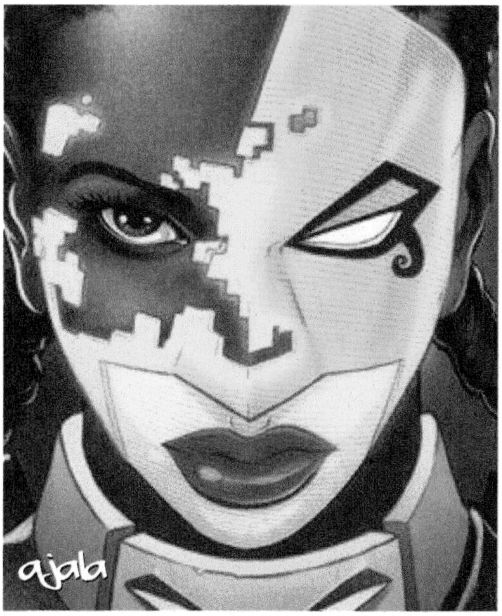
ajala

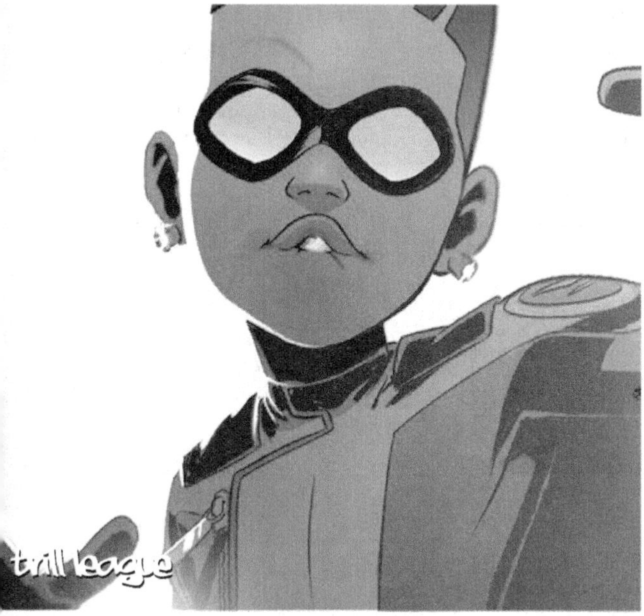
trill league

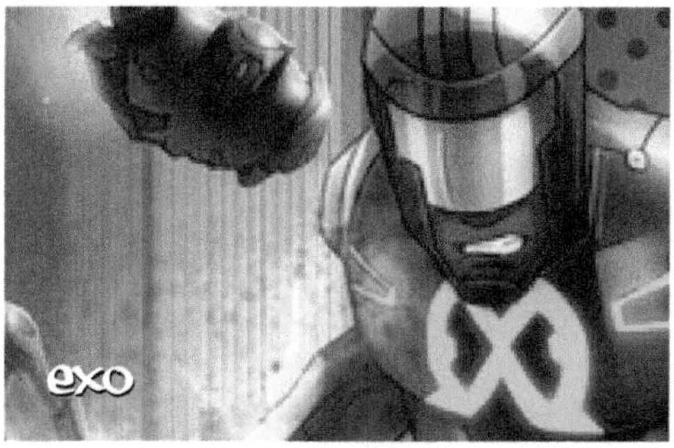
exo

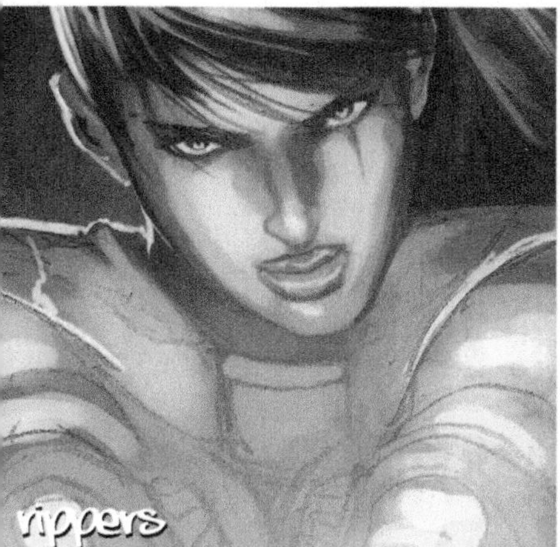
rippers

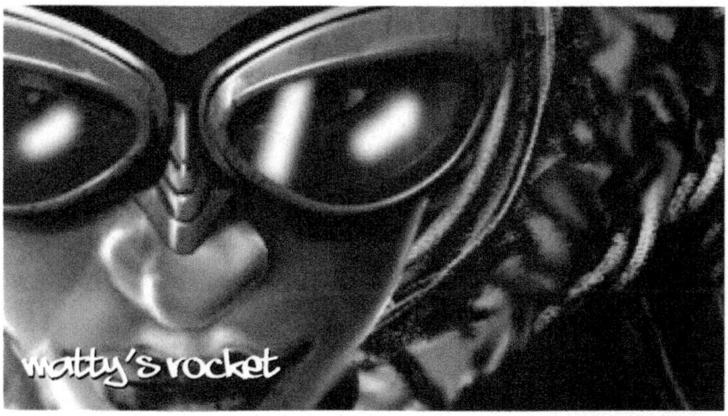
matty's rocket

and more... fall 2015

4 pages 16 bars
a visual mixtape

THE DOCTOR IS IN...

The Master of the Unknown returns to Griot Enterprises!

A revealing vision of the true nature of Voodoo follows the unpredictable travels of Dr. Jovan Carrington, and unfolds a tale of Black history, revolution and vengeance.

Includes the **Voodoo Child, Family Ties, School Spirit** and **Blind Faith** arcs of the first series!

AVAILABLE NOW!
PRINT: www.indyplanet.com
DIGITAL: www.drivethrucomics.com

www.griotenterprises.com

www.griotenterprises.com

WITCHDOCTOR

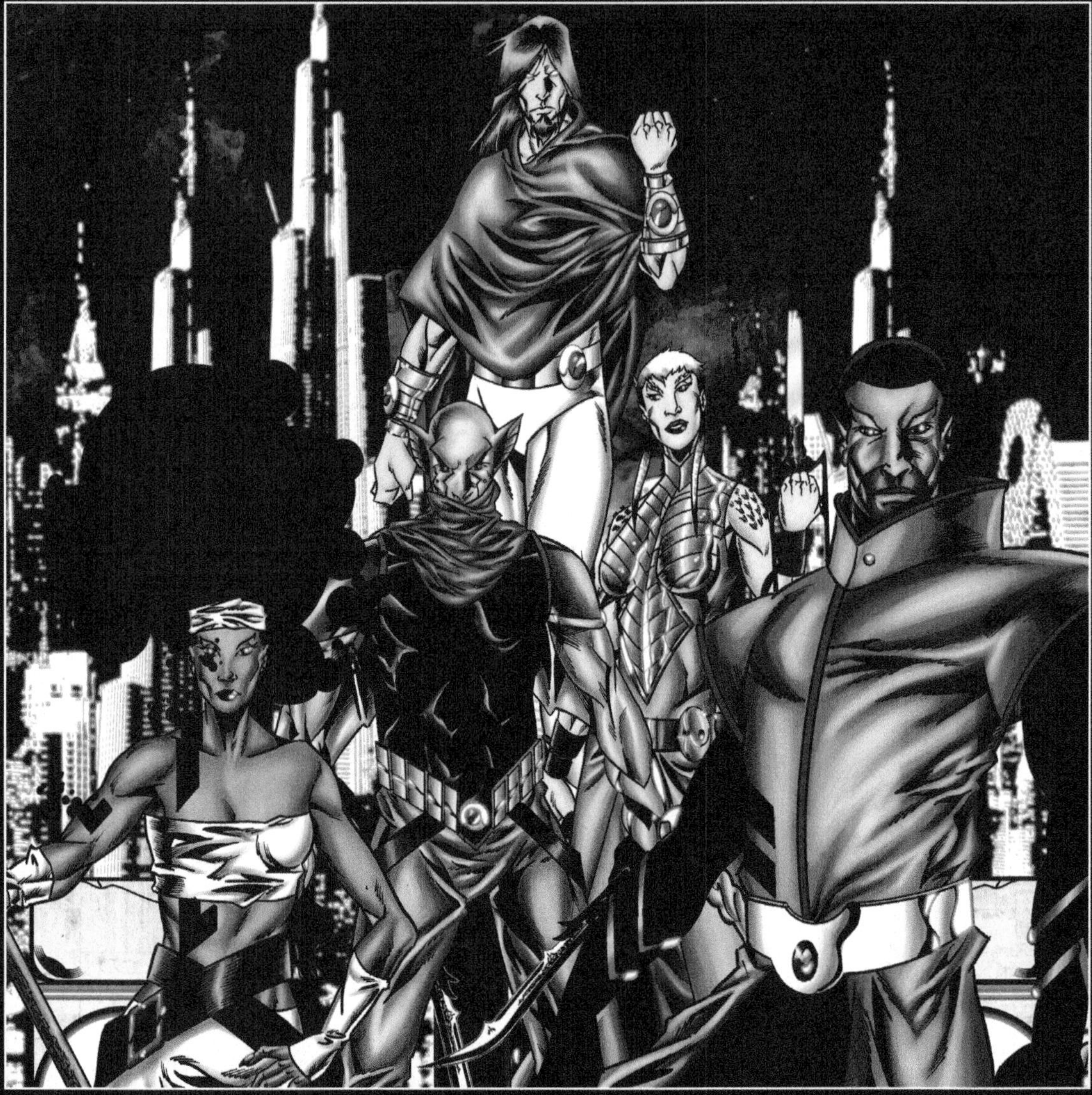

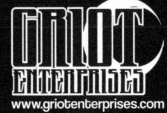

we tell great stories...

We have seen many great African American superheroes in comics, but we never saw an iconic African American superhero team. We didn't have our Justice League, our Avengers. We, as comic book fans of color, young and old, didn't have a universe where our heroes reside...

... **Griot Enterprises** fills that void.

Griot Enterprises' core form of communication is the comic book, a uniquely American art form. But creating a good story is only half of the battle. In order to give a story life, it must be told to as many as possible.

Griot is dedicated to producing product that is at once familiar to the current comic book community, but is not afraid to tackle new concepts and format to reach an audience outside of the typical comic book realm.

Comics foster reading comprehension and can be an effective delivery system for lessons and concepts in all subjects. Griot is dedicated to the use of comics for education.

The entertainment industry has many innovators. Unfortunately, it has a greater number of imitators. Griot respects its audience and our strong sense of commercial viability. We remain true to our vision and our work while creating a financially viable product. We take no shorts. We create innovative concepts, establish newtrends, and produce high-quality products.

Superheroes, Science Fiction, Westerns, Kung-Fu Action, Gritty Urban Drama, Historical Pulp Fiction... We've got it all.

A Griot concept will always be worth the selling price!

Jiba Molei Anderson, MFA
CEO - Griot Enterprises

www.griotenterprises.com
© Griot Enterprises and the respective creators

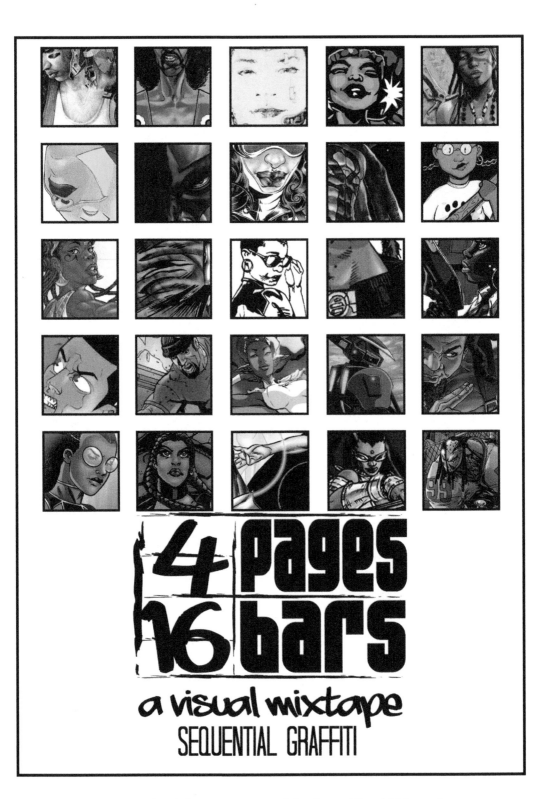

4 pages 16 bars

a visual mixtape
SEQUENTIAL GRAFFITI

A poster book featuring some of the finest **Visual MCs** and **Literary DJs** comics, animation, and speculative fiction have to offer... This is the EP to the mixtape.

BLAXIS

on sale now!

CPSIA information can be obtained
at www.ICGtesting.com
Printed in the USA
LVOW05s2247180717
541838LV00014B/48/P

9 781941 958186

3